JOSEPH F.]

JOSEPH F. LAMB

A Passion for Ragtime

Carol J. Binkowski

Foreword by Patricia Lamb Conn *and*
Robert J. Lamb

McFarland & Company, Inc., Publishers
Jefferson, North Carolina, and London

Frontispiece: Joseph F. Lamb, circa 1915 (courtesy Patricia Lamb Conn).

LIBRARY OF CONGRESS CATALOGUING-IN-PUBLICATION DATA

Binkowski, Carol J.
    Joseph F. Lamb : a passion for ragtime / Carol J. Binkowski;
foreword by Patricia Lamb Conn and Robert J. Lamb.
        p.   cm.
    Includes bibliographical references and index.

    ISBN 978-0-7864-6811-9
    softcover : acid free paper ∞

    1. Lamb, Joseph F. (Joseph Francis), 1887–1960.
    2. Composers— United States— Biography.   3. Ragtime
music — History and criticism.   I. Title.
ML410.L24556B56 2012
786.2092 — dc23
[B]   2012007920

BRITISH LIBRARY CATALOGUING DATA ARE AVAILABLE

On the cover: Joseph F. Lamb in 1908, the same year that
"Sensation" was published (courtesy Patricia Lamb Conn);
background image a fragment of the piano score for "Hi,
Everybody," a Lamb song from the 1935 production of the
minstrel show (courtesy Patricia Lamb Conn); rose © 2012
Shutterstock

Manufactured in the United States of America

McFarland & Company, Inc., Publishers
  Box 611, Jefferson, North Carolina 28640
  www.mcfarlandpub.com

For my husband, Richard,
with deep gratitude for all the years of his
unwavering support and encouragement

Table of Contents

"We found him!"—Rudi Blesh (1949)

Acknowledgments

Researching and writing Joe Lamb's biography has been a rewarding experience, and I was extremely fortunate to have encountered many wonderful people along the way who generously shared their time, resources, and expertise — all of which helped to make this project a reality.

My heartfelt thanks to Patricia Lamb Conn and to her husband, Bill Conn, for their friendship, generosity, time, and wonderful recollections. Pat offered unique personal reminiscences and details as well as access to letters, memorabilia, and photographs pertaining to Joe Lamb, all of which were an enormous asset to my research. I am so truly grateful.

My deepest appreciation and thanks to Robert and Joan Lamb, as well, for their warmth and hospitality. They graciously provided stories, photographs, and distinctive glimpses into the past — helping me to further understand Joe Lamb and his world.

A resounding thank you to Marjorie Freilich-Den who took the time to speak with me about her excellent master's thesis, "Joseph F. Lamb: A Ragtime Composer Recalled," and generously permitted me to reference and quote from material therein.

Also, sincere thanks to Carol Scotti for offering me her willing permission to reference and quote material from her late husband Joseph R. Scotti's dissertation, "Joe Lamb: A Study of Ragtime's Paradox."

Much gratitude to Mary Van Gieson and George A. Van Gieson for allowing me to use family letters, miscellaneous writings, and photographs — all extremely valuable resources.

A number of individuals enthusiastically shared their personal experiences, resources, and expertise. I am so grateful to each one: Max Morath for generously providing research materials, photographs, and valuable insights; Stella Laufer-Turk for recollections and information pertaining to the dedication of the Joseph F. Lamb school; Sue Keller for details on her creation of the folio and recording *A Little Lost Lamb* and Howard Vigorita for the photograph of his CD cover design; Glenn Jenks for the Joseph F. Lamb Rose story and photograph; Ted Tjaden for information regarding Lamb's Canadian publications; Nan Bostick for an overview of early San Francisco music publishing; and John Broven for locating the rare second volume of *The Classic Rags of Joe Lamb*.

Sincere appreciation to Denise Gallo and Karen Moses at the Library of Congress Music Division for knowledgeable assistance with the Joseph F. Lamb Collection; Randall McMillen at the Charles H. Templeton Collection, Special Collections, Mississippi State University Libraries, for assistance with classic sheet music cover materials; Rick McRae at the Sibley Music Library, Eastman School of Music, for assistance with the John Stark photograph; Margaret Chevian of the Providence, Rhode Island, Public Library, for information on J. Fred Helf; and Elaine Simpson at Park Lawn Cemetery in Toronto for details on Harry H. Sparks.

In addition, many thanks to Jewel Seehaus-Fisher and Rick Snyder for their patient and insightful reading of drafts; as well as to Larisa Migachyov, Trebor Tichenor, Bernard Kalban, Lowell Mate, Edward A. Berlin, Larry Karp, and the late Michael Montgomery for their time and interest.

Also, much appreciation to the Music Reference Department at the New York Public Library for the Performing Arts at Lincoln Center, the Montclair Public Library, the Montclair Historical Society, the Brooklyn Historical Society, and the United States Copyright Office for their help.

Many thanks to my father, A. Robert Knobloch, for reading and commenting on my drafts and, as always, for being so supportive. With gratitude to my late mother, Dorothy H. Knobloch, for listening to the music.

Also, thanks to my daughter, Daria Binkowski, for her willing technical assistance.

Last, but certainly not least, my deep gratitude and thanks to my husband, Richard Binkowski, for his continued patience and encouragement with this book as well as with all of my creative endeavors in writing, music, and life.

Foreword: A Few Words from the Lamb Family

Thank you, Carol.

At long last, a book about my dad, Joseph Lamb, my favorite ragtime composer. These pieces were my lullabies, way back when. I learned some things even *I* never knew before, especially things that happened before he married my mother.

Recently, I was amazed to hear how many compositions he'd written when they were played by many performers at a concert in Columbia, Missouri. He's written many more, too.

Now we can all enjoy his many rags and songs, forever.

Patricia Lamb Conn • West Haven, Connecticut

My earliest memories of my father and his music are hard for me to pin down because I was very young. I recall my mother singing soft melodies and hearing my father playing the piano. One thing I do remember is my father rocking my little brother in his bassinet and playing the piano at the same time. My father's first love was his family and the second was the music which he composed. Sometimes after supper, he would sit at the piano with a pencil in his mouth and some blank music sheets in front of him and would play some chords and strains that were running through his mind; he would play a few notes a couple of times and then write them down on paper. This could go on for hours until he had them all written down so he would not forget them. He never stopped composing music.

Music was a very important part of our family's tradition. As we grew older, we would all gather around the piano after supper and sing all types of songs which my father bought in the city and brought home. Being a very humble man, he gave away many sheets of music he wrote, never asking for any compensation. He only wanted to see his music published and for people to enjoy it. Eventually his talent, passion for music, and genius for harmonization became recognized as a gift to ragtime music.

I am very proud of my father and of what he passed on to the music world. I hope his legacy and his music will be preserved for future generations.

Robert J. Lamb • Manchester, New Jersey

Introduction

In 1980, just after the houselights dimmed and the audience settled to a hush at Broadway's John Golden Theatre, I first became acquainted with Joseph F. Lamb's music. No traditional overture signaled the opening curtain of this production of *Tintypes*. Instead, an ascending arpeggio from a lone piano, haunting in its minor key, introduced a stunning composition, the gentle sound of strings quietly joining in. Squinting eagerly at my program, I discovered that this beautiful music was entitled "Ragtime Nightingale" and had been written in 1915 by Joseph F. Lamb. I was clueless, though, never having heard of him. In the following days, I investigated both composer and composition; however, it would be many years before I had the opportunity to learn about both on a deeper level and, subsequently, to begin work on this biography.

Joseph F. Lamb (1887–1960) composed with enthusiasm and drew deeply from a variety of sources, his inspiration coming from all kinds of music, cultures, traditions, and the everyday — reflecting his joyous curiosity about the world around him. He was always humming an original musical phrase or tapping out a fresh rhythmic pattern, eager to use them in a new composition — one with distinctive melodies and harmonies artfully blended, one with the potential to linger more than a short while in a listener's memory. Lamb's approach was distinguished by an eclectic creativity that reflected American music and the culture of his era and offered rich insights into it as well.

In researching and writing about any individual's life, work, and times, it is impossible not to learn things that are beyond the surface facts and events. Joe Lamb taught me much about ragtime and popular music, history, the many facets of creativity, and appreciating the important things in life. Along the way, I also met many individuals who were generous with their time, knowledge, and resources. And, of course, there was always Lamb's wonderful music, a captivating soundtrack for it all. This has been a journey that I never could have imagined back in that darkened theater during the opening notes of *Tintypes*.

3

Music was everywhere when Lamb was growing into young adulthood, perhaps even more so than in our current culture. Now we are able to electronically access sheet music and recordings by the thousands in the comfort of our own homes, all within mere seconds. We can transfer our favorite music onto a small listening device for our jogging and commuting hours. We can be entertained by musical performers on the screens of our computers, and we can print out sheet music from the same machine to play or sing for our own amusement while other family members occupy themselves with their own computers and chosen hobbies. With all of this technology, ours has become a more solitary existence, both musically and otherwise.

A century or more ago, it was a different story. Families gathered after dinner for regular musical evenings together, singing and playing instruments. The centerpiece was the piano that was in almost every parlor. It did not gather dust; it was played daily. Shoppers frequented department stores and specialty shops where they could hear concerts as well as readily purchase real sheet music after a demonstrator played its melodies on the house upright. All of this was enjoyed by enthusiastic crowds.

Bands and other ensembles played on the streets and in parks. Everyone went to vaudeville and variety shows, and those who didn't could catch up on some of the latest songs at one of many social or local events. Readers would open up their Sunday newspapers and a beautiful musical supplement would tumble out. Mailboxes were crammed with thick publications ranging from *The Etude* to *The Musician* to *The Intermezzo* — each one a treasure of articles, reviews, and playable music — including duets — ready to be shared with family and friends. Those who lived on quiet streets could be invited in by a neighbor to an elegant afternoon musicale and tea presented by the daughter of the house and her friends, a performance which might be reviewed in the next issue of the local newspaper. And those who walked the city's busy avenues might distinguish the voice of an eager song plugger singing his heart out above the everyday cacophony, hoping to make his publisher's latest melody an unrivaled hit. There was no escaping music; it was all around. Joe Lamb breathed in this musical atmosphere during his youth, and it remained with him for life.

With the exception of brief employment on Tin Pan Alley as a young man, Lamb's working career was spent outside of the professional music world. He commuted to Manhattan from New Jersey and, later, from Brooklyn, spending time composing during his leisure hours. He was not, as the song goes, "living a ragtime life."[1] He was removed from the surroundings where ragtime was initially a focus, with its music regularly shared and performed by groups of itinerant pianists. And in an era when many of the classic ragtime figures were African American and emanating from the Midwest, Lamb was a white man living in the East.

Later, and despite his reputation for composing a group of fine classic ragtime works, Lamb faded into obscurity in the aftermath of the ragtime era. Joe Lamb was not in hiding; he was just busy with everyday details, unaware that his whereabouts, or even his identity, were ever in question. He never knew until later in life that he was one of ragtime's "big three." Most important of all to him was his family, and he was content to enjoy time with them, seeking neither fame, nor money from his music.

When Rudi Blesh and Harriet Janis, two very determined researchers, finally discovered his whereabouts in 1949, they were able to put to rest the assumption that Lamb's name might have been pseudonymous for Scott Joplin—an ironic twist since Joplin had been a champion of Lamb's work and the one ragtime composer with whom Lamb had a friendship. And, then, at a later age, when many other composers would have been content with reputations based on their youthful output alone, Lamb began composing anew, attracting fresh recognition and acclaim. Without even realizing it, he had defied the odds of achieving success in a number of ways, leaving a substantial collection of enduring works whose lasting beauty and musical quality are the embodiment of his own distinctive style as well as fine examples of the creative possibilities within the classic ragtime form. Joe Lamb was a ragtime original.

I didn't discover Lamb's music until later in my own life. I grew up during a surge of interest in honky-tonk style piano, listening to the recordings of Knuckles O'Toole, "Garters" Grady, Pianola Pete, and others, which my mother was fond of playing on our new "hi-fi" system. Here were old-time songs (and old-time sounding songs) played with peppy tempos on tinny uprights. It was all ragtime to me, and I was captivated. The upbeat piano performances of Tiny Little and Jo Ann Castle on *The Lawrence Welk Show* were mandatory viewing in my house. (Their grand finales with signature show-stopping glissandos were not to be missed—something I tried to emulate at the keyboard myself in an effort to thrill relatives at family gatherings).

Like millions of others in the early 1970s, I went to see the hit film *The Sting*, happily purchasing the soundtrack album and adding Scott Joplin to my list of favorites. Here was a different kind of ragtime—both buoyant and thoughtful, with some classical overtones. A subsequent gift of Vera Brodsky Lawrence's collection of Joplin rags offered me a closer look into this world of ragtime. It was different than the sound of Pianola Pete's spirited rendition of "Wait Till the Sun Shines Nellie," his banjo player happily chiming in, on the by now well-worn hi-fi. Yet, somehow, they were related. I was discovering that the word ragtime took in a lot of territory, and it was a bit difficult to define in the bargain. There was much to learn.

Joseph Lamb wasn't part of the equation yet. I didn't know about Milton

Kaye's recordings of his compositions in the 1970s, and I had just missed an opportunity to join a co-worker for a performance of *Push Comes to Shove*, the dance production in which Lamb's "Bohemia Rag" was prominently featured. It wasn't until that evening at *Tintypes* that he entered the picture.

During the next few years, I became acquainted with more of Lamb's works through a singular recording here or an item on a concert program there. When I began attending ragtime festivals, though, I started to understand the scope of works that this man had composed.

In 2005, I had the pleasure of meeting Patricia Lamb Conn at the annual Scott Joplin Ragtime Festival in Sedalia, Missouri. At this particular event there was a segment devoted to her father with a performance of selections from the newly released folio and CD, *A Little Lost Lamb*, compiled by Sue Keller, which contained an appealing array of Lamb's previously unpublished works. Pat was asked to say a few words during the proceedings.

There was a large audience that day, and it was only by chance that Pat and I happened to walk out of the concert hall together. I was glad to have the opportunity to speak with her about the new CD and folio. I also recognized her accent as one from closer to home and after laughing about the coincidence of meeting each other so many miles away, we continued our conversation — one that was to last through subsequent festivals and led, several years later, to a discussion of my interest in writing this biography.

Pat warmly welcomed me into her home on numerous occasions where she, along with her amiable husband Bill Conn, talked about Joe Lamb and his life. She also generously shared with me a wealth of letters, photos, and other memorabilia.

Later on, I had the pleasure of meeting Lamb's son, Bob, and his wife, Joan. They also gladly invited me to visit them, kindly sharing their own reminiscences, photographs, and memorabilia.

During this time, I was often asked, Why Joseph Lamb? Why a biography? Simply stated, I found Lamb's music greatly appealing and grew curious about the man who had written it. I wanted to know why he had been so far out of the spotlight and yet came to write compositions which later turned up in places ranging from regional music festivals to the Broadway stage. I became engrossed.

One thing that piqued my curiosity about Lamb was that his musical achievements and path to recognition did not fall into a readily definable pattern — at least not by modern standards. I'm always intrigued by individuals who don't fit into a predictable mold.

With little in the way of traditional musical training or exposure to the performing network of ragtime composers, Lamb became recognized as one of the genre's "big three" along with Scott Joplin and James Scott. He learned ragtime through the study of printed sheet music, an unusual method for its time, and drew his musical inspirations from a wealth of sources. His music was also part of a life that held other interests and activities, carpentry and drawing among them; and somehow he made them all seem unified. Lamb's eclecticism, resilience, and ability to balance it all were intriguing. Beyond this, he didn't care about being famous or hitting the million mark in sheet music sales. He loved music, especially ragtime, and wanted to compose it well — and he just wanted people to enjoy his compositions.

Just as in anyone's life, one road leads to another sometimes by chance, sometimes by plan, but Lamb's life held much of the former. His friendships with both Scott Joplin and music publisher John Stark were important as well as serendipitous. There were others — some names forgotten, others not — who were significant to Lamb in coincidental ways, as well. All of it put together creates an absorbing story — an American story at heart and one closely intertwined within its historical and cultural fabric.

On a personal level, the era in which Lamb initially began composing has always fascinated me. It was one of excitement and innovation, of history and hardship. It was a time, too, when my own ancestors were making their way in Brooklyn and Manhattan — places where Lamb had lived and worked — and despite the need for economic conservation and while living in buildings where space was in short supply, they still had pianos. Many years later, also quite by chance, my family and I moved to a town near Montclair, New Jersey, where Lamb grew up — further adding to my curiosity.

My mother had studied piano in her youth and especially enjoyed hearing it played on any occasion. In later times, during a long illness, she found enjoyment when I played songs of all types from the past, and I distinctly recall her listening serenely when I played Lamb's "Ragtime Nightingale," composed in the year that she was born. My father enjoyed listening, too, and derived a measure of contentment as he watched my mother become absorbed in the music. He also became interested in Joe Lamb's story and its historic times and places.

In writing any biography, one must make choices. Should it focus on analyzing the individual's work? Offer a comparison with others in the same field? Provide a strictly details-only approach to life's events? The list could go on. I have chosen to focus on the man himself and the times in which he lived, intertwining this life with details about his music as well as the people and places that helped give texture to it all.

This is a chronologically organized book, and one that continues on for more than half a century after Lamb's death to provide a larger context, one in which his compositions have endured — spilling over into other art forms, showing up in the most curious of places, and touching the lives of new generations.

I discuss specific compositions as they relate to Lamb's life and times, of course — with references to published commentary as well as my own obser-vations — but this is not a musicological study. Nor is this a comparative or critical analysis of Lamb in relation to Scott Joplin, James Scott, or any other composer — although, naturally, there is information about these individuals as they relate to Lamb and to the musical picture of the times.

Mine is just one of many approaches to telling the story of Joseph Lamb and his music, and I sincerely hope that others will want to write about him from their own viewpoints. There are many to choose from.

There are full-length biographies of Scott Joplin as well as of James Scott, the other two members of the "big three." Although Joe Lamb has been the focus of many excellent articles as well as of two fine, unpublished scholarly works, there has not been, to my knowledge, any published book-length work to date. Lamb deserves consideration as an important part of our American ragtime heritage — a frame of reference for new generations to create their own fresh musical interpretations while maintaining a connection to past traditions. And in a larger sense, our American history is always illuminated by a look at its music and its creators.

During my research, I had the good fortune to have had personal contact with Joe Lamb's family, members of the ragtime community, and fine research institutions. In addition, I was provided with a number of primary sources, including correspondence written by Joe and Amelia Lamb, as well as by their brother-in-law and two of their nephews. I was also granted permission to draw upon material from the research works of Marjorie Freilich-Den and the late Joseph R. Scotti. Having access to all of this information was priceless. More specific details are provided in the acknowledgments section.

Researching and writing this book has been an educational and rewarding journey for me — a true joy in so many ways. My hope is that others will expe-rience a bit of this joy and find Lamb's story an enjoyable read. If this offers additional insight and contributes to the preservation of ragtime music and its history — Lamb's, of course, in particular — then I will be more than content.

Joe Lamb's music is timeless and will continue to offer enjoyment for generations to come — whether it is a buoyant rendition of "Champagne Rag" performed by an onstage ensemble for an audience of hundreds or the haunt-ing melody of "Ragtime Nightingale" played by a lone pianist to the delight of an evening stroller passing by an open window at twilight.

*   *   *

I have tried to the best of my ability to present all of the information in this work as accurately and completely as possible. I apologize for any omis-sions or errors that may have occurred; they are mine alone and are certainly unintentional.

Note: There are some photographs, quotations, and references in this work that pertain to theatrical productions, styles of music, and specific songs common to the accepted culture and performance customs of long bygone times. Some of these are of a regrettably stereotypical nature and are included only for the purpose of presenting historical facts and information relevant to the eras discussed. No offense is intended in any way.

Prologue

A dancer.... A derby.... Some sly introductory notes....

A performer takes the spotlight, moving in mischievous harmony to a jaunty two-step called "Bohemia Rag." Quirky, sexy, witty, innovative. With the flavor of an era and a music both bygone and timeless. Yet with a glimpse into a new frontier of artistic possibilities.

Push Comes to Shove* ... Its musical setting pairs ragtime and classical: Joseph Lamb and Franz Joseph Haydn. An eclectic sound for an eclectic, cutting-edge masterpiece of dance.

Audiences are wild with enthusiasm. Critics are astounded. The choreographer will make history. And in the next few decades this work will be performed around the world.

Haydn's name is in history books, on recordings, atop thick musical scores. His compositions resonate from the stages of major concert halls.

But what of Joseph Lamb whose "Bohemia Rag" took center stage with a ballet great, a groundbreaking choreographer, and a classical icon?

Who was this man and what is the story of his music?

---

*Choreographer Twyla Tharp's *Push Comes to Shove*—with music by Joseph F. Lamb and Franz Joseph Haydn—was premiered by the American Ballet Theatre with Mikhail Baryshnikov in 1976 at the Uris Theatre in New York. During subsequent decades it has been performed around the world—from Stockholm to Zurich, and from Tokyo to Washington, D.C.

One

Setting the Stage (1887–1899)

"Home at Montclair"— George Inness landscape painting

On December 6, 1887, President Grover Cleveland delivered his third address to the United States Congress in which he urged the reduction of high protective tariffs as a means of balancing the growing Treasury surplus. This was a condition, he firmly emphasized, which required "immediate and careful consideration."[1] The issue was not new, having roots in the Civil War years; yet it was one that had attracted attention because of its increasing economic and political complexities.

Under ordinary circumstances, James Lamb — an independent building contractor and carpenter in Montclair, New Jersey — would have been eagerly awaiting news concerning the president's remarks. He had strong Republican leanings and was well known for his enthusiastic debates with friends on political topics.[2] Since this was a Democratic presidency and the focal issue concerned the health of the country's economy, Lamb was surely looking forward to spending the coming weeks discussing the finer points of Cleveland's address, particularly with his friend and neighbor Thomas Hughes who was, himself, a Democrat.[3] And then there was the added local interest factor, the president's native town of Caldwell being just a few miles up the road.

At the same time Julia Lamb, an admirer of good music, was hoping for some bit of news about the new Mrs. Cleveland. The president's marriage to the young and beautiful Frances Folsom had captured headlines the previous year, and the first lady's aptitude for the piano had not gone unnoticed.[4] Their wedding at the White House was a landmark event, with the additional distinction of having had musical selections performed by the United States Marine Band under the direction of John Philip Sousa.[5] Thereafter, Mrs. Cleveland became a figure of more than just passing curiosity.

On this particular December 6, however, political and musical issues were far from James and Julia Lamb's thoughts. This was no ordinary day in the Lamb household, nor were the days that followed. News of the Clevelands in forthcoming headlines would have to wait; for on the exact same day as the president addressed Congress, Julia Lamb gave birth to their fourth child — Joseph Francis.

Young Joseph would inherit many things from his parents that would last him a lifetime. From his father came a strong affinity for discussing politics as well as a remarkable talent for carpentry and building. From his mother came a love of music. As he grew, Joe would enjoy all of these pursuits and excel at them. Music, however, was destined to become his passion — with ragtime close to his heart.

Deep winter, with its festive holidays, approached quickly, and a sudden burst of cold weather during those early December days of 1887 sent Montclair families scurrying to buy everything from heavier clothing to new stoves. Some rushed to nearby Newark to admire the lavish Christmas displays at Hahne & Company's famous department store while, locally, boys flocked to the frozen surface of Crane's Pond to skate for a carefree afternoon.[6] Yet most people increasingly relished the comfort and warmth of their homes as shorter, more wintry days settled in. Soon all the world would resemble *Home at Montclair*, the evocative, snowy landscape by beloved local artist, George Inness, who had moved to the town in 1885.[7] And James and Julia Lamb also remained close to home with their three older children and their new baby, Joseph, as he began to adjust to his comfortable house and to his beautiful hometown.

Montclair was an appealing community and an ideal place in which to grow up. Its distinctive character was well defined after becoming a separate township in 1868, when its break from neighboring Bloomfield became official. By this time, the Greenwood Lake Railroad line began making multiple stops there, ensuring Montclair's popularity as a residential choice for businessmen and their families who needed easy commutability to New York City and, at the same time, wanted a lovely, quiet atmosphere in which to live. Despite the town's close proximity to the more urban environments of both Newark and New York, it continued to maintain its pastoral essence over time. Joe Lamb always loved it. "I was born in Montclair, N.J. (in the country)," he wrote many years later, "and *am* stuck on it."[8]

While the Montclair of his boyhood possessed a country-like charm, it also had a finely organized sense of community, culture, and sociability — offering much in the way of variety to its fortunate residents. In winter there were sleighing parties, and on summer evenings the lovely tree-lined streets invited strolling under the charming glow of gas lamps.[9] With the arrival of the 1890s, downtown Bloomfield Avenue became an active destination and was home to such diverse businesses as Mrs. A. Maynard's Fashionable

Trimmed Hats as well as Baker and Confectioner William Niederhauser's Ice Cream Saloon,[10] the latter of certain interest to Joe and his friends. And the town provided a relaxing day's respite from nearby city life for visitors in their horse-drawn carriages. As a contemporary observer enthusiastically noted: "There is no section of New Jersey where more fine drives abound than in the vicinity of Montclair."[11]

The town's cultural life was a busy one, and some of its activities were chronicled by S.C.G. Watkins, a dentist who lived a short distance from the Lamb family. An astute observer of the local scene, he reported on its many artistic groups. According to him, the Montclair Glee Club, founded in 1885, performed "two first-class concerts each year, equal to New York City's standards"; and its Dramatic Club, organized four years later, also ranked "favorably with professional players."[12]

The New York Philharmonic Club performed to a full-capacity crowd at Montclair Hall in 1887,[13] establishing an ongoing relationship with the town that continued in the years to come. Opportunities for musical instruction were also abundant. Local teachers were often featured on page one of *The Montclair Times*, their advertisements filled with enthusiasm, such as the one for violinist E.N. Treadwell that read "Lessons Given Until Ten O'Clock P.M."[14] There was even a Montclair College of Music regularly advertised; it was located in Pillbury's Building and directed by the estimable Professor A. Wehner.[15]

A range of popular offerings—from programs by humorists and musicians to minstrel show entertainment—blended into the mix, both in town and within sister communities. Some of these shows were presented by professionals and others by many enthusiastic amateur groups. Audiences in 1895 alone had varied possibilities to choose from—a women's banjo duo at a Club Hall musical tea,[16] a minstrel show by the neighboring Bloomfield Young Men's Catholic Union—with its hilarious concluding sketch titled "Fun in a Cooper Shop"[17]—or a performance by John Thompson at the Montclair Opera House where singing, dancing, and music were featured along with his acclaimed comedy.[18] There was even a Wheelmen's Orchestra and Minstrel Troupe nearby, a group that advertised their performances frequently.

By the time young Joe was in grammar school, Montclair was the solid center of an especially thriving cultural life and had close access to even more possibilities. It was "an important town," as Joe's sister Anastasia was to comment in later years, "one of the most important towns in that part of New Jersey."[19]

The Lamb family's home was located at 113 North Fullerton Avenue (now 111), located just a few blocks from the town's main avenue. Joe joined three older siblings there — James (1872–1941), Katharine (1878–1948), and Anastasia (1884–1976). Two other sisters had died as infants.

Although the Lambs originally lived on William Street, their family's desire for additional space prompted James Lamb to put his superb building knowledge and carpentry skills to good use in constructing a new house in 1885, two years prior to Joe's birth. This home offered a welcoming environment in which Joe and his siblings could spend a happy youth, its two-and-a-half stories plus basement providing the room that the family craved.[20] Set on a generous piece of land that also included a carpentry shop and a barn, the house and its expansive yard were a favorite haven for Joe and his friends while growing up. Childhood friend Paul Hughes later reminisced: "There was more room on the Lamb property ... we generally made our headquarters there."[21] Joe fondly recalled that the Hughes and Lamb families "lived four doors apart and ... were very close friends. So as soon as two people [Joe and Paul] could know each other we did."[22]

Joe, Paul, and other neighborhood friends gathered at the Lamb house where they learned to build canoes, kites, and other challenging creations, trying them out with zeal and sometimes dramatic results, such as the accidental crashing of their well-crafted sled into a fence on its inaugural voyage.

Joseph Lamb's boyhood home in Montclair, New Jersey, built by his father, James Lamb (courtesy Robert and Joan Lamb).

The boys' afternoons were filled with more antics—target shooting on the barn or using whatever was available to shake chestnuts free from the trees, an occasional broken window in their legendary repertoire of mishaps.[23] It was a boyhood filled with normal, energetic, outdoor adventures.

The Lambs were part of a large Irish community in Montclair, a slice of the multifaceted cultural mix that helped to define the town's character. Ireland's potato famine of the 1840s and its ongoing social and political turmoil brought a huge influx of people into the United States for a number of years, and many of these individuals came to New Jersey to seek work there as domestics, on the railroads and canals, or in other labor-intensive jobs. They eventually developed solid ethnic communities of their own in a variety of places. Montclair's "Irishtown" section was one of them. Its residents were well known for their local contributions,[24] including the building of the Church of the Immaculate Conception in 1856. This congregation thrived to such an extent that construction on a new and larger church began in the 1890s in order to accommodate its growing population. The project was ultimately completed and dedicated in 1909.[25] The church became one of the leading religious centers in town.

The Lambs were devout members at Immaculate, and James Lamb was elected to its board of trustees. Joe served as an altar boy at the church in his younger years and also attended its affiliated grammar school, a small educational community that met in the basement of the building. Even as an adult and long after moving from New Jersey, he continued in this family tradition of being an active participant in the neighborhood church community. It was always an important component of his life.

Joe Lamb's Irish heritage was a source of pride and occasionally served as an inspiration for musical subjects, contexts, and lyrics—just as it did for other popular songwriters of the day. These ethnic themes and characters appeared during his early songwriting years, as seen in "Sweet Nora Doone," who is more completely described as "Irish lass is Nora Doone, Belle of County Tipperary"[26] as well as in "Three Leaves of Shamrock on the Watermelon Vine," in which "Pat McCarty sings his songs in Irish brogue."[27]

Many Irish immigrants rose to places of importance within Montclair, and Joe's father was among them. James Lamb (1846–1900) came from Drogheda, Ireland. An older brother, Hugh, immigrated first, changing his name from Lambe (originally with an "e") to Brady (that of his employer) before leaving Ireland in order to avoid being detained and conscripted into the British army. He came to New Jersey, homesick with nowhere to go, and was befriended by a jeweler in Bloomfield, who gave him a job at which he remained for several years prior to going into the building business.[28]

James Lambe—having also changed his name to "Brady" as his brother had done and for similar reasons—followed him to the United States several years later. Although there are no records of this, he immigrated possibly by 1862 or "sometime in the 1860s,"[29] according to family letters. He kept the name Brady for several years, long enough to have a family Bible embossed with the name "James T. Brady."[30]

The New Jersey State Archives has a record of a marriage between James Brady and Julia "Hanniberry" (Henneberry) in Montclair on May 4, 1871,[31] supporting the fact that James did, indeed, use the name of Brady.

Also, there are records of both a Hugh Brady and a James T. Brady serving in two separate New Jersey regiments in the Union Army during the Civil War.[32] (James Lamb's cemetery marker displays a medallion attesting to his service in the Grand Army of the Republic,[33] although the census records for 1900 indicate that he only came to America in 1870[34]; and the newspaper account of his death in 1900 specifies that he "came to Montclair thirty years ago"[35] but did not say that he "immigrated." The name change could well have accounted for the discrepancy in these dates.

James went to work for his brother before setting up his own business and, although Hugh kept the name Brady, James later returned to his given last name (dropping the "e") upon the advice of a lawyer.[36] James Lamb went on to become a successful building contractor in Montclair. His talents had to have been superior in this field because he was responsible for the construction of a number of lovely homes in the most prestigious areas of town where the houses were grand beauties set on large, grassy plots of land. He, himself, owned and rented out a half dozen houses—including several on Midland Avenue as well as those on Lorraine Avenue and Christopher Street—a testament to his enterprising nature.[37] One of these homes was leased to Thomas Manley, a member of the Montclair Art Colony whose famous community of fourteen artists worked in the locale from the 1860s through the ensuing six decades.[38] The group included the acclaimed landscape painter George Inness as well as sculptor Jonathan Hartley.

James Lamb had a real appreciation for the arts coupled with a generous nature because he was known to have accepted some watercolors from Manley as payment for due rent[39]—the type of understanding and support that can make all the difference to an artist during lean times. (Manley was not only a landscape artist but also created etchings for print publications.[40] Some of his work was later acquired by the revered Montclair Museum of Art.) Young Joe inherited the same generosity of spirit that his father possessed, a quality he demonstrated all during his life through his interactions with family and friends as well as with new acquaintances.

Despite a full schedule of work projects, James Lamb still found time to serve as an active member of several local groups, including the Montclair

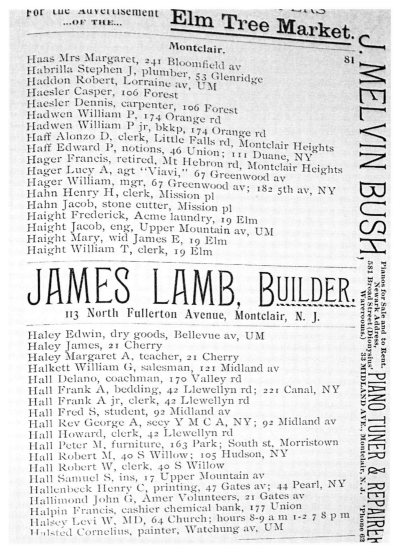

For the Advertisement
...OF THE...

Elm Tree Market.

Montclair.

Haas Mrs Margaret, 241 Bloomfield av   81
Habrilla Stephen J, plumber, 53 Glenridge
Haddon Robert, Lorraine av, UM
Haesler Casper, 106 Forest
Haesler Dennis, carpenter, 106 Forest
Hadwen William P, 174 Orange rd
Hadwen William P jr, bkkp, 174 Orange rd
Haff Alonzo D, clerk, Little Falls rd, Montclair Heights
Haff Edward P, notions, 46 Union; 111 Duane, NY
Hager Francis, retired, Mt Hebron rd, Montclair Heights
Hager Lucy A, agt "Viavi," 67 Greenwood av
Hager William, mgr, 67 Greenwood av; 182 5th av, NY
Hahn Henry H, clerk, Mission pl
Hahn Jacob, stone cutter, Mission pl
Haight Frederick, Acme laundry, 19 Elm
Haight Jacob, eng, Upper Mountain av, UM
Haight Mary, wid James E, 19 Elm
Haight William T, clerk, 19 Elm

JAMES LAMB, BUILDER.

113 North Fullerton Avenue, Montclair, N. J.

Haley Edwin, dry goods, Bellevue av, UM
Haley James, 21 Cherry
Haley Margaret A, teacher, 21 Cherry
Halkett William G, salesman, 121 Midland av
Hall Delano, coachman, 170 Valley rd
Hall Frank A, bedding, 42 Llewellyn rd; 221 Canal, NY
Hall Frank A jr, clerk, 42 Llewellyn rd
Hall Fred S, student, 92 Midland av
Hall Rev George A, secy Y M C A, NY; 92 Midland av
Hall Howard, clerk, 42 Llewellyn rd
Hall Peter M, furniture, 163 Park; South st, Morristown
Hall Robert M, 40 S Willow; 105 Hudson, NY
Hall Robert W, clerk, 40 S Willow
Hall Samuel S, ins, 17 Upper Mountain av
Hallenbeck Henry C, printing, 47 Gates av; 44 Pearl, NY
Hallimond John G, Amer Volunteers, 21 Gates av
Halpin Francis, cashier chemical bank, 177 Union
Halsey Levi W, MD, 64 Church; hours 8-9 a m 1-2 7 8 p m
Halsted Cornelius, painter, Watchung av, UM

J. MELVIN BUSH,
Pianos for Sale and to Rent.
Newark Address,
581 Broad Street (Dionysius'
Warerooms.)
33 MIDLAND AVE., Montclair, N. J.
PIANO TUNER & REPAIRER
'Phone 62

An 1898 local directory featuring builder James Lamb as well as J. Melvin Bush, whose music store was to become a fixture in Montclair.

Club,[41] a town social organization that was formed shortly before the time of Joe's birth. The grand official opening of the Club's spectacular new premises was held in 1889 — with a thousand guests who enjoyed dancing, dinner, and a Hungarian gypsy band. The event was among "the sensations of the year"[42] in the surrounding area.

Originally designed as a men's club, the building was open to the families of members on Mondays when they were welcome to use its game rooms and other facilities. The club also housed a five-hundred-seat hall which was the site of concerts, lectures, dances, and theatrical events of all types. It was said that "half the town's social activities"[43] took place at the Montclair Club. Since James Lamb was an active participant in the life of the organization, it is sure that Joe was familiar not only with its expansive premises but also with its vast array of events, musical ones included. In addition, James Lamb was a member of the Athletic Club,[44] its first president being George Inness, Jr., also a painter like his well-known father.[45]

At home on North Fullerton Avenue in the carpentry shop behind the house, James Lamb passed along his knowledge of carpentry and mechanics to Joe and his boyhood friends. It was here that young Joe acquired high-level skills that remained with him for life. His brother, James, Jr., was also a skilled carpenter and, like their father, chose a career as a builder. Joe, however, enjoyed carpentry exclusively as a hobby, although his work exhibited the superior quality of a professional, and he approached all of his projects with great care and enthusiasm. In later years, his sons and son-in-law would often comment about his knowledge and excellence within this area. As an adult, Joe Lamb continually used these carpentry skills in a practical manner for the benefit of his entire family. Even during his retirement years when getting ready for a trip to the family vacation home, he wrote to a friend about the necessity of being prepared for carpentry projects at his destination, cutting short his letter writing because he was worried that he would "never get my tools packed."[46]

Joe's mother, Julia Henneberry (1848–1919), was from Kilkenny, Ireland. She and her husband met after immigrating to the United States and were married in 1871. Julia had a strong appreciation of music, something that she passed along to her children. She had sung in a choir in her native country[47]—one of the few distinguishing details about her that remains. The rich musical tradition of her homeland, though, remained dear and served as inspiration within her family.

Although Julia did not continue on with any musical pursuits herself after coming to Montclair, she encouraged her daughters to study piano. Both took to their lessons with an enthusiasm similar to that of other young women of the time throughout the country. This was surely the age of the piano.

For the Lambs and thousands of others like them in the later nineteenth century, the parlor piano was an important part of the family household. Gaining a domestic stronghold not long after the Civil War, the piano was said to have been only slightly less significant to a home than the kitchen stove.[48] Owning a piano was many times equated with a rise to middle-class respectability—a visible symbol of having achieved the American dream of a better life. This was especially important to immigrant families after struggling to become established in a totally new part of the world. And some portion of the repertoire played on these pianos—from familiar ethnic songs to solo compositions—provided a comforting reminder of the homes that they had left behind. Long before radio and television, these families and their friends gathered around the piano to sing and to play popular waltzes, parlor pieces, and classical compositions—all part of an ordinary evening's entertainment. The Lambs were no exception.

Even President and Mrs. Cleveland figured in this trend. In honor of their wedding in 1886, William Steinway of the Steinway Company presented the president and his bride with the beautiful gift of an elegant piano[49]—a delight for the first lady, who enjoyed playing this instrument. Mrs. Cleveland also helped to further the studies of young women who sought serious musical careers in what was a highly male-dominated profession.[50]

Like Mrs. Cleveland, young women around the country took to studying the piano with keen interest and incorporated this skill into their regular social lives. The pages of the Montclair newspaper were consistently filled with news and reviews of home and church concerts in which women participated, the piano usually an important feature of these events. A December 1895 afternoon "musicale" at a Harrison Avenue home received a detailed review, praising a Miss Noyes for her "brilliant execution" at the keyboard in performing the works of Schubert and Moszkowski as well as for her "intelligent and sympathetic" efforts as accompanist to four other performers.[51] Reviews of this nature were quite common.

Playing the piano, a refined musical pursuit, was believed to elevate the minds of young women and infuse their homes with a sense of harmony, ultimately providing a lovely sanctuary for both husband and family. Simply stated, the ability to play the piano made a woman more attractive as a potential wife and in nineteenth-century America, it was hard to put a price on such a valuable by-product of musical skill. Even Grover Cleveland praised the charms of piano music as a way in which a woman could reach "the heart of her future husband."[52] On the practical side, too, women with musical training could also earn money by teaching piano; and if the advertisements in the Montclair newspaper were any indicator, women were certainly applying their musical knowledge for commercial gain.

Piano manufacturers had begun to reap huge economic rewards from this trend, and competition among them soon reached an all time high. The Columbian Exposition of 1893—better known as the Chicago World's Fair— was the scene of an enormous piano conflict, even before President Cleveland touched the button that raised the flags to signal its official opening. Numerous manufacturers from different regions of the country had planned to display their products at the impressive exhibition site. They were enraged, however, over the proposed judging system that was the basis for granting coveted awards and medals,[53] the acquisition of which were of incalculable value in future marketing endeavors for these firms. All manner of heated controversy followed. From this, it was clearly evident that there were serious financial and reputation building issues at stake within the industry, amply fueled by a public in love with the product.

All over the country, families could buy a piano at a local store or select one from rows of piano showrooms in big cities, their tempting advertisements regularly splashed across the pages of magazines and newspapers. Even remote farm dwellers were never too far off the beaten track to buy a lovely instrument from the wagon of a traveling salesman.

The Montclair Times continually published advertisements for piano firms ranging from Mason & Hamlin and Fischer Pianos in nearby New York City, to the Newark-based Lauter and Dionysius companies. As the years progressed, these advertisements became more numerous. A family had a wide range to choose from in purchasing a suitable model for their home. The Lambs would have had no trouble in obtaining an instrument that could serve as the centerpiece of their parlor and one on which their daughters could practice the pieces assigned to them at their regular piano lessons. A piano — with its bench crammed with collections of printed music — was always there during young Joe's formative years.

"When I was a kid my folks had a Sohmer Square Grand,"[54] he reminisced, recalling the appealing sound of this piano, already a part of his home before he was born. Sohmer was a well respected manufacturer, and the presence of this instrument in the Lamb household showed that they placed an important emphasis on music as a part of their family life.

Both of Joe's sisters were serious piano students, having studied with a Professor Hatterslee who taught at St. Elizabeth's Academy and also played the organ at the cathedral in Newark.[55] Katharine — known as "Kate" — the older of the two, also took lessons with several other top teachers in the Montclair area, including a Mrs. Marrin.[56] Like many local musicians, she became a professional piano teacher, "not because they [the Lambs] needed the money, but [because] Kate wanted to do something."[57] Also a fine organist, she performed frequently at the Church of the Immaculate Conception and, as noted in *The Montclair Times*,[58] was eventually responsible for the Christmas service music there. According to her nephew, Kate was "paid $150 p.a. for playing the Immaculate Conception organ"[59] and was later awarded a silver crucifix by Father Mendl, upon his return from an Austrian trip, for her contributions to the church through her music.[60]

Anastasia—nicknamed "Sta"—earned a scholarship to study music at St. Elizabeth's based upon her accomplishments at the keyboard. She was the closest to her younger brother in age, and he named his first published composition in her honor during his teenage years. Sta may also have proven to be more of an adaptable pianist than originally surmised, later on playing other than the strictly classical repertoire learned during her youthful studies, which had been a mix of "serious and light classical" and included "Bach, Beethoven (sonatas etc.)."[61] However, beyond this, Sta had to have possessed an ability to read and improvise from some form of lead sheets used for standard popular music when she performed as an alternate pianist in an ensemble formed by her brother and her future husband.

With a piano in the house and two sisters who continually practiced their lessons, young Joseph Lamb had a front row seat from which to hear good music as well as an excellent opportunity to develop strong musical interests. He was magnetized by the piano, despite the fact that this was a quiet pursuit in contrast to his usually energetic outdoor activities with friends. Like many boys of the time, however, he was not sent for formal piano lessons. It seems clear, though, that Julia Lamb understood and supported her son's musical leanings. (Later, when he paid tribute to her, it was through music. Beneath the title of early his waltz "Mignonne" were the words "respectfully dedicated to my mother."[62])

As a young boy, Joe continually listened to the classical repertoire that his sisters practiced, absorbing its many styles and sounds—the harmonic textures, melodies, rhythms, and phrase structures that distinguished each work. His curiosity was intense.

But he was compelled to do more than just sit quietly and listen. By the time he was eight years old (his nephew

Anastasia Lamb (circa 1908–09), one of Lamb's two sisters who showed him the notes on the piano (courtesy Mary Van Gieson).

stated that it could have been as early as age six),[63] Joe approached his sisters with repeated requests to be shown the notes on the piano. Kate and Sta treated these requests with good humor. They were older than Joe, however, and were busy enough with their own studies and activities to be unable to spend too much time with him, the type of time required to provide systematic piano instruction. Later, Sta's son Paul remembered his mother commenting that she and Kate didn't teach Joe but "they'd always answer any of his questions and show him anything."[64] But his most pressing request was to be shown what the notes were on the piano, and this is what his sisters did for him.

Joe remembered that he got his "first crack at learning the notes and their relation to the keys on the piano"[65] at the family's lovely square Sohmer grand. Sta and Kate also gave him a book that they had used in their own beginning piano lessons. He accepted this gift with his characteristic enthusiasm, delving into it with gusto "instead of doing homework,"[66] he confessed. Although Sta and Kate pointed him in the right direction, the young boy plunged into learning on his own. He was content to work by trial and error, totally absorbed in the process of figuring out the notes and their contexts. He continued to study not only using the book but also becoming acquainted with other printed music as well as with the musical magazines belonging to his sisters.

Soon Joe decided that in addition to learning to play the piano that he, too, wanted to take some of those mysterious symbols and form them into something of his own. He wanted to compose. Early on it was obvious that he possessed an innate ability to absorb and remember much of what he heard—something that was true both then and in later years—drawing on it in a variety of innovative ways to build upon and enrich his own work. As a composer, he would put all of it to use, experimenting at first and then developing his own style that grew from his innate creative gifts as well as from his exposure to an eclectic mix of musical elements.

At first, Joe's musical manuscripts looked like dots on the paper or, more accurately, in his words, "just little round black notes."[67] These notes were not punctuated with time signatures or rests or any of the usual markings associated with printed music or even with a roughly drafted composition. Note values were non-existent. There was no indication that these markings were produced by someone who had taken piano lessons or had any theoretical training. "I sort of doped out something on the piano," Joe said, and "wrote them [the notes] on paper."[68] It was a start.

Joe would then repeatedly ask Kate and Sta to look at these notes and to play them on the piano. Of course it made little sense at first. To his sisters' credit, though, they obligingly agreed to keep trying to decipher his early attempts at creating songs and little compositions, giving him a sense of how the paper markings could translate into real sound.

Joe persisted and, in time, those little round black notes began to coalesce into something more unified and recognizable. These youthful experiments in composition, not to mention the boy's determination, must have made an impression on both Kate and Sta. Joe later recalled a somewhat prophetic comment made by one sister to the other: "maybe Joe will write music some day."[69] He would — and before too much time was to pass.

By this time, the Lambs had replaced the square grand with a new Sohmer Upright Grand. This brand of piano was a popular one and well advertised in music periodicals since the firm specialized in selling their instruments for home use. Sohmer declared that it prided itself on using the best materials and finest craftsmanship possible, always striving to preserve the firm's integrity — it was part of the "Sohmer Creed."[70] This was the time when Joe began working more seriously at playing the piano and developing his penchant for composing. "Then I started going in earnest,"[71] he later said, fondly remembering that new piano and how he eventually composed some of his famous rags at this instrument.

Throughout Joe's youth, Kate and Sta subscribed to a popular magazine — *The Etude* — a highly respected publication issued by the Theodore Presser Company of Philadelphia. It reached homes all over the country for more than half a century, its beautifully rendered covers bearing the likenesses of famous composers, contemporary performers, and musical themes — all hinting at the treasure trove of information within. *The Etude*'s pages were crammed with articles, tips for dealing with technical and performing issues, reviews of all sorts, advertisements for pianos and teachers, and relevant musical news. But its most popular feature was the large selection of playable music that was offered in each issue. According to famed music journalist and contemporary observer Henry T. Finck, the magazine had a million readers and did "more to educate America musically than any individual except Theodore Thomas."[72]

The Etude in particular — and other magazines issued by publishing firms and pedagogical groups — helped to spread the appeal of the piano even further. Joe Lamb mentioned *The Etude* in later years because of his access to it through his sisters. With his unflagging curiosity and habit of closely studying any subject of interest, he assimilated valuable information from its pages — consciously and subconsciously. (He said that Ethelbert Nevin's "Nightingale Song" — something he saw in *The Etude* — was among the several inspirations for his famous composition "Ragtime Nightingale."[73]) The magazine also helped to build his piano playing skills. His nephew, Paul Van Gieson, later said that Joe "did do exercises, etc., from the Etude."[74] Beyond this, Joe's seriousness about studying classical music published in the pages of this magazine and elsewhere was reflected in his remembrances of playing some Mendelssohn as well as Bach in his youthful days. ("I liked Bach,"[75] he later confessed.) He suggested that such classical music might have "had something to do with the kind of Rags I wrote."[76] He managed to blend the two styles, both in his playing as well as in his composing. However his sisters, well trained in the classics, later attempted to play some of his ragtime compositions, and the resulting effect sounded "like a hymn."[77]

The wide selection of repertoire provided in *The Etude* during Joe's early years offered ample resources to draw upon during a lifetime of composing. During the closing years of the 1890s alone, the magazine published such traditional pieces as Chopin's Prelude, Op. 28, #15 and Bach's "Little Prelude in D," as well as piano arrangements of works ranging from the "Star-Spangled Banner" to Wagner's "Prize Song" from *Die Meistersinger*. Then there were such enduring favorites as Foster's "My Old Kentucky Home" and Cecile Chaminade's "Scarf Dance."[78] These and countless other compositions offered inspiration in many forms, from little rhythmic motifs and harmonic ideas, to a lingering phrase or stylistic turn that could later combine with something else to serve as a springboard for a new musical creation.

By the late 1890s, Joe was improving his piano technique and composing skills while still enjoying the carefree days of his Montclair boyhood. He was also aware of other musical styles during this time in addition to the classical music played by his sisters. These trends in popular music and culture were reflected in the wide variety of entertainment available at the Montclair Club and other venues as well as at civic, church group, and social events; and some of them were closely associated with new developments within the music publishing industry.

Popular music and culture were being dramatically transformed, and some industrious young pioneers filled with enthusiasm and entrepreneurial drive were a major force in this phenomenon. By the time that Joe was born, some important transitions had already taken place. Established, traditional music publishers such as Oliver Ditson and William A. Pond had been the norm, their reserved and low-keyed approaches to marketing keeping their businesses afloat but a bit out of the wider mainstream focus. These firms were content to concentrate, for the most part, on such repertoire as piano waltzes, marches, and arrangements of opera themes. By the 1880s, though, things began to change.

Some enterprising young men began shifting the emphasis of their companies in order to issue popular songs that were singable, playable, of current interest, and more appealing to a larger audience. Frank Harding was among the first, cultivating a group of songwriters who offered their manuscripts to him for a mere $10 apiece. Soon, the trio of Witmark brothers successfully launched their landmark business after a grassroots-type beginning in 1886 with the sale of their sheet music for "President Cleveland's Wedding March." These young men (all under the age of eighteen at the time) had marketing savvy and seized their opportunity by choosing something topical for a song, releasing it at the just the right time, and promoting it with vigor.

Suddenly it seemed that everyone was writing songs and opening publishing firms. Former button, shoe, and corset salesmen were abandoning their jobs for careers in songwriting and publishing, sure that they would strike it rich in the rapidly commercializing world of popular music. And many of them did. It seemed that almost anyone could write and sell a song. Music appeared to be pure gold.

"Take note of public demand,"[79] counseled another pioneering songwriter/publisher, Charles K. Harris. His mega-hit "After the Ball" sold millions of copies and was enthusiastically received on the New York stage and at the Chicago World's Fair. Some of those copies reached the Montclair of Joe's boyhood. The song's sad and sentimental words and music resonated in many a parlor there after dinner. Harris gauged what the public wanted and aggressively sold to his audience. This straightforward formula caught on.

And so, the world of music publishing began to change, and it would continue to do so alongside American life itself, with its introduction of electricity, new theatrical forms, nickelodeons, crazes for bicycles, horseless carriages, phonographs, and many other inventions and trends. It was a time of exciting transition, and popular music represented it all — keeping the lingering nostalgia of the Victorian age while, at the same time, embracing the young, the new, and the modern in songwriting and composition. Music reflected and permeated all phases of life.

Popular repertoire was now regularly enjoyed by young and old. In Montclair itself, stated a contemporary observer, the town's "young people grouped about the piano singing such new songs as Hot Time in the Old Town, Band Played On.... My Wild Irish Rose."[80] Songs like these could be heard on thousands of pianos in American homes, and they were also beginning to be heard "on wax cylindrical records, by one of the wonders of the age, the graphophone, or phonograph."[81]

The writing, publishing, and distributing of popular music had more and more turned into an enormous profit-driven industry, feeding the buying public's continual appetite for the most current of songs and instrumentals. This was the music heard in theaters, vaudeville houses, restaurants, local halls, on the street, in department stores, and at friendly gatherings. It was music that could be brought home and played on the piano for all to enjoy — accompanied by singing as well as by additional instruments. There were sen-

timental songs, tributes to people and inventions, marches, comic fare, minstrel songs, and dances in the popular cakewalk style — something that had
become the rage during the last decade of the century. For a young boy such
as Joe with clear musical acumen, there had never been a better time to become
acquainted with all types of musical styles and subjects — and to begin composing.

The new publishing firms that introduced this music to the public had
a pushy and aggressive approach, one that engaged in hard-driven marketing
practices and shrewdly incorporated attractive artwork and photographs on
the covers of the sheet music to enhance its visual appeal. This would further
turn the popular music world around with its definite emphasis on the business of making money quickly through a strong combination of advertising
practices. These new firms were uniquely American in style, with high energy
and ingenuity, capable of introducing a greater volume and variety of music
to the public in a rapid turnaround time.

By the turn of the century, these companies had congregated in a fairly
well delineated area of New York City eventually referred to as Tin Pan Alley.
Popular music publishing would never be the same. And even at a very young
age, Joe was aware of it all.

There was also another American phenomenon starting to draw the public's attention during this time, as well. It was a unique musical style that had
been continuously evolving in honky tonks and social clubs, especially those
across the Midwest. The sound was rhythmic and magnetic and joyous. It
was ragtime.

Ragtime captured a wider public attention during the 1893 Chicago
World's Fair but this was more on an unofficial level. On the premises of the
fair itself, much was made of music and the wide variety of offerings there.
The Musical Courier devoted generous space to describing concerts featuring
repertoire composed by Gounod, Rossini, Liszt, and Sousa, as well as Algerian,
Russian, and Irish works — not to mention music performed in honor of the
poet, Thomas Moore's birthday. "There is no music under the sun that cannot
be heard in Chicago in these days,"[82] stated the fifth in a series of letters entitled "Music at the World's Fair." The word ragtime wasn't mentioned —
exactly.

However the author of *The Musical Courier* letter made an interesting
observation in response to Antonin Dvorak's famed comments about what
he felt should be the basis of true American music — negro melodies. "There
is a large germ of truth in Dr. Dvorak's assertion as to the inevitable influence
negro melodies are to exert on our national music," wrote W. Waugh Lauder
in his letter from the fair. "The minstrel troupes have settled that for us.... Is
it not strange that no one has thought of giving real old-time minstrelsy at

or near the Fair? ... We had better get right down to business and hear and study these tunes."[83] Perhaps the author was aware that this and other sounds of music were just within reach.

Scott Joplin, Ben Harney, and other ragtime figures were said to have been in Chicago but no records have yet been found of their performances of ragtime inside the official boundaries of the fairgrounds—one quite reasonable explanation being, as suggested by scholar Edward A. Berlin, that this style of music had not at that point "found its name."[84] Instead, ragtime was likely performed at nearby saloons and other popular (and occasionally less-than-straight-laced) venues, where crowds would have naturally gravitated and subsequently discovered this musical sound that was too infectious to be ignored. Its popularity was going to spread even further, and Tin Pan Alley was ready to welcome it warmly.

Drawing from cakewalks, marches, folk melodies, coon songs, and an amalgam of rhythmic and structural influences, ragtime's captivating style and sound were still evolving and were often difficult to precisely define. The style had syncopation but not all syncopation was ragtime. Nevertheless, Tin Pan Alley would eventually push beyond the boundaries of any of this form's reasonable definitions in order to suit its own economic ends, succeeding in marketing almost any piece of music as ragtime and driving the public crazy for all of it. There would be ragtime instrumentals, songs, and dances, and a staggering array of variations within each category. Was it all really ragtime—even if it contained the word "rag" in the title? Tin Pan Alley didn't care, and much of the public who bought this music over the next decade or so didn't seem to care either.

By the time Joe turned ten years old in 1897 and was spending some serious energy at the piano, ragtime was on the rise. During January of that year William Krell's "Mississippi Rag" was published, and it led the way for other compositions similar in style or with "rag" as a part of their titles—many of them now beginning to be heard onstage in music halls and in other entertainment venues in larger cities. Ben Harney—composer of such popular works as "Mr. Johnson, Turn Me Loose"—proclaimed himself the "Inventor of Ragtime,"[85] and became a star attraction at Tony Pastor's music hall in New York. (Such entertainment venues were not just limited to New York City either. The Paramount in Newark, New Jersey, nearby to Montclair, opened in 1895 as a vaudeville theatre, one of many similar houses that were thriving everywhere.) Tin Pan Alley and ragtime were now beginning to join forces and, with the popularity of the piano at an all-time high, the whole combination would soon be unbeatable.

In the meantime, Joe's hard work was beginning to pay off. Now he possessed fairly proficient skills at the piano,[86] and he was getting a sense of various musical styles, working at developing his own take on them in his continuing attempts to compose. A number of factors came together to Joe's advantage. He was fortunate to have had serious exposure to classical music, to live in a town that had a wide range of musical and cultural offerings and was nearby to New York, and to be coming of age when many new developments were taking place in popular music as well as in the world at large. Now when his sisters sat down at the piano to play what he had written, it was a different story than it had been earlier. "You could have knocked me over with a feather," recalled Joe years later, "when it sounded like what I had in mind."[87] He continued to progress and his compositions took a recognizable shape. He even began writing lyrics.

Around the same time, two men who lived far away from Montclair were on the threshold of making musical history. Itinerant pianist and composer Scott Joplin and music store entrepreneur and emerging publisher John Stark met in the town of Sedalia, Missouri. The deal they struck would reverberate through the music world and down through history with the publication of Joplin's famous "Maple Leaf Rag" in 1899. It came to be known as a classic ragtime composition, not just any Tin Pan Alley variation or imitation.

This deal would change the lives of both men, while helping to bring real ragtime further front and center in the public eye. Eventually everyone would want to play "Maple Leaf Rag"—from the home pianist to John Philip Sousa's band. And even though Joe Lamb hadn't even quite entered his teens yet and lived far from the site of this momentous event, it would change his world, too.

"Maple Leaf Rag" was destined to become one of the most popular ragtime titles of all time. Both Joplin and Stark would leave Sedalia and begin their individual treks east as their mutual success widened, settling first in St. Louis and then in New York. It was a musical, commercial, and personal journey for each. And the young man from Montclair, New Jersey, with a growing passion for the piano and for writing music was now at the beginning of his own journey — one that would eventually lead him into ragtime and directly into the orbit of John Stark and Scott Joplin.

Two

From New Jersey to Canada (1900–1904)

"Walper House Rag"— Joe Lamb's first titled rag

The young people of Montclair danced a festive cakewalk in celebration of the opening days of the New Year 1900. It was the joyous conclusion to a minstrel show organized for the benefit of Mountainside Hospital's building fund, and the large audience that filled Montclair Club Hall was delighted by the "jokes, popular songs, banjo [and] buck and wing,"[1] not to forget Issler's Orchestra of Newark that provided music for the evening.

Cakewalks had been the rage for several years, and their popularity spilled over into the new century. A dance with complex origins in the African American culture, it evolved into a vivacious parody of the stiff formality of white ballroom dancers. The cakewalk, though, was eventually embraced by everyone, including the population it originally satirized. Onstage as well as at public and private functions, everyone strutted with exaggerated steps and eccentric movements as couples marched in promenade formation.

Vaudevillians Dora Dean and Charles Johnson helped ignite the cakewalk craze in the early 1890s. Several years later, the famed team of Bert Williams and George Walker successfully used it in their own shows, achieving even greater notoriety after humorously challenging William K. Vanderbilt to a cakewalking contest, after it was learned that the railroad heir had hired an instructor to teach him the dance.[2] Teddy Roosevelt was to eventually lead a cakewalk promenade at the White House, and, on one of their tours, John Philip Sousa's band created a frenzy among the French as they danced to its sound by the Eiffel Tower.

Cakewalk music was comprised of upbeat, syncopated tunes. Everyone wanted to try writing in this style. *The Etude* magazine — usually more traditional in its content — published the "South Car'lina Tickle: Cake Walk" by Adam Geibel in its 1898 holiday issue.[3] Even the classical composer Claude

31

Debussy composed "Golliwog's Cakewalk" as part of his famed *Children's Corner Suite* a few years later in 1908. People loved the cakewalk, and some of Lamb's earliest compositions showed the influence of this style, as well.

A top enduring favorite in this category was the 1897 hit song "At a Georgia Camp Meeting," written by the Tin Pan Alley songwriter and publisher Kerry Mills. Joe Lamb may have had more than his usual curiosity about this hit tune, since Mills was listed in the Montclair directory beginning shortly after the turn of the century.[4] He remained in the town through the following decade during which Joe Lamb still lived in Montclair.

Although the cakewalk and its appealing music lingered into the opening years of the century, it was already overlapping with ragtime, the two styles often referred to synonymously because of their use of syncopation. The term "rag" was gaining increasing attention from the public, though, and it was used on a freewheeling basis by songwriters—both correctly and not so—because of heightened public interest in the style. "Mississippi Rag" was already in print, and Tony Pastor and other theatrical impresarios increasingly featured ragtime performers. "Classic ragtime"—a segment of the form that would occupy its own distinctive place—would begin to enter the mix on a larger scale in the short-term future.

While cakewalks were usually written with dancing in mind, ragtime was not quite so focused, although it was also used for dancing. Real ragtime was more difficult to define as a form than the cakewalk—complex in structure and composed with instrumental performance in mind, with a name that was attributed to a wider range of compositions. Some of it leaned towards classical compositions in many ways. However, both cakewalk and ragtime forms danced together on their own through the turn of the century; then the cakewalk graciously drifted to the sidelines and allowed ragtime to take a larger share of the spotlight—just around the time that Lamb was achieving a more significant grasp of the piano and a greater acquaintance with theory and composing techniques.

At the same time, the range of other popular repertoire was continually expanding. Coon and ethnic songs, sentimental ballads, cakewalks, parodies, marches, waltzes, rags of all sorts, and standards were joined by new styles and variations on existing ones. The heyday of popular music had arrived, and the music publishing business had pyramided impressively.

The heart of the industry, once centered near Union Square in New York, was now located along West 28th Street between Broadway and Sixth Avenue and its nearby environs. It supposedly received the name Tin Pan Alley in the New York *Herald* sometime in 1903 from songwriter, newspaperman, and local character Monroe Rosenfeld who said that the noise up and down the whole street sounded like the clanging of tin pans. (This explanation is the most popular, although there are several variations.) Reminiscing about this lively and notorious district, veteran songwriter and publisher Charles K. Harris said: "My memory will always cling around dear old Tin Pan Alley.... What a lane of hilarious melody!"[5] Yet by the time this area actually received its famous name, it was already sowing the seeds of its restless move northward.

This popular music phenomenon was getting increasing recognition. *The Music Trade Review*'s first January issue of 1900 concentrated mostly on discussions of classical music and developments in piano manufacturing, accompanied by copious advertisements for related products.[6] One year later, however, the same publication included numerous items about the popular music world — where to obtain full scores and orchestrations for *Floradora*, listings for Weber and Fields' "two splendid burlesques," and news of the success of Sol Bloom's "Coon, Coon, Coon" as performed by Johnson and Dean.[7]

Advertisements for traditional piano companies were now just pages away from glowing publicity items for such popular Tin Pan Alley firms as M. Witmark & Sons; Shapiro, Bernstein & Von Tilzer; and F.A. Mills (the publishing company owned by composer Kerry Mills). The Alley was on the rise and fascination with popular music along with it.

These ongoing developments kindled the eager musical curiosity and imagination of young Joseph Lamb — from the culture and content of the music to the growth of the business that published it. There was no way to avoid knowing at least something about the continually developing musical scene of the time, and Lamb embraced it with a whole heart. By now, his little round black notes had transformed themselves into complete pieces of music, his first unpublished songs dating from the year 1900. They reflected the diverse influences from which Lamb drew, including *The Etude* and its usually sedate repertoire as well as the definitely popular Tin Pan Alley style.

"Meet Me at the Chutes" — a lighthearted piece in waltz time about Coney Island — was a composition for which Lamb wrote both music and lyrics in 1900. Songs about this popular Brooklyn locale — whose fame as an entertainment and amusement center was well known beyond its immediate boundaries — were already in print. Among them was the tune, "At Dear Old Coney Isle" (1897) by Charles B. Lawlor, who had also composed the melody for the famous "Sidewalks of New York" in 1894. Lamb was aware of the musical and popular interest in the place and of the trend to immortalize this and other specific locales in song. (In an ironic twist on his choice of topic for this early work, he would years later reside in an area neighboring this famous amusement center.)

"Meet Me at the Chutes" referred to the popular "Shoot-the-Chutes" water slide in Coney Island's Sea Lion Park, the late 1890s predecessor to the famous Luna Park, which opened in 1904.[8] The song is about a couple who plan to travel to Coney Island — a trolley ride from the city, as described in the verse — and meet at the chutes for an evening's amusement. Although the opening lyrics suggest that the young man needs to convince his sweetheart about what a lovely time they will have, by the end of the chorus the young woman is totally caught up in the spirit of things, singing: "I'm your little girl/You can call me your pearl/If you meet me at the chutes."[9] The subject of Coney Island was one that Lamb would revisit again as did other song-writers, its promise of fun mirroring both the spirit and the music of the years prior to World War I.

In the same year Lamb wrote "Idle Dreams," a short piece for piano. This composition is evocative of the dreamy mood suggested by its title. It possesses an interesting feature that foreshadows Lamb's approach in his future composing. He begins in the key of F sharp — certainly not one of the easier keys to work with as a newer pianist and composer. In later years, how-ever, he wrote in similarly difficult keys for the simple reason that this was how the music best appealed to him. Nevertheless, in 1900, at an early time in his composing efforts, this was an impressive challenge and illustrates his deep commitment to working with different musical nuances and complex-ities.

It is possible that Lamb composed something else during this year as well, further underlining his keen youthful observations of trends in theater and performance repertoire. During a visit to his home almost half a century later, researchers Rudi Blesh and Harriet Janis spied a cover containing a "florid hand-lettered title" which read "COONTOWN FROLICS Two-Step by J. Francis Lamb," underneath which was written "One of Lamb's Famous Hits."[10] (It appeared as if he had been experimenting with a change in his name's presentation, possibly inspired by local Montclair music store pro-prietor, J. Melvin Bush, or perhaps even an early acknowledgement of others who used this style, including J. Fred Helf, a prolific songwriter/publisher for whom Lamb would eventually work years later.)

Lamb's title page for this work was dated 1900. Later, he said that he couldn't find the composition and wondered if only the cover might have existed.[11] Yet the words on this cover alone showed that he was aware of the many current types of popular music, including coon songs, and showed a willingness to experiment by composing in this genre, something he again tried several years later.

Coon songs were popular during Lamb's boyhood — syncopated in sound and regrettably stereotypical in their portrayal of black individuals and cul-ture. They were, however, a regular staple of the minstrel show and vaudeville stage and used by both black and white performers. This song genre even reached Broadway in such productions as the 1898 Cole and Johnson hit show, *A Trip to Coontown*. The wave of popularity for this style served as inspiration for Lamb. In addition, the "famous hits" phrase on the cover recollected by Blesh and Janis showed that he knew the types of advertising jargon that appeared on popular sheet music and in its related promotional materials.

Despite the emphasis on classical music in the Lamb household because of his sisters' studies, Joe Lamb had ample opportunity to be exposed to other types of music — popular genres included. For one, there was Montclair's own music store operated by J. Melvin Bush. This business was consistently advertised in Montclair newspapers and directories throughout Lamb's youth, emphasizing pianos for sale and for rent in addition to its well-stocked supplies of sheet music, piano rolls and, eventually, "talking machines." Bush himself was a versatile entrepreneur and musician. In addition to running the store at 501 Bloomfield Avenue (near the corner of North Fullerton Avenue), he was a respected organist at the First Presbyterian Church and "well known in musical circles."[12] Previously he had risen through the ranks at the C.A. Dionysius piano store in Newark, buying out their stock and moving to Montclair in 1900.[13] And, as if that were not enough, he lived in the neighborhood near the Lambs—first on Midland Avenue and later on North Fullerton Avenue itself. Lamb had easy geographic access to the store and its proprietor. Bush's was a town fixture and a good resource for the musically inclined.

Perhaps one of the most direct ways, though, in which Lamb would have become familiar with current song trends was through the newspapers. Sheet music was inserted into the Sunday supplements of the larger papers, a system that was championed by William Randolph Hearst to widen the circulation of his paper, *The New York Journal*. Although it was not unusual to find songs in some publications prior to this, Hearst raised it to an art beginning in the mid–1890s and thereafter and, not surprisingly, coinciding with the rise of Tin Pan Alley. The public was always in the market for new music since the piano was in its heyday as a prime source of home and local entertainment.

Hearst wanted to sell newspapers and beat out the competition; and songwriters were only too happy to join forces with him to spread their own names and increase the sale of their sheet music in the stores. He embraced this system with gusto, creating two new Sunday sections that carried music. Although the *New York World* and the *Herald* also jumped on the musical supplement bandwagon, Hearst outranked them all. He was a master. From vaudeville and burlesque to musical theater, he printed works by three hundred composers over a sixteen-year period — the songs of George M. Cohan, Reginald DeKoven, Chauncey Olcott, Bob Cole, and many others, with a repertoire covering topical songs, coon songs, ballads, and more.[14] Readers of

The New York Journal could open its pages to find anything from Victor Herbert's "The American Girl March" (for piano) and May Irwin's famous "Bully Song," to "Coney Island," "My Creole Sue," and "Poor O'Hoolahan."[15] Never one to stint on going all out, Hearst also tempted readers with beautiful artwork and photos on the sheet music covers—a tactic already effectively employed by Tin Pan Alley in order to make the music even more irresistible.

By the turn of the century, inserting musical supplements was an established practice used by almost two dozen major newspapers countrywide,[16] and one that continued for years. These supplements offered Lamb a fine opportunity to study popular repertoire of the day and to become acquainted with a vast range of styles. With his family's interests in politics, business affairs, and cultural matters, newspapers were certainly regular reading matter in the household. Given Montclair's thriving newsstands and proximity to New York, these papers were readily available. Several Montclair news dealers were located nearby to the Lamb family home, including Hooe's at 449 Bloomfield Avenue and Rudensey's at 82 Walnut Street, and these establishments were noted for the number and variety of publications that they carried.

General magazines also printed pieces of music and might have been another source of inspiration for the young composer. The *Ladies' Home Journal* was known for championing music as well as for publishing compositions in their pages from the early 1890s through the 1920s. Charles K. Harris wrote of winning a $500 prize from the magazine in a contest for the best ballad by an American composer.[17] Other periodicals followed similar practices—from family and cultural publications to those with religious and political themes. Both classical and popular type repertoires were featured,[18] again offering a wealth of material for study. Kate and Sta would surely have expressed an interest in some of these magazines, and their younger brother would have gravitated to the music immediately.

Music was everywhere in 1900, aided by a newspaper circulation of more than 15 million daily and a roster of 1,800 published magazines in the United States.[19] Lamb had numerous opportunities to hear, buy, and see music of all sorts, and his passion resulted in growing accomplishments at the piano and in composition.

This beginning of the new century was an exciting time, one of innovation and change. Music was evolving in many exciting ways, and it joined literature, invention, reform, fashion, and theater in breaking new ground. The International Ladies' Garment Workers Union was founded; and the shirtwaist became a fashion staple. Carrie Nation attacked her first saloon in the name of temperance; and the shocking novel *Sister Carrie* came from the pen of Theodore Dreiser—brother of songwriter Paul Dresser. The public was already in love with images that moved on a screen but now Eastman Kodak released its popular new Brownie camera with a price tag of one dollar so that anyone could freeze an image in time. Risqué Floradora girls debuted on Broadway; and vaudeville shows, both high class and low, continued to pack in audiences on ever-widening travel circuits. Life was changing quickly, and it was doing so on a grand scale.

Life was also changing for the Lambs. Although things seemed to be going smoothly for them at the year's beginning, events were about to take a sad turn for the entire family. In an almost chilling clue to the future, Lamb's friend Paul Hughes remembered that as kids they "often went to the drugstore in Montclair Center to get medicine for Joe's dad, who was ill for quite a time."[20] Then, in October of 1900, James Lamb passed away at the untimely age of 54. *The Montclair Times* called him "one of Montclair's most respected citizens" and "a self-made man" who rose to well-deserved success in his thirty years within the community.[21]

His loss was devastating for all. Joe Lamb was only twelve years old at the time. His generous and loving father was gone. James Lamb had been an important influence in his life in many ways, particularly as a fine example of a good family man, a role that his son would assume with devotion himself in later years.

Lamb experienced a troublesome time after his father's death. An adventurous boy by nature and just entering his teen years at the close of 1900, he was in the throes of understandable grief. His siblings were older and involved in their own lives, with less time to devote to their younger brother. Julia Lamb soon realized that controlling her youngest son was becoming a challenge, particularly at a time when she was coping with her own grief and adjustment to life as a widow. She felt that he needed a strong male presence to guide him during the next few years and to ensure that his energies and emotions followed a positive direction.

As a result, Julia decided to send him to St. Jerome's College in Berlin (now Kitchener), Ontario — a Catholic prep school and seminary in Canada. Although there has been much speculation over the years that Julia might have wanted her son to become a priest, this was not really the case. She just wanted to be sure that he developed a sense of discipline within a "cultured masculine environment."[22] It is not known why Julia chose a school at such a distance — and a Canadian one at that. The move might well have been suggested by a clergyman at the local church since the Lambs were devout members there, and Julia and the entire family must have relied strongly upon this community for spiritual and emotional support after James's death.

Although an exact month has not been pinpointed, Lamb later stated that he arrived at St. Jerome's in 1901.[23] Presumably the months following his father's death and the early portion of 1901 would have been devoted to completing the current school year in Montclair while allowing Julia time to arrive at her decision to send him to Canada. Then there would certainly have been details to finalize such as settling admissions and transportation matters.

An advertisement for St. Jerome's College published in 1904 stressed its location on the "main line of Grand Trunk Railway."[24] This would have made the school quite accessible from distant points such as New Jersey as well as to and from major cities in Canada, including Toronto. The school flexibly admitted students at any time during the year and offered academic, commercial, and arts programs in preparation for higher degrees and professional studies as well as training for the seminary — all for $140 annual board and tuition.[25]

Lamb was a small young man for his age, looking younger than his thirteen years as 1901 arrived. Making the trip to Canada to live so far from home was surely overwhelming, even for a spirit as adventurous as his. He had enjoyed living in Montclair and was secure in the house where he had grown up surrounded by family and friends. Now he was off to live in a town that was seventy-five miles outside of Toronto — not only in a far country but also in an area with its own entirely unique ethnic concentration and culture. It was a different world from the one of the tree-lined street on North Fullerton Avenue, where sweet melodies were played on the Sohmer piano in the parlor. St. Jerome's promised to be a distinct change from the familiar streets of Montclair, New Jersey, and one that did not please the young, grief-stricken boy at the outset.

Lamb was terribly homesick after his arrival in Canada and might have also been feeling a bit rebellious at this turn of events in his life. At one point early on, he wrote to his mother saying that if she did not send him the money for transportation back to Montclair then he would walk home instead. Years later his wife jokingly commented that she was surprised that he didn't actually make good on this threat because of his strong-willed nature.[26]

Fortunately, Lamb eventually settled into his new surroundings, his characteristic resilience, adaptability, and curiosity taking over. He soon made good use of the chance to explore not only his new home but also its unique musical life as well. Lamb reminisced long after his departure from St. Jerome's: "The only foreign country I ever visited is Canada.... I love Canada."[27] It was a country that would weave in and out of his musical world throughout his life, holding interesting opportunities and warm memories.

St. Jerome's was located in Berlin, Ontario, Canada — a close sister village to Waterloo. Although the land for both of these villages originally changed hands several times, it was eventually settled by Pennsylvania Mennonites at the beginning of the 1800s. They sought a locale where they could worship freely. Each of the villages was formally incorporated by the mid-nineteenth century. Because of its German-Mennonite roots and spirit of religious tolerance, a multi-faceted German-speaking population gravitated to the region. All of these settlers brought a rich heritage of language, culture, and music there as well as their fine skills as craftsmen and farmers.[28]

By the time Lamb arrived at St. Jerome's, the Berlin-Waterloo area was thriving and filled with manufacturers, being particularly well known for its furniture and leather industries, as well as for a diverse array of individual businesses. A "made in Berlin" label signified excellence, and this reputation spread far beyond its local boundaries. The success of these firms was enhanced by the town's proximity to the fine transportational network provided by Canada's Grand Trunk Railway,[29] a system that had been extended to Berlin in 1856 and one that allowed the area to prosper commercially. An active and well-run city by the opening years of the twentieth century when Lamb made his home there, Berlin boasted twenty churches, three public parks, five banks, and according to the pamphlet, "Busy Berlin," published in 1901, only one policeman to patrol the quiet, almost problem-free streets.[30]

By this time, approximately three-quarters of the population were of German heritage, a unique cultural stamp in Ontario. It was an ethnic group that enjoyed music with great enthusiasm. Band music was especially popular, and singing schools and their associated choral societies held large festivals that were well attended.[31] It was enough to draw the curiosity of a homesick boy in a new land who loved music, something to occupy his attention and help in the adjustment process—and something that would add to his storehouse of musical knowledge.

Lamb was busy not only with his schoolwork but also with exploring his new environs at every opportunity, observing many of its unusual (to him) cultural features. He began to carefully absorb and analyze the sound, style, rhythms, and content of the omnipresent German music. Years later he spoke about the extent of the Germanic culture in Berlin outside the walls of St. Jerome's. According to him, it permeated "darn near everything going on outside of the educational phase.... Folksongs, games and everything."[32] Although he may not have taken a liking to all of these cultural components (he reportedly hated sauerkraut[33]), he was certainly intrigued by its musical features.

Lamb eventually adapted to life at St. Jerome's. Although he had no calling to become a priest, he did set his sights on a career in electrical engineering, influenced by all of the superb training that he obtained from his father in the building business. As a result, he concentrated on the school's pre-engineering studies program. A small, wiry boy with years of outdoor adventures in the spacious surroundings of Montclair behind him, he also gravitated towards athletic activities; participating in some of the special events at St. Jerome's. At the American Thanksgiving Sport Program, he placed well in various running and jumping events.[34]

Lamb made friends at school, too, and obviously became an integral member of his class group, even taking part in the customs that were created by the students themselves. One experience in particular stands out under the heading of memorable youthful capers and showed his enthusiasm for being a congenial part of his peer group. St. Jerome's school guidelines dictated that students had to do without butter at their meals once a week. The enterprising boys, of course, dreamed up their own system to bypass this rule. Each week a different student volunteer would go into town to buy butter and bring it back for all. When it was Lamb's turn, he was so excited to run back to school with his purchase, something he did with enormous speed, that he smashed into a wall and broke his nose.[35]

When not engaged in adventures with contraband food, Lamb continued to compose and became even more serious about gaining skills at the piano. He was already quite accomplished. According to his sister Sta, he began taking piano lessons from a priest at the school but quit several weeks into the

Detail from a class photograph taken at St. Jerome's. Joe Lamb is on the bottom row, second from right (courtesy Patricia Lamb Conn).

program, saying that he was learning nothing and didn't want his mother to spend the money if it was not worthwhile. He was also later quoted as saying that he did not study piano at St. Jerome's at all,[36] perhaps because of the short duration of the lessons.

In a letter he wrote during adulthood, he related a more specific story about his inquiries into taking piano lessons with the music professor at the school, taking with him on the day in question, a Canadian march entitled, "The Maple Leaf Forever." As Lamb remembered, the professor "asked me what I was doing with it. I told him I was playing it. He told me if I wanted to take lessons from him I couldn't play anything like that. Well, that was that! So I didn't start."[37] Instead, he continued to play the piano and to write music on his own. His determination had already taken him quite far, and a nephew later wrote: "It was while at St. Jerome's he got to play well."[38]

Not only was Lamb aware of the German music in Berlin but he also had been keeping current with developments in popular music in general, synthesizing everything he had learned up until that time — popular, classical, traditional, ethnic. Now he fluidly experimented with different styles of composition, including both instrumental and song forms.

Two of his pieces, dated 1901, are titled "Mignonne" and "Lenonah." "Mignonne" is a composition for piano, subtitled "Valse Lente." It contains the inscription: "Respectfully dedicated to my mother."[39] It is possible that these works were written around the time that Lamb was either about to leave Montclair or was newly arrived in Canada. Dedicating a composition to his mother would have been natural, given the fact that he was far from home and would have missed her while at St. Jerome's. There is no explanation as to why "Mignonne" was so titled (although *The Etude* had featured Joseph Rheinlander's "Mignonette," Op. 122, in December of 1896, which may have been of some inspiration). However *mignonne* means "sweet" or "cute" in French — and this may simply have been his characterization of Julia Lamb herself. An appealing waltz for piano, "Mignonne" is a lovely musical tribute, yet one that remained unpublished for over a century.

"Lenonah" is a waltz song, one in which the narrator speaks of a declaration of love made under an oak tree in Mexico. At first glance, the title would suggest an Indian motif, however the name "Lenona" is spelled without the final "h" in the lyrics. Love songs were always popular, and an international setting made them all the more appealing. Any locale could turn into the setting for a song, as demonstrated in some of the *New York Journal*'s 1900 Sunday supplements which included "Sweet Fleur-de-Lis (Lily of France)" as sung at Proctor's Fifth Avenue as well as "In Naples Fair" which made the rounds of the vaudeville circuit.[40] The Mexican theme might have been suggested by his brother's many travels to the west as well as the popularity of adventure

Popular Music

Issued in Star Edition of
Popular Ten Cent Music

FOR SALE AT ALL MUSIC STORES

Yes or No · · BALLAD *William Westbrook*
(Give me your answer to-night.)
The seasons sensational ballad by the composer of "A Handful of Maple Leaves". The grandest ballad yet published. Sales will reach 100,000.

VIOLETS · · THREE STEP *Eugene Claire*
A graceful Three-Step that may be used effectively as a dance or piano solo.

The Irish Minstrel CHARACTERISTIC MEDLEY *Carl Kahn*
A clever and Amusing Irish Medley by the composer of the famous "Kamona" depicting Prof. B'owball, The Irish Minstrel, in his walk from Limerick to Dublin.

If I Had You · · BALLAD · *Leonard & Dore*
A New York Success of dainty construction with a pretty waltz Chorus.

Amy and I, · · · · *William Westbrook*
A dainty waltz song by the writer of "Handful of Maple Leaves."

On the War Path, A RUSSIAN RETREAT *Wallace Grant*
A great characteristic patrol, depicting the Russian Cossacks in full retreat.

When the Frost has turned the Maple Leaves to Gold,
Fenton S. Fansher
Another song success by the popular writer of "Where the Shading Maples Grow."

Celestine, · · WALTZES · *Josef F. Lamb*
Unsurpassed in rythm or beauty of melody. 27,000 copies sold

Verona, · SPANISH INTERMEZZO · *Clarence H. St. John*
A Spanish Serenade that is creating quite a stir with lovers of this style of arrangement.

Father on thee we call, · · *Eugene Claire*
A pretty sacred song. Sung by the eminent singer, Conductor Ruthven Macdonald, of Cooks Church.

The Gondolier, · INTERMEZZO · *W. C. Powell*
One of the most popular instrumental numbers published.

Down where the Congo Flows, · *Chas. Shackford*
A Congo love song sung with great success by Leo Kriger.

Hurry a Little, CHARACTERISTIC TWO-STEP *Chas. Cooper*
A warm member that will make you ginger up and keep you shifting with delight.

Mem'ries, DESCRIPTIVE SONG *Llyod G. Williams*
Three beautiful pictures in word and song never to be forgotten.

The Gibson Girl, A TONY TWO-STEP *Chas. E. Bodley*
A dainty number that may be well termed "tony," as it is in the better class and catchy all the way through.

Prayer and Passion, NOVELETTE · *Herbert Neviu*
A perfect tone picture and one of the most popular classics written in years. A grand number for Church, Home or Sunday Recreation.

O Happy Day!. · *Llewellyn Morrison & Carl Goten*
A sacred song that is being sung by noted artists of the continent

His Way, · · *Llewellyn Morrison & Jules Faber*
Another sacred song success, by the writers of "The Pearly Gates and Golden." This song is bound to strike a responsive chord in every heart.

Where the Shading Maples Grow, · *Fenton S. Fansher*
Just a little heart song that is sure to please.

In Memory of Jack, · · *Fenton S. Fansher*
True to the memory of her soldier boy a pathetic story is told. A song that is being featured by the leading singers of vaudeville.

Kamona, · · Intermezzo, · · *Carl Kahn*
This composition known as "Kamona" has swept the country with remarkable speed and, despite the simple title is recognised as the most meritous work of its kind written in a decade.

I'm wearing my heart away for you, · *Chas. K. Harris*
The composer's name is sufficient recommendation and the above is among his best efforts.

The Organist's Last Amen, · · *Harry A. Edwards*
One of the best descriptive songs ever written portraying a sad but beautiful story in melody and song.

Rose, My own Canadian Queen, · *Purdy & Fansher*
A pretty story of devotion. A song that is sure to be a winner.

Which Way did the Angels Go? · *Herbert H. Powers*
The reigning success. 90,000 copies sold.

Where the Dreamy Humber Flows, · *Eugene Claire*
A charming song that is meeting with unbounded success where ever sung.

There's Nobody Just Like You, · *Gardenier & Penn*
A sweet little song by the composers of "The Honeysuckle and the Bee."

The Pearly Gates and Golden, · *Llewellyn Morrison & J. Faber*
A grand sacred song of masterly arrangement for which we predict an enormous sale

Dance of the Butterflies, · · *Percy Furneaux*
A dainty characteristic number full of grace and melody that can be used effectively as a schottische.

Outside the Gates of Paradise, · *Harry Herbert*
A worthy successor to the "Holy City." A song that commands the attention of lovers of a better class of music.

Lead Thou O Kindly Light, or · *Jules Faber*
"Please Sir does God Live here."
A beautiful semi-sacred song of the little innocent who sought the modern church as God's home, only to be disappointed.

A Handful of Maple Leaves, · · *Wm. Westbrook*
The song of the century,. 20,000 copies sold

Old School Chums, or · · · *William Westbrook*
Shall I meet my lost love in the High School above.

In a Garden of Love, · WALTZES · *Gerald Salfield*
A fascinating sweet flowing melody. A charm in itself.

The Bonnie Briar Bush, MARCH TWO-STEP *Ian Kilmaster*
Played by the famous "Kilties" Band to repeated encores. Also introduced in the famous play of the same name.

He Sleeps in the Transvaal To-night, · *J. Cecil Rolls*
A beautiful pathetic song dedicated to the mothers of Canada whose sons have stirred the world with their heroism.

Ask Your Dealer
FOR THE
"Star Catalogue"
IT'S A GEM

HARRY H. SPARKS
MUSIC PUBLISHER
TORONTO, · · · · CANADA

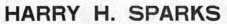

An advertisement for Lamb's first publisher, Harry H. Sparks. It is assumed that the cameo photograph near the firm's logo is of Sparks (courtesy Patricia Lamb Conn).

stories set in the southwest and Old West — all of which had some Mexican influences. (Lamb certainly would have spent hours reading to pass the time en route to Canada and to seek some diversion from the recent life-altering events that he had experienced.) Most interesting about "Lenonah" is not the setting of the piece but the brief little hint of syncopation in the introductory bars.

Once settled in school, Lamb's compositional output increased — songs, two-steps, waltzes, and miscellaneous pieces. His seriousness about composing took a huge step further as he approached the Harry H. Sparks Music Publishing Company in Toronto in order to sell some of his work. He had to have been well motivated and possessed of a mature self-confidence to make this move as a young teenager. Lamb did not personally meet Harry Sparks until much later[41]; and, therefore, might have initially dealt with other members of the Sparks firm or else corresponded with Harry Sparks by mail in order to arrive at an agreement about the sale of his compositions.

The Harry H. Sparks Music Publishing Company of Toronto was in business from 1900 through 1910. During the years that Lamb lived in Canada, the company was located at 306 Yonge Street, conveniently near other musically related establishments such as Whaley, Royce & Company as well as The T. Eaton Co., Limited, both musical instrument and sheet music dealers.[42]

Sparks issued more than two hundred popular compositions with many falling into the dance, march, and sentimental song categories, although local and patriotic themes were not neglected.[43] Titles in the Sparks catalogue ran a wide gamut from a two-step called "The Gibson Girl," to "On the War Path," to "The Organist's Last Amen."

Judging by the actual dates of publication, the Sparks firm paid Lamb up front for his compositions but didn't publish them until later on — after he returned home to New Jersey.[44] He received $5 for "Celestine Waltzes," a composition dedicated to his sister Anastasia — Celestine being her confirmation name — in acknowledgement of her early help at the piano.[45] It was his first sale and was eventually published in 1905, a year after he returned home, as was "Lilliputian's Bazaar: A Musical Novelty." Scholar Joseph R. Scotti suggested that this latter piece contained some syncopation and could be one of the earliest examples of the composer's budding ragtime sensibility.[46]

"Florentine Waltzes" followed the initial two compositions, appearing in print in 1906. The cover showed the composer as "Josef" F. Lamb, the spelling of his first name a likely attempt to appeal to the local German population in Berlin, Ontario — the first of a number of his compositions from this time period to do so.

Sparks published the works of many composers — or so it seemed. It is possible that a number of them, including Sparks himself, wrote under several pseudonyms to make the firm appear more active and successful, not an uncommon practice during the time. Given the fact that the "H." in his own middle name stood for "Herbert," it is likely that the composer Harry Herbert, whose compositions appear frequently in the firm's advertisements, was Sparks himself. Harry Herbert's output included such titles as "Only a Picture Postcard" and "Outside the Gates of Paradise."

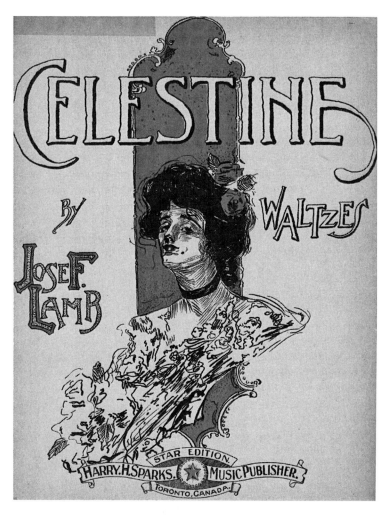

Lamb's first published composition, issued in 1905 by the Harry H. Sparks firm in Toronto. It was dedicated to his sister, Anastasia, for her musical help when he was a child (courtesy Patricia Lamb Conn).

Lamb also used various "Sparks" pseudonyms, including Earl West and Harry Moore. (Later on, "The Ladies Aid Song" was identified by Canadian researcher Ted Tjaden as a possible Lamb composition, since it was penned by Harry Moore. This is a unique treasure, if so, because it was published by the Canadian firm of Musgrave Bros. & Davies after the Sparks firm closed.[47])

Lamb joined the ranks of other Sparks composers, who were an eclectic group. Among them were Arthur Wellesley Hughes (1870–1950), a runaway from Ontario who joined the circus and went on to a varied and accomplished career as a composer and arranger.[48] Americans Charles K. Harris, composer of the mega hit "After the Ball," and Clarence H. St. John, creator of the popular "Coal Smoak," also had works issued by Sparks, although they were not necessarily their most famous titles. It appears as if there was a fluid interaction between composers and publishers in the two countries.

Sheet music published by the Sparks firm cost 10 cents each in the much publicized Star Edition. Accompanying back-page advertisements were lavish in their praise for Lamb's work. The "Celestine Waltzes" was said to be "Unsurpassed in rhythm or beauty of melody" with "27,000 copies sold." "Entrancing" described the graceful "Florentine Waltzes," and "The Lilliputian's Bazaar" was said to be "making a decided hit everywhere." Lamb had to have been thrilled to have had his work accepted for publication as well as to have been paid for it — all while still a young teenager. When the pieces were eventually issued, it was doubly exciting for the young man to see his work in print and to be so highly complimented for his efforts.

Lamb continued to keep up with current musical trends and one of the most popular of these focused on native American Indian subjects. Charles N. Daniels was the first to compose in this vein, his work, "Hiawatha (A Summer Idyl)," becoming a favorite in 1902. It was written under his frequently used pseudonym, Neil Moret.[49]

Daniels was well known, and his name was listed as "arranger" on the cover of Scott Joplin's early work, "Original Rags," of 1899 — a move that helped the then young composer gain some notoriety by association, a gesture that Joplin would, in turn, emulate when his own fame became established. Obviously Daniels, writing and working under any of his names, was a musical figure of great appeal.

After "Hiawatha" was published, a number of composers gravitated to Indian themes. Lamb was among the earliest. He wrote "Muskoka Falls—An Indian Idyl" in 1902, a piece that possesses the unmistakable suggestion of Indian drums in its opening lines.

The title itself refers to the name of a large, scenic region approximately a hundred miles north of Toronto. "Muskoka" was derived from Indian names, although there are different explanations as to the exact source, usually referring to the name of a chief of one of several possible tribes (the Obijwa, "Musquakie,"[50] or the Chippawa, "Mesqua Ukee,"[51] among them).

Muskoka became a sought-after tourist area and vacation resort by the late 1800s as accessibility to the area grew through a combination of railway and, particularly, steamship transportation. In 1901, the same year that Lamb began his schooling at St. Jerome's, the Muskoka Navigation Company, a forerunner in the area's steamship tourism business, built the sumptuous Royal Muskoka Hotel, helping to further seal the area's popularity as a vacation destination.[52] This drew increased attention to the region as even more visitors became attracted to its vast beauty and, of course, its lovely waterfalls. It eventually became known as the "Waterfall Capital of Canada."[53]

Combining the newly popular Indian musical theme with the name of this fashionable Canadian area attraction, Lamb created his unique composition. He did not complete the entire piece, though. It was not unusual for him to occasionally put a composition aside for later revision or completion and, with youthful enthusiasm, his attention would then turn to a new work. In the case of "Muskoka Falls," the piece was only partially finished and was not published. The manuscript was subsequently stored away with Lamb's other papers and effects, only to claim renewed interest a century later.

Among Lamb's other unpublished compositions from his time in Canada is one called "Dora Dean's Sister," dated 1902. The title alone shows his knowledge of popular performers as well as of musical trends. Dora Dean was a famed black stage performer along with her husband Charles Johnson. They were respected for presenting a high-class act and were a part of the well regarded Keith Vaudeville circuit. Together they helped to ignite the popularity of the cakewalk. Dean was so well known that several songs were written about her, including "Dora Dean: The Sweetest Gal You Ever Seen" (1896) by the hit composer and performer Bert Williams.[54] Not only was Lamb aware of Dora Dean and the associated songs written for her, but he also decided to write with perhaps a bit of humor, as well, since his title refers to her "sister." The composition has the sprightly sound of a comic vaudeville song but there are no lyrics, indicating that perhaps Lamb planned to return to this work later on.

In 1903, he wrote a piano piece, "Midst the Valleys of the Far Off Golden West" (also unpublished). Although western themes were in vogue, this was also the year that Lamb's brother permanently relocated to California. The western motif would have captured his attention on its own but the family connection intensified it. This also indicates that he was well aware of what was happening back in New Jersey as well as with his family as a whole.

Lamb's first real attempt at writing ragtime also came in 1903 with his "Walper House Rag," the title drawn from the name of a famous hotel in

Berlin, Ontario—certainly far from the ragtime epicenters of the day. A local historic landmark, an inn had existed at the site since 1820. This was a popular meeting place as well as an Indian trading spot early on, changing ownership several times. It was eventually bought by Curry Walper in 1886, only to suffer a devastating fire six years later. Abel Walper subsequently built a beautiful four-story edifice with a tower the following year.[55] (The hotel still contains many restored original features.)

St. Jerome's used the hotel as a temporary dormitory for a while during the time that work was being completed on their campus residential facilities and, therefore, Lamb was well acquainted with the place. Walper House served as a natural inspiration for him, similar to many composers who titled their works after places with personal history or significance.

Although "Walper House Rag" is written more in the style of a cakewalk, it was the first officially titled "rag" in Lamb's growing list of works. It showed that he had more than a passing knowledge of both forms and was aware of the growing enthusiasm for composing and performing ragtime. (Even before he left Montclair, the form was so popular that it prompted the Witmarks to humorously write in their new house organ in 1898, that "one can almost expect to hear it [ragtime] at a grand concert during the rendition of a Beethoven Sonata."[56]) "Walper House Rag," however, remained unpublished for a century.[57]

Lamb did not neglect other Canadian themes in his work. The same year that he composed "Walper House Rag," he also created "Golden Leaves (Canadian Concert Waltzes)," an ambitious piano piece in the style of *The Etude*'s lighter classics, with arpeggios, turns, tremolos, and a grand finale. Another piece, "Le Premier — French Canadian March" is unfinished, with only the melody existing in manuscript form. Still, it shows that he was interested in different compositional forms as well as in his surroundings—this time, in the larger spectrum of Canada's ethnic heritage. Lamb visited Quebec at some point and mentioned becoming fairly proficient in French, due to his studies at St. Jerome's.[58] He also picked up some German while living in Berlin, Ontario. This eclectic cultural experience influenced some of his musical works and also was of help in his later non-musical career.

Although Lamb presented works of his own to the Sparks firm for consideration, the publisher also approached him, in turn, to set a number of existing poems and lyrics to music. This resulted in a group of sentimental songs such as "If Love Is a Dream Let Me Never Awake" and "Dear Blue Eyes: True Eyes"— both with words by Llyn Wood. Lamb would study these poems for their themes and "get the rhythm of the words" and then "the music would always come."[59] Sparks did not publish these works until several years after Lamb left Canada.

Lamb's musical skills were a versatile asset to Harry Sparks. Aside from composing complete songs as well as setting lyrics to music, he also created the piano arrangement for Charles Wellinger's "Twilight Dreams," published in 1908. Wellinger was the same age as Lamb and was a composer and eventually a member of a dance orchestra in Hamilton Ontario.[60] The nature of this particular composition, though, was enhanced by Lamb's unique and rapidly developing arranging skills. With Lamb's aptitude for harmonization and flair for introducing classically influenced devices to advantage, he would later on be identified and sought out for his abilities in arranging. Sparks was among the first to discover his gift in this area.

Lamb was obviously interested in the rhythm of words. His copy of Tennyson's *The Princess* (containing his name, that of St. Jerome's, and a date of February 9, 1904, on the inside cover) has careful pencil markings indicating the meter of specific passages.[61] Also discovered inside the cover of this book was a sketch containing Lamb's initials. It depicts a young woman in Victorian hairdo and dress (similar to that shown on the cover of "Celestine Waltzes") and was found years later among Lamb's effects. He enjoyed drawing and might have completed the sketch for fun or maybe in the hopes of suggesting a future sheet music cover — or even creating one himself.

Lamb finally met Harry Sparks and developed a friendly relationship with him that continued long afterwards. However this meeting did not take place until after Lamb had graduated from St. Jerome's. Sparks "had published several [works] before I even met him,"[62] he said later on. He remembered both Sparks and his wife, Maude, as a warm and loving couple, and he felt they were as much friends as business connections, a pattern that he was to duplicate in the future with the publisher of his classic rags. The occasion for this meeting was a return trip to Canada for a vacation (where he must have returned several times, including on the occasion of the cornerstone laying for a new portion of the St. Jerome's building).[63] Visiting Harry Sparks was at the top of his list of potential destinations. "My first thing was to meet him,"[64] he admitted.

Lamb must have made quite an impression on Sparks as he was building his list of titles in the firm's catalogue of composers. And, in return, Sparks made quite an impression on Lamb for providing him with the opportunity to become a published composer — and arranger. But it was the personal side of Harry Sparks that really touched him. When he arrived for dinner at the publisher's home, Spark's immediately introduced his wife of many years, saying: "This is my wife and sweetheart." Lamb remembered this vividly years later, commenting that Mr. and Mrs. Sparks "lived the kind of a life together that you would expect from an introduction like that."[65]

Lamb continued to stay in touch with the publisher (who died in 1939 at the age of 68).[66] He also later mentioned seeing Sparks's son, Dr. Balfour Sparks, in 1933 as well as in 1959,[67] indicating that he had extended contact with the Sparks family, as well.

Lamb always maintained fond memories of Harry Sparks, and his compositions continued to be published by the firm until it closed its doors in 1910. By then, however, Lamb had long returned home and was busy with new phases of his life.

Three

A Montclair Homecoming and
California Adventures (1904–1906)

"East is East; and West is San Francisco"— O. Henry

President Theodore Roosevelt pressed a golden telegraph key in Washington, D.C., on April 30, 1904, to signal the official opening of the Louisiana Purchase Exhibition—otherwise known as the St. Louis World's Fair. Although other dignitaries were personally on hand at the ceremonial festivities on Roosevelt's behalf, his exuberant presence was surely missed.

Despite Roosevelt's absence, the crowd of almost 200,000 was certainly thrilled at the sight and sound of John Philip Sousa and his band filling the air with their stirring rendition of "The Star-Spangled Banner" prior to joining forces with a four hundred-voice choir to perform "A Hymn to the West," one of three specially commissioned works for the Fair. This piece contained music by Harvard University's John Knowles Paine and lyrics by poet Edmund Clarence Stedman. A four-mile parade followed that included twenty marching bands.[1] Thereafter, music continued to be an important part of this fair. There were extensive competitive band tournaments with $30,000 in prize money at stake,[2] and Sousa and his group performed frequently. There were also choral group contests, a light opera day, and even a demonstration of a lamp that transmitted music.[3]

This was a fair that would attract exceptional notoriety for its many striking features—from its architecturally stunning buildings to its impressive cascading waters, and from its Eskimo Village to its eclectic music. Music reigned high on the list of wonders—in quality, quantity, and diversity. On a given day such as on June 16, visitors could tap their feet to the First United States Cavalry Band's rendition of Bodewalt Lampe's cakewalk, "Creole Belles," or contemplate Mrs. Mary Chappell Fisher's performance of Bach's Prelude in B minor as performed on the six-manual organ in Festival Hall[4]— the largest such instrument in the world and one that would later enjoy lasting fame in Wanamaker's Philadelphia Department Store. The festive atmosphere in St. Louis, with its special musical emphasis, had a significant impact on the whole country.

Lamb returned home to Montclair from Canada soon after the opening of the Fair. The same young boy who had threatened to walk home only a scant few years before had ultimately embraced both school and surroundings, receiving an education in the cultured environment that his mother had envisioned. He was no longer a boy, but had grown into a fine young man. In addition, the singular atmosphere he experienced in Canada also broadened his exposure to different sounds and styles, further enhancing his musical resources. And now, as a paid composer whose works would soon be in print, Lamb was ready to delve even further into writing music. From the continuing growth of Tin Pan Alley to the musical and cultural overflow of excitement from the Fair, there had never been a better opportunity to begin devoting time and energy to composing in earnest.

All the world was humming "Meet Me in St. Louis, Louis," whose happy melody had been composed in honor of the Fair by the versatile Kerry Mills and published by his Tin Pan Alley firm, F. A. Mills. Lamb was humming this tune, as well. Already popular for his cakewalk, "At a Georgia Camp Meeting," Mills was classically trained and had formerly served as a violin professor at the University of Michigan. His eclecticism and song output would have appealed to Lamb.

Mills had an Upper Montclair address on Lorraine Avenue and would eventually reside for a number of years on picturesque Upper Mountain Avenue, as well.[5] Aside from the popularity of Mills' songs and his varied background, the local Montclair geographic connection surely piqued Lamb's interest, and it is not impossible that the two crossed paths at some point, either in their hometown or else on Tin Pan Alley within the next few years.

Because of Montclair's proximity to New York, it was not unusual to see popular figures there, either as residents, such as Kerry Mills, or as guests. Lamb's friend and future brother-in-law, George Van Gieson, wrote years later that the famous songwriter and performer Paul Dresser would occasionally visit the "Montclair Church to help entertain."[6] Dresser was especially known for his song "On the Banks of the Wabash" as well as for his partnership in the Tin Pan Alley firm of Howley, Haviland & Dresser. His appearances had to have been prior to 1906, the year in which Dresser passed away and, most probably, not many years before this. Van Gieson doesn't provide a date range but he does speculate on what the quality of Dresser's voice must have been like in his "younger days."[7] Van Gieson would have had to have been old enough to attend the shows in order to make such valid assessments of the performances, placing the time of Dresser's visits during the first several years of the century. Even if he did not attend any of these events, Lamb had to have been aware of Dresser's appearances in Montclair through Van Gieson, since the two were close friends and also had a musical association.

In the meantime, and far from Montclair, Scott Joplin was in St. Louis drawing inspiration from the Fair in person, particularly from the series of fountains called the Central Cascade whose water flowed dramatically in front of the 3,500 seat Festival Hall, a site even more spectacular at night as multi-colored lights played upon the aquatic show. He composed a new rag, "The Cascades" (1904), in its honor, a work that joined his growing body of ragtime pieces that already included "The Easy Winners," "The Entertainer," and "The Strenuous Life" (in honor of that strenuous dynamo, President Theodore Roosevelt). Joplin was well known in St. Louis musical circles, particularly at Tom Turpin's popular Rosebud Café which served as host to ragtime composers and performers, many of whose works would become familiar to Lamb.

The fair drew tremendous interest from other songwriters as well, with titles such as "Strolling 'long the Pike," by Bennett and Feist, and "Piking the Pike" by Penn and Stone. There were also instrumentals, including "The Pike" by Becucci and "A Night on the Pike" by Heinzman. In addition, James Scott's "On the Pike" would not only tie into this theme but it would also be a lasting work from the repertoire of this era. However, "The Cascades" was quite the popular one among this group, and it was reported to have been played frequently at the Fair.[8] All of this interest and compositional productivity highlighted the close ties between music and important national events such as this.

While Joplin was in the St. Louis vicinity and the fair was in full swing, Lamb was becoming reacquainted with the once familiar surroundings of Montclair and welcoming the promise of a lovely summer ahead. He was free from studies and all academic pursuits at this moment, although he planned to attend the prestigious Steven's Institute of Technology in Hoboken, New Jersey, in the fall where he had been accepted into the engineering studies program. His passion and aptitude for mathematics and technical subjects had set him in this direction. He admitted years later how much he liked math, a subject he equated with syncopation as both being the "really important things in life."[9] Lamb must have possessed a fine academic record in order to gain admission to Stevens, a well-respected school with an acclaimed engineering program and varied courses in the sciences and humanities.

That was several months in the future, though, and in the meantime, a well-intentioned neighbor asked if Lamb would be interested in a summer job as an office boy in a wholesale dry goods firm. The deal comprised of a salary of three dollars per week and, of course, a chance to commute to New

The Intermezzo
A MUSICAL MONTHLY

JUNE, 1905

Subscription, $1.00 a Year   Single Copies, 25 Cents

PUBLISHED BY
THE INTERMEZZO CO.
210 OLIVE STREET   ST. LOUIS, MO.

The 1904 St. Louis World's Fair embraced all music and had a long-lasting impact. Its Palace of Liberal Arts is shown on a magazine issued by Lamb's future publisher, John Stark, still in St. Louis and observing the Fair's musical aftermath in 1905 as Lamb journeyed to California.

York City "with the big shots"[10]—a tantalizing prospect for the young man. He immediately accepted the offer. This would change everything.

Lamb reaped a number of benefits from working in a city filled with music. Tin Pan Alley was busy churning out hits, and some publishers had already become so successful that they were beginning to move further north into larger and more modern quarters, closer to the equally nomadic theater district. Tin Pan Alley was always adaptable.

Given his youthful curiosity, passion for music, and daily commute to the city, Lamb gravitated to Tin Pan Alley and other appealing geographic areas of New York during this time. Since Tin Pan Alley was at the heart of the popular music world commercially, if not always artistically, he was continually exposed to the numerous and creative ways that music was always being advertised and sold. Publishers were now making full use of all the valuable components of the physical piece of sheet music itself, beyond just the melodies and words featured. Here was a potent blend of art, music, and advertising in one beautiful package, the power of which William Randolph Hearst had long recognized in his newspaper supplements.

In addition, the reach of music had extended far beyond the offices of publishers, places of entertainment, and newspapers, and into the major retail department stores. If songs were such highly saleable merchandise, then why not promote and sell them in places where the entire general public shopped? Just in case some absent-minded musical consumers were not aware of music specialty stores, they were sure to enter one of the large retail establishments in the city. Here was an excellent opportunity for "pushing" songs to an even wider audience and, at the same time, department store retailers could tempt sheet music customers with their considerable stock of non-musical merchandise. Everyone emerged a winner.

Naturally, Lamb frequented the popular sheet music counters at these department stores where demonstrators would play songs for customers upon request—leaving nothing to chance in mining an opportunity to sell. Whether or not customers were able to play the notes as written when they arrived home, they would buy the music because they liked the sound of it in the store, or else appreciated its beautiful appearance, its featured cover performer, and its spectacular advertising. And, of course, they were lured by that most time-honored of all retail practices—the promise of a discount. Macy's and, a few years later, Gimbel's began putting their sheet music on sale on Saturdays at seven or eight cents per copy, and this was one place where Lamb enjoyed becoming acquainted with the current song hits and, eventually, with ragtime.

Since Lamb was already frequenting the department stores to buy music, then he was naturally aware of the other varied musical offerings available at these locations. Department stores had long realized the value of marrying music and business—just as Tin Pan Alley had done. They just approached consumers in a different way.

Now, not only did department stores feature sheet music counters but they also offered regular concerts right in the store itself during the day and at other special times. This was ostensibly done to educate the public in fine music but it was also designed to encourage them to enjoy a pleasant visit and to linger in other sections of the store. This also attested to the importance of music in everyday life. With each passing year during the first decades of the twentieth century, these concerts and events multiplied in number and became more elaborate.

Some stores even possessed concert halls of their own. Small ensembles, player pianos, and phonographs were also employed to ensure that music was always being heard. And it was a varied musical menu, too, ranging from the classics to light operetta selections to marches. The resulting positive effect on customers couldn't be ignored. They remained in the store, thought well of its proprietors, socialized, and made more purchases. En route to the sheet music counter, Lamb was treated to a delightful mix of music that added another eclectic influence to his own work.

Lamb was buying music at Macy's[11] and would later add Gimbel's to his list of designations. There were so many New York stores to visit when buyers were musically oriented. The sumptuous Siegel-Cooper was a favorite place to shop. Early in 1904, it advertised "40,000 Copies of Sheet Music" to be sold at an "Amazing Price."[12] Their stock included repertoire from coon songs and two-steps to comic opera favorites.[13] Then there was Woolworth's, whose founder loved music so much that he commissioned the composition of "The Woolworth March" for orchestra — a piece played at all of the chain's special events.[14] Added to this were stores and displays operated by publishers throughout the city (and in other cities across the country as well). Help & Hager and, eventually, John S. Stark were among the many that both published music and sold it to the public — individuals who would figure prominently in Lamb's life in a few short years.

Ragtime had edged its way into more mainstream sheet music markets in 1904, not only with Joplin's works but also with compositions by others such as Tom Turpin with his "Saint Louis Rag." And it was a special year for enduring popular hits, too, including George M. Cohan's "Give My Regards to Broadway" and "The Yankee Doodle Boy." There was plenty of variety, and music was available and eagerly embraced by all.

Lamb browsed, and listened, and bought. Then he continued with his usual approach: studying the printed notes, learning the music, and scrutinizing the forms, styles, structures, and subjects of the works. This was a good foundation for further creating his own unique style. He had been doing this all along—from his boyhood through his time at St. Jerome's but, by now, he was more fluent in the process.

His perseverance as well as his meticulous methods laid the groundwork for a lifelong approach to composing, one which closely resembled the careful process necessary for completing a carpentry project. He appreciated the raw materials of carpentry, such as the singular characteristics of various grains of wood—choosing the type that would best suit a project both practically and aesthetically. He then planned accordingly. When he began to work on the project itself, it was with methodical and measured precision. His family all later agreed that he aimed for perfection.

Lamb approached composing in the same manner as he did carpentry. He had an instinctive understanding of the raw materials of music—harmonies, melodies, and rhythms—and he chose them to best reflect the finished product that he envisioned. Carefully organizing all of these components, he aimed at a composition of high quality. Both his carpentry and his music blended knowledgeable choices as well as careful precision and, finally, drew sensitively upon artistic gifts.

In the case of music, however, he had not received the same training as he had in carpentry. "It's definitely not academics," he later said; "it must be intuitive."[15] Despite these intuitive musical talents, though, Lamb also continued to work hard at learning the intricacies of musical forms and styles. He purchased and analyzed a large quantity of sheet music. This, in turn, built upon the material that he had gleaned from Kate and Sta's music books and magazines. All of it was valuable knowledge to be used in composing but it would also ensure his popularity at social functions since he could perform an eclectic variety of music that he had learned.

Once the young man gained a taste of working in the city atmosphere with its everyday excitement and musical discoveries—in addition to earning money in the bargain—there was no turning back. When fall arrived, the lure of a salary and the opportunity to continue exploring vibrant New York, with all of its wonderful music, won out. He remained at his job instead of beginning school at Steven's Institute. The job "seemed to overshadow being an engineer,"[16] he later confessed. He reminisced about the experience and spoke humorously of his move up the ladder from office boy to messenger and beyond. "I started at $3.00 per week and in 10 months I was getting—you guessed it—$3.00 per week."[17] After calculating the cost of the daily commute and lunch expenses for his six-day work week, his take-home pay was not as princely a sum as it originally seemed. And, at a cost of up to ten cents per title, some of his earnings also went into Tin Pan Alley's deep pockets as a result of sheet music purchases for his collection, a tempting expenditure for the young man.

Although 1904 seemed to be a quiet year in terms of composing, Lamb was still writing and putting aside manuscripts for the future. Among his unpublished songs from that year were "Tell Me That You Will Love Me as I Love You" and "The Ivy-Covered Homestead on the Hill." Although the latter piece was a sentimental song of the type still popular at the time, it drew from Lamb's personal feelings while he was still in Canada. "I was many miles away from loved ones dear," read a portion of the lyrics, "I will soon return to mother."[18]

Lamb also experimented with pieces for solo piano, including "Lorne Scotts on Parade — March" and "My Queen of Zanzibar." This latter locale seemed to be a popular one as Will D. Cobb and Gus Edwards wrote "In Zanzibar — My Little Chimpanzee" in the same year. Also around the same time, Fenelon E. Dowling and Mary Dowling Sutton composed "My Star of Zanzibar." Exotic locales were still popular.

While Lamb was definitely enjoying the excitement of New York and its musical scene, he was growing restless at the sameness of his regular job duties. He also hadn't seen much of his brother, James, in quite a while and was anxious to reconnect with him. Now that Lamb had spent time back in Montclair with his family and friends from earlier days, his brother would naturally have been on his mind, especially since it was only a few short years since their father had passed away. Young and full of spirit, this was also a good time for a new adventure. After approximately ten months on the job, he decided to give California a try.

James Lamb, Jr., had also been sent to a seminary school in his youth, although it had been years before and was located in Pennsylvania. He was quite a bit older than his brother and had spent time making "many trips around the globe,"[19] picking up work along the way to fund his travels and to maintain his daily life. It was the stuff of adventure stories. He returned to Montclair to work with their father in the building business, afterwards embarking on his travels.[20] He saw much of the world and, as Joe Lamb remarked: "He would travel to some place he had in mind, get a job there and make enough money to go somewhere else. That process was repeated as often as he got the wanderlust."[21] His travels included a cross-country tour of the United States as well as some time in Ireland, among many other destinations.

After their father died, James Jr. and his wife went to California where he went into the building business for himself, disappointed that his mother left the management of the Montclair business with the shop foreman instead of him.[22] However, given the fact that he was truly drawn to California, this was an appropriate turn of events. Now Joe Lamb would follow in his brother's footsteps with a cross-country trip of his own.

James Lamb, Jr., was later described by his nephew as "a big, intelligent, amiable guy."[23] He had relocated to California in 1903[24] and was now settled and raising a family in the San Francisco area. In addition to wanting to visit his brother, Joe Lamb would have also looked forward to experiencing this new and exciting part of the country, especially since he had already lived far away from home during his school years and had grown used to traveling long distances.

One of his unpublished pieces, written in 1903 while he was still in Canada, was titled "Midst the Valleys of the Far Off Golden West," appearing to have drawn some inspiration from his brother's new home territory. The young man could now see it firsthand, with all of its fabled romance and adventure.

As early as the spring of 1905, Lamb headed west. This trip promised excitement on a number of levels. Of course, the young man was looking forward to seeing his brother once more, but aside from this, California and the great American west was something that had been in the forefront of novels, entertainment, and the public interest from at least the turn of the new century. It had also been emphasized during the previous year's St. Louis Fair where, among other western attractions, was Zack Mulhall's Wild West Show featuring guest star, Apache Chief Geromino.[25] More interest in the west was also being sparked with the opening of the Lewis and Clark centennial event in Portland, Oregon, slated for the fall of that year. The entire west coast was a much publicized part of the country.

For Lamb, there was, of course, the added adventure of traveling by train to California. Although he was an experienced train traveler because of his schooling in Canada, he now embraced the opportunity to go cross-county on a trip that was of his choosing and without a school program waiting at its conclusion. And he was fascinated with trains, too—everything about them. "As a kid," he confessed, "I used to draw pictures of engines, take pictures of them, and even make models of them."[26] In his letters years later, he even gives in-depth descriptions of various railroad systems, routes, and terminals that he remembered while in California.[27] And he was fascinated by all of the components of the trains themselves. "I always did love those big engines," he said, adding that "I don't think the Diesels will ever inspire awe like the old steam jobs."[28]

Lamb even composed on the subject. "The Engineer's Last Goodbye" (written under the pseudonym of Harry Moore) was published by Harry H. Sparks in 1908 but in all probability had been written prior to this. The lyrics recounted the sad story of an engineer who said farewell to his wife before perishing as the only casualty in a train collision, a theme that paralleled the story, and the subsequent ballad, of the famous Casey Jones who died in a wreck in 1900. Lamb's song was "Dedicated to the Railwaymen of America."[29]

At the end of his train journey, Lamb was reunited with his brother. James Lamb liked California a great deal and had visited there several times. After getting married, he and his wife chose San Francisco as their home.[30] This was a city that Joe Lamb would enjoy, too, spending much time visiting its sights.

San Francisco in 1905 was a city of contrasts. It still exuded the atmosphere of its wild former days — the pioneer spirit blending with the rambunctious ghosts of the Gold Rush, its hoards having passed through the city en route to striking it rich. Lamb wrote of "evidence of the old west hanging around" and the city being "quite open, especially the Barbary Coast."[31] In this area, mixed legends of dance halls, smuggling, bawdy houses, and shanghaiing still lurked mysteriously in the air — a legacy of the gold rush era.

On the practical side, there was shabby wooden housing, industrial pollution, and notorious crime. The streets were a cacophonous mixture of horse-drawn conveyances and pedestrians, streetcars and an isolated automobile — an emerging addition to the scene.[32]

However, there were also some beautiful examples of Victorian architecture, new hotels, shopping, and restaurants that attracted crowds. It was also a wonderful cultural center with thriving legitimate arts such as theater and opera. Literary figures gave it a creative energy, and places like Coppa's restaurant, frequented by Jack London and others, served as centers of bohemian culture and conversation. All of it made this city a favorite of celebrities from Sarah Bernhardt to Enrico Caruso.[33] And plans for development and beautification always seemed to be in the works.

San Francisco was exciting, with enough of a contrasting atmosphere from New York to offer a unique chance to explore something new. Since Lamb was an inveterate walker, he could enjoy strolling throughout the city, absorbing its atmosphere, history, culture — and its music.

Lamb's stay in California was more than just a brief visit; it lasted approximately ten months in duration — roughly equivalent to the time he spent on his first job in New York. James Lamb, Jr., like their father, was a building contractor and, just prior to his younger brother's arrival, had moved from San Francisco to Marin County to be near a number of his ongoing work projects. Lamb was able to stay for a little time in his brother's vacated San Francisco apartment while adjusting to his new surroundings and finding work.

Lamb visited his brother and his family in Marin County on weekends. His niece, Kitty, remembered him well, even though she was an extremely small child at the time. Music topped the list of her early reminiscences of her uncle. "He was just a young fellow," she commented, "playing the piano wherever he could find one and having a great time."[34]

Musical socializing was frequent during the time that Lamb worked for the wholesale housewares firm of Harry Unna Company, his first job in San Francisco, located at 113 Battery Street.[35] Lamb reveled in the weekly parties given by the young people in his office there, making friends within this group. Lamb found these individuals, and sometimes even their families, quite intriguing, his anecdotes remaining fresh in his memory even decades later. He recalled a "swell outing" one afternoon to a chicken ranch in Petaluma that was owned by the sister of a colleague; and also fondly remembered traveling with another work friend to Twin Peaks—a place with lovely, windswept views of the city—to "telegraph to each other on wire fences."[36] California was filled with new friends and adventures, and Lamb welcomed each one of them with enthusiasm.

Music was an important part of his time there, and he continued to develop his keyboard skills while building his repertoire and storehouse of musical knowledge. Lamb happily performed at the weekly parties of the Harry Unna crowd, just as Kitty remembered him doing at family gatherings. "I was the popular one," he said, "because I was the only one who could play the piano."[37] The guests thoroughly enjoyed the entertainment. Although there is no record of his exact repertoire, it had to have been a mix of popular songs of the day gleaned from visits to music counters and stores, interspersed with a few of his own songs and piano compositions. And he would have honored song requests from the party guests. If he didn't know a particular song, it is certain that he learned it before the next gathering, adding more titles to his diverse and growing repertoire.

Like New York, San Francisco had numerous music stores and sheet music counters in addition to the regularly featured Sunday supplements in the *Examiner* and other city papers. There was plenty to choose from.

One of the most well-known of the music stores in San Francisco was Sherman Clay. Lamb certainly would have visited here on more than a chance occasion. Leander Sherman came from Boston in the post-Gold Rush days and eventually built a successful business selling fine instruments and music. He sponsored concerts in the store's own hall and was known to major artists from Adelina Patti to Paderewski.[38] Here customers could "enjoy the best of everything" musical.[39]

But more than this, the firm became increasingly focused on the publishing side of the music business just before the turn of the century, particularly due to the efforts of Edward P. Little, who because a major figure at Sherman Clay and was well respected within the music publishing world at large in the western part of the country. It was Little who discovered and published Sydney S. Barker's "Johnny-Jump-Ups" in 1905 under Sherman Clay's imprint — said to be "San Francisco's first rag."[40] Joe Lamb would have taken notice immediately. It was obvious that he was already acquainted with ragtime, and any new publication in the genre would have intrigued him.

There were plenty of other music stores to seek out, as well — respected ones with fine reputations and extensive stock, such as Kohler & Chase, a store that dated back to the Gold Rush era.[41] Now music publishers Reese and Fuhrman ran a music counter there.[42] Others included Henry Grobe, with his extensive collection of all musical items, Eilers' Music Company, and Clark Wise & Company — with a "live music" counter operated by Florentine Music.[43] The latter establishment was admired for the "excellence of the sheet music department."[44] (In an interesting coincidence, one of Lamb's early compositions, which was published by Harry Sparks in 1906, was titled "Florentine Waltzes.")

The Wiley B. Allen Company was a firm that had long been based in Portland, Oregon. However it opened a store in San Francisco in 1901 on Market Street with an attractive array of pianos as well as other instruments for sale — and, also, they carried "a large stock of sheet music."[45]

Lamb had many such places to visit and since they were all well known, it would not have taken him long to find these stores and develop his favorites among them.

Although sheet music counters were a part of large piano and musical instrument stores, by 1900, sheet music departments were beginning to infiltrate regular department stores as well. And they all provided some sort of entertainment. The famous Emporium on Market Street, a centerpiece of the city's shop-

Kohler & Chase

The oldest and largest Piano and Music House in the city.

SOLE AGENTS FOR
KNABE PIANO
—"The best in America," so declare all the great foreign artists.

SOLE AGENTS FOR
CRITERION MUSIC BOX
—The world's best music box.

All grades of Pianos and Organs at bottom prices. Repairing and tuning by expert workmen. We have our own shop and repair and manufacture Brass Musical Instruments

28=30 O'Farrell St.
SAN FRANCISCO

An early advertisement for a historic San Francisco music store that was popular at the time of Lamb's visit in 1905.

ping area, hosted weekly concerts under its sumptuous landmark dome. Decades later, Lamb referred to this shopping mecca, one that was to exist, although in a slightly different form, into the next century. He joked to a friend in California that he "could have easily spent [his] surplus cash somewhere else, for instance — at The Emporium."[46] All in all, there were instrument stores, sheet music displays, and concerts enough to keep the young man busy with the art that he loved.

Once, while in the middle of the music area of a department store, Lamb started to play the fife, delighting a crowd there.[47] What he played remains a mystery but years later, his daughter remembered him saying that he could at least play "Yankee Doodle" on just about any instrument. Perhaps he played this song on that particular day. The incident illustrates Lamb's love of music, and it also confirms that he frequented music shops and counters in the San Francisco area often enough to have been comfortable with the culture there, enabling him to perform — even on the fife.

Lamb continued to learn new repertoire, play piano, and develop his compositional skills. While in California, he worked on composing "Ragged Rapids Rag: Ragtime March and Two-Step," a piece that, like "Walper House Rag," showed his early interest in experimenting with the form. According to Joseph R. Scotti, while the composition possessed elements of early ragtime and was titled "rag," Lamb did not refer to it as such, possibly because it was written prior to his becoming acquainted with and assimilating the more complex ragtime style of Scott Joplin.[48] In line with this theory, Lamb wrote that he "hadn't started writing rags yet [in California] but it came soon after that — after I got back home to Montclair, N.J."[49] Yet he was already becoming familiar with the style and laying the groundwork for his later concentration on this form.

During 1905, he also composed "The Eskimo Glide" and "My Little Glow-Worm." This was the same year that the popular song "The Glow-Worm" appeared, with its lyrics translated from German into English. This surely influenced Lamb to try writing something on the subject from his own perspective, again showing his keen awareness of the current musical trends and his willingness to use them as a basis to perfect his own compositional techniques.

Aside from music, Lamb was enjoying everything about California. He rode the ferries, trains, and trolleys, making special mention of the California Street Trolley, which ventured out to the Cliff House by the water and "really hit it up."[50] An old landmark, the Cliff House had been refurbished in 1896. Its eight stories were Victorian in splendor, and its many amenities included dining rooms, art galleries, and an outdoor veranda. The two-hundred-foot high observatory tower offered magnificent views of the water, and nearby were extensive facilities for recreational bathing and entertainment.[51] This was a wonderful day's excursion that appealed to the young man.

He and his friends also explored other places on foot, climbing some precarious cliffs at Fort Point to see the S.S. Alameda that had been grounded on the rocks[52] on September 30, 1905.

He even spoke highly of the climate in the San Francisco area — particularly since he did not like heat and humidity — as "[suiting] me to a T."[53]

Lamb held several unique jobs aside from the one at Harry Unna's during his time on the west coast. He mentioned working for Pacific Plating and Metal Works in San Francisco at "either Third or Fourth and Mission" where he did some sort of office work and also helped to install partitions and rails in offices.[54] He must have excelled at this because of his father's training and perhaps also with some additional tutelage from his brother.

One of the young man's jobs was working for a leather goods firm in San Francisco, an interesting coincidence since Berlin, Ontario, had also been noted for its leather goods industry. Part of his job was to transport animal hides to various locations via the city's famous trolley cars. This task caused much dismay for the cars' conductors who realized that the hides not only took up extra valuable room but they also had an unmistakably unpleasant aroma. With no small degree of amusement, Lamb would wrap himself in the hides and stand in the trolley in order to minimize the space he invaded and also to lighten the frustration of the conductors as he transported this unusual item.[55]

For a while, Lamb lived on Walnut Street in Berkeley with a cousin who was also his godfather. James Lamb, Jr., had been quite close to this cousin in their New Jersey days, and he might possibly have been Frank Brady, the relative who was later mentioned as having followed James to California.[56] This cousin was a building superintendant for the firm that constructed California Hall on the Berkeley Campus. (California Hall served as the school's administration building until 1941.) Lamb lived in Berkeley during the time he worked briefly at Breuner's,[57] a furniture store that had originally been formed to sell to people traveling through California during the gold rush days. It is possible that Lamb worked at the Oakland store. He mentioned that he was fired from this job,[58] and perhaps this was when, after working hard for six days a week, he wanted to have one day of fun — so much so that he took off one Saturday to go to a Stanford football game, thereby risking his job.

Toward the end of his visit out west, Lamb joined his brother and his family in Ross Valley for a while. At this point he was not working, and Ross Valley was a beautiful place to explore, one that was filled with visitors in the summer but empty in winter. James Lamb and his family lived on a dirt road and owned several bungalows on the property. These he rented out. Lamb commented that the locale was a perfect one for "riding Tony Marshall's bronco."[59] (Marshall was a railroad engineer and member of a prominent family in that area.)

While in Ross Valley, Lamb vividly recalled climbing to the top of Mt. Tamalpais one day to see a spectacular sunrise — it remained vividly in his memory years later as being "worth the trip."[60] One of the most dramatic places in Marin County, this mountain rises almost from the sea level to a height of over 2,500 feet and was considered a sacred place by Native Americans. The views were, of course, breathtaking — the panoramic landscape far-reaching. His extended and wonderful trip, however, was drawing to a close.

Lamb headed back to New Jersey, arriving home by the first week of April in 1906. He had a fairly peaceful train ride home from the coast and years later both specifically and fondly recalled a musical incident en route. The car was empty, except for Lamb and one other man who boarded the train at Tracy. Because of all the obviously available space, the porters met in their car and, according to him, "we had some real colored harmony to soothe us ... we had those concerts for three nights."[61]

Lamb especially enjoyed this distinctive type of harmony and later referred to "the old Colored Spirituals" that he heard at a camp meeting ground outside of Baltimore where he frequently visited in order to hear similar performances. "That was music," he wrote, concluding that the singers were probably not able to read the notes — "but could they harmonize? [sic]!"[62] Lamb placed great emphasis on the importance of harmony and drew deep inspiration from the train porters and camp meeting singers. Later, his piano rags would contain beautiful, lush harmonies with intricate inner voices, a uniquely distinctive quality of his work.

A short couple of weeks later, Lamb was settling back home in Montclair after his evenings of enjoyable concerts on the train. At the same time, and back across the country in California, the famous tenor Enrico Caruso was also happily settling into his San Francisco hotel after a performance of *Carmen*.

The next morning, though — April 18 — Caruso woke abruptly to horrifying sights and sounds, "buildings toppling ... masonry falling ... screams."[63] Earthquake. It was the sound of San Francisco's historic 1906 disaster. It just one short burst of time, the buildings, streets, trolley cars, stores and all that Lamb had so lightheartedly enjoyed for the previous few months crashed into ruins.

Joseph Lamb had been home safely in Montclair for a scant couple of weeks. His brother and family were far enough from the disaster to have remained unharmed. The timing of his return, though, was startlingly fortunate and something that his niece Kitty says that "he never got over."[64]

Nevertheless, Joe Lamb's stay in California was an interlude that he always remembered with fondness. In his words: "The short length of time I spent out there was certainly full of excitement and fun and stands out in my life as something special."[65]

Four

An Unforgettable Meeting
(1906–1908)

"Well, here's your man"— Sarah Ann Stark

Joe Lamb would find a kindred spirit in John Stark. Despite a substantial difference in their ages and life experiences, they shared a number of musical interests and personal values, not the least of which was their mutual zeal for the serious instrumental ragtime form. Once Stark arrived in New York, it was inevitable that the two men should meet and forge a bond that would be lasting.

John Stillwell Stark (1841–1927) was a combination American pioneer and Renaissance man. His early background held little clue that he would eventually achieve a distinguished place in music publishing with a name that was to be remembered into the twenty-first century, long after many of his peers were forgotten.

Born to a large family in Kentucky and orphaned young, Stark worked on his brother's farm in Indiana, a livelihood that he returned to in rural Missouri after serving as a bugler in the Union Army and settling down with his young wife, Sarah Ann, to start a family. Later he entered the new business of ice-cream making, peddling this popular treat and, subsequently, pianos and cabinet organs from the back of his trusty Conestoga wagon. Pleased with the success of his musical instrument sales, he eventually moved his family to the city of Sedalia, Missouri—deep in the "cradle of ragtime"— where he bought a music store, sold pianos, and even ventured into a little music publishing.[1] Stark possessed versatility and integrity, and he was a natural born entrepreneur.

Similar to Lamb's father, John Stark not only had his own business but he was also a thoroughly devoted family man. As in the Lamb family, music played an important role for the Starks. Two of their children were well-trained musicians. Eleanor became a serious concert pianist, continuing her studies in Europe. Etilmon was a violinist, composer, and arranger who eventually wrote some ragtime works. And like Joe's brother, James, who pursued their father's career path in the building trade, so did Stark's other son, William, follow in his father's footsteps into the music publishing industry.

By the time that he had seriously established his business and publishing endeavors in Sedalia, Stark was fast approaching his sixth decade and only on the threshold of making his real mark in the music world. St. Louis and New York were still in his future. Age was never an inhibiting factor for John Stark, a philosophy that Lamb would also embrace in his own later years.

Stark's New York office was already up and running for about eight months when Lamb arrived home from California in 1906. Musically, New York was the place to be. From classical to popular, music was performed in stores and parks, in concert halls and restaurants, and in homes and on theater stages. This particular year ushered in the Victrola style phonograph and introduced George M. Cohan's popular "You're a Grand Old Flag." Victor Herbert's famous operetta *The Red Mill* premiered, noted for such memorable melodies as "In Old New York" and "Moonbeams" as well as for its moving electric sign, the first used in a Broadway theater. The pianist Arthur Rubinstein made his U.S. debut at Carnegie Hall, and Tin Pan Alley composer Paul Dresser died, leaving behind his sentimental song "My Gal Sal" to become a hit without him.

John Stark (as depicted in a music periodical from 1915) was the publisher of Lamb's famed classic rags, which earned him a place among ragtime's "big three" (courtesy Sibley Music Library, Eastman School of Music).

And this was also the year that Lamb began working in New York once more, commuting from Montclair with his friend and future brother-in-law George Van Gieson. At this time, Lamb found employment with the Syndicate Trading Company at 2 Walker Street.

Syndicate Trading was formed by Abel Swan Brown in 1880 as a purchasing company for department stores. Its main office was in New York but it had branches in four major European countries. Brown was a multi-faceted individual who had lived, among other places, in Passaic, New Jersey, not far from Montclair, where he was not only highly active in community endeavors but was also host to many musical gatherings in his home, his interest kindled by his own accomplishments on the violin.[2]

Although Brown had passed away a few years before Lamb joined the firm, his eclectic influence lingered. At some point, Syndicate Trading took on some publishing and book distribution,[3] apparently as an offshoot of its regular business. It issued works of classic authors, published adventure novels, and, later, advertised in trade publications as a buyer of remainders of saleable books.[4] Although it is not known what type of job that Lamb held with the company during this time, he was certainly exposed to the varied world of business on both national and international levels, something that he would find useful in his future employment.

As always, Lamb was still busy in his leisure time making the rounds of various sheet music outlets in the city — from publishers' offices to department store music counters. He was eager to check out the latest song hits of all types, especially ragtime. He was also soon to become acquainted with John Stark's establishment, among others.

During this time, sheet music was everywhere and not only was the public intrigued by its beautiful style and content but it couldn't help but be fascinated by the internal politics relating to the places where it was sold. Much entertainment could be drawn from the rivalries between some of the department stores and the publishers themselves.

War had broken out between the elegant Siegel, Cooper & Company at Sixth Avenue and 18th Street and the famous R. H. Macy & Company, located in its new home on West 34th Street and Broadway. A price cutting feud erupted that was equivalent to a duel at dawn, during which a coveted piece of sheet music could be bought for a mere six cents per copy at Macy's. There was nothing like a good discount to attract buyers. Business was never better.[5]

This situation was hurting the music publishers, though, and they were not taking it lightly. A group of Tin Pan Alley firms had already banded together to form The American Music Stores, Inc., an organization that had contracts with approximately fifty department stores in the United States for the sale of sheet music at their counters. Now these publishers were watching their profits float away while the giants continued their duel and a happy public leaped at the opportunity to stuff their piano benches with bargain priced treasures.

This group of publishers— Feist, F.A. Mills, Charles K. Harris, Witmark, and Howley, Haviland & Dresser — launched a plan to catch the attention of the warring giants and bring business, and their balance sheets, back to normal. They enlisted the aid of Rothenberg & Company, an establishment on West 14th Street that billed itself as "New York's Fastest Growing Store," striking a deal whereby Rothenberg's would sell hits at one cent per copy, thereby undercutting the larger names and drawing away business. The plan backfired when a riot started at Rothenberg's after the stock quickly ran out.[6]

The publishers did make their point, though, and the message was clear: sheet music was a hot commodity and everyone wanted to be in on it, but a more upstanding approach had to be taken in its sale. Lamb surely noted these proceedings with interest. There had never been a better time to compose and sell if department store giants considered music worthy of a war and if riots broke out during public sales.

Despite the fact that Lamb visited a number of stores and larger music counters (and he admitted that he liked a bargain price as well as anyone else), Stark's still evolved into one of his favorite haunts, its stock of ragtime sheet music serving as a strong magnet. During his frequent visits there to buy sheet music, he usually stopped to chat with the music publisher himself as well as with his wife, Sarah. As a result, the three soon developed a cordial relationship. Their mutual reverence for "classic ragtime"— a term coined by Stark — was a focus of the conversation. And Lamb's love of this style of music and his frequency as a customer at Stark's store soon earned him a special discount as well.[7]

As an added benefit, the firm was housed at 127 East 23rd Street in a busy and fascinating area located only a few blocks away from the unusual Fuller Building. Better known as the "Flatiron," this building was completed in 1902 and unofficially defined the beginning of the modern age of the skyscraper in New York. Lamb had no doubt originally seen the building when he was employed at his first job after returning from Canada in 1904, particularly since it was not far from Tin Pan Alley. He certainly became acquainted with its musical connections as well as with the slang and stories that were a part of its growing lore.

Located at Fifth Avenue and 23rd Street, this innovative architectural landmark was constructed in the shape of a pressing iron, hence its popular name. The building alone was enough to draw visitors to the area, its exterior a marvel of the age and, almost immediately, it drew notoriety in the form of sheet music. "The Flatiron (The Fuller) March and Two-Step" of 1903 by J. W. Lerman, was issued by one of the building's resident music publishers, N. Weinstein. Thurland Chattaway's piano piece "Trombone Sammy," of 1905, amusingly depicted the instrumentalist of the title accidentally splitting the Flatiron in half with his slide.

The building's eclectic roster of tenants included the Fuller Company itself, overflow offices for several Tin Pan Alley firms, and the indefatigable pulp magazine czar, Frank Munsey who published *Munsey's Weekly, The Argosy*, and *Railroad Man's Magazine*. It also housed the Flatiron Restaurant and Café which, in addition to its extensive cuisine, also featured music, advertising it prominently in its menu.[8]

The wind-blown corner by the building was supposedly responsible for coining a new phrase—"Twenty-three Skiddoo"—used by the local police to scatter groups of young men who gathered there hoping for the breeze to catch a passing hemline or two. (In 1906, there was even a comic song by Miller and Boecher called "23-Skiddoo!"[9]) The word "skidoo," meaning to "go away," first came into common slang use around 1903 when the Flatiron was becoming populated both inside and on its famous corner.

Lamb had to have been acquainted with the phrase since he used it in his lyrics for "Sweet Nora Doone," published in 1907, in which the faithful Nora tells some potential suitors that "they must 'skidoo,' [she] doesn't wish to hear their blarney."[10] The musical accompaniment is a simple waltz, its chorus containing a few octaves and some broken chords, indicating that it was among Lamb's earlier works. According to the title page, both the words and music were penned by Harry Moore, one of Lamb's several pseudonyms from his Canadian days. The song was published by Harry H. Sparks in Toronto, its cover containing a signed photo of Eddie Piggot, with no indication as to whether he performed this song or not.

Although a number of the "Sparks" compositions were written during Lamb's time at St. Jerome's and published later on, he might have written this particular piece upon returning home (either after Canada or California) and becoming acquainted with the popular new slang. Since Lamb did maintain contact with Harry Sparks after leaving Canada, it is likely that he continued to send additional works for publication. This could have been among them. In either event, Lamb kept up with the current "Flatiron" jargon and humorously inserted it into his lyrics, demonstrating his keenly observant nature.

The Flatiron was in close proximity to Stark's and even though the building where he was located lacked the architectural singularity of the Flatiron, it was still destined to become a stellar landmark in Lamb's life. John Stark was an anomaly on the New York music publishing scene since he championed the pure style of the ragtime instrumental form, unlike the majority of firms whose focus on money far exceeded their artistic considerations. If they could call something "ragtime" and it sold, then that was all that mattered. Stark's approach was refreshingly different. And in keeping with this spirit of not running with the crowd, he also maintained his publishing firm just outside the mainstream of Tin Pan Alley.

Ragtime fever was increasingly captivating the country, with Scott

Joplin's "Maple Leaf Rag" having grown on the popularity list since its initial 1899 publication by Stark in Sedalia. Its catchy themes resounded on uprights everywhere. And its familiar strain didn't just come from the keys of that most popular of instruments; it could be heard in a variety of arrangements— and places. Teddy Roosevelt's daughter, Alice, insisted that it be performed by the United States Marine Band at the White House. And five-string banjo virtuoso Vess Ossman turned out a hit recording of the composition in 1907. "Maple Leaf Rag" was a consistent winner, and Lamb later confessed that it "hit me good and proper."[11]

In the intervening years after the publication of "Maple Leaf Rag," Joplin had penned other gems including: "The Entertainer" (1902), "The Cascades" (1904), and "The Ragtime Dance" (1906)—all issued by John Stark. It had been a busy time for Scott Joplin, now referred to as the "King of Ragtime Writers." And in 1907, the lovely "Gladiolus Rag" appeared, a piece that Lamb called "the most beautiful rag I have ever heard."[12] This composition, however, was published by Joseph W. Stern & Co., perhaps a foretaste of the rift that was to grow between Joplin and Stark in the following years.

Joe Lamb himself was fast becoming more immersed in ragtime; he took to it with a natural instinct. Like John Stark, he valued the "classic" form and with his characteristically methodical approach, he accumulated a vast quantity of sheet music and began analyzing it with his usual intensity, just as he had done as a boy with the piano lesson book from Sta and Kate. He played these rags and examined their structure, style, and singular features. And classic ragtime had a defined structure, despite the fact that individual composers incorporated their own modifications into the form. Using his analyses as a method of self-education and as a starting point for his composing, Lamb worked at creating his own special sound within the ragtime form, and this included a number of creative variations that eventually helped to identify his style.

During this time, also, Lamb continued to enhance his musical education in other ways. He owned a copy of the 1907 edition of *A Catechism of Music* by J. Jousse.[13] This little book not only presented basic information on scales, intervals, and transposition but it also featured an addendum that contained sections on modulation, forms of composition, piano technique, and—most notably—accent and syncopation. Lamb probably used this as a supplement to his close analysis of printed sheet music along with the information that he continued to glean from *The Etude* magazine and other similar publications.

Even John Stark issued a monthly musical publication called *The Intermezzo* of which he was editor. Like *The Etude* and other publishers' house organs, it offered printed music by well known names such as Scott Joplin as well as less popular composers who wrote in styles ranging from marches to waltzes. Editorials voiced opinions on music and other topics, and there were advertisements, notices, and jokes, although the subject of ragtime did not gain as much space as that of the traditional classics. For a subscription of $1.00 annually, readers could find music and articles in their mailboxes, and John Stark could keep his publishing company and sheet music in the public eye. By the time that Stark was in New York, subscribers were also told that they would receive a special bulletin each January listing all publishers' latest hit compositions. Stark then offered these hits at "10 cents per copy and postage, or 11 cents net," commenting that his firm would "save you money on anything you want in the sheet music or music book line."[14] Aside from being a savvy music publisher, Stark was also a quintessential salesman.

Lamb would have read this publication, noting Stark's respect for the classics as well as for other types of music. Since he not only grew up surrounded by classical music and *The Etude* magazine but also gravitated to ragtime and other genres, he would have had much to discuss with Stark, a man of similar tastes.

Although Lamb purchased as much of Joplin's music as possible, he also sought out the works of others, including the compositions of James Scott. Scott was a native of Neosho, Missouri, and ultimately became one of the "big three" names of classic ragtime along with Joplin and Lamb himself. (In an interesting coincidence, Lamb's niece and her husband lived in Neosho many years later.[15]) Scott, an enterprising young composer, worked at the Dumars music store in Carthage, a firm that eventually published some of his pieces including "On the Pike" of 1904, written in honor of the St. Louis World's Fair. He also played piano and steam calliope at a popular local park.[16] But it was when he journeyed to St. Louis in 1906 and was in contact with Scott Joplin that his wider fame became assured. Joplin introduced the young man's work to John Stark who published Scott's "Frog Legs Rag" that same year, a composition that was to become another of Lamb's real favorites.

John Stark was a central figure for Joe Lamb's further exposure to the ragtime world, particularly since he published the compositions of Joplin, Scott, and others who wrote in the classic rag style. Also, while browsing through the music for sale, he enjoyed talking with both Mr. and Mrs. Stark, a down-to-earth and friendly pair. All of this further intensified his enthusiasm and contributed to his passion for ragtime.

While active in New York and interested in its cultural world, Lamb continued with his life and musical pursuits in Montclair, as well. It was a busy time for the town. Although Montclair was emerging into the modern spotlight, it still maintained the charm of yesteryear, with advertisements for automobiles and horse blankets sharing a page in the local newspaper,[17] and where talking machines increasingly took space there, as well.[18] A new mountaintop hotel there, The Montclair, attracted auto parties and tourists.[19] Celebrities wove into the life of the place as Annie Oakley exhibited her skills at the local gun club,[20] the world renowned local resident Mme. Schumann-Heink sang with Damrosch, and pianist Josef Hoffman prepared a concert at the Outlook Club.[21]

In the midst of it all, Lamb cofounded the Clover Imperial Orchestra in Montclair, a small ensemble that specialized in performing at local social events. The group consisted of his friend, co-founder, and future brother-in-law, George Van Gieson on the violin, Frank Rogghe on the trumpet, Al Myers on drums,[22] and Lamb, himself, at the piano. Although Lamb was always modest about his pianistic skills, he must have been quite accomplished by this time. His sister, Sta, alternated with him at the piano, and it is possible that this is how she became acquainted with her husband-to-be. (Van Gieson mentioned that he met Sta when he was around twenty years old,[23] and this would have placed the date at approximately 1908 by which time the group, which may have been founded as early as 1906 and sometime after Lamb's return from California, was up and running.) In a letter Lamb wrote to Van Gieson in later life, he tells him how much he valued his friendship, commenting somewhat humorously: "I can well understand why I agreed to start an orchestra with you thereby making it possible to have you accepted into the family."[24]

This musical group played at halftime during games at Montclair High School, as well as for parties, civic events such as hayrides,[25] and Knights of Columbus affairs. Van Gieson mentioned that they "were willing recipients of remuneration"[26] for their efforts and humorously reminisced at a later date that the group prided itself on its slogan: "Music Furnished for all Occasions!"[27] Town directories list a "Van Gieson's Hall" at the corner of Valley Road and Bellevue Avenue — one of a number of halls in Montclair at the time — and it is possible that the orchestra might have even appeared there at functions, given George Van Gieson's extended family connections within the town.

This enterprising young ensemble were certainly known to the J. Melvin Bush Music Company as well which, in addition to its sales of instruments and sheet music, also locally advertised "Music for Entertainments, Parties, Receptions."[28] Not only would Lamb have frequented this store to buy sheet music but he also would have known Bush as a neighbor at some point, since the man was listed in the Montclair directory as a piano tuner at 133 North Fullerton Avenue, just up the street from the Lamb family home. In addition, Lamb later mentioned that his family's piano was always well maintained, and their neighbor would have been a logical choice to have completed the tuning and technical work for them. Bush was a well known figure within the community and could have put the young group in touch with possible sources of musical engagements.

The repertoire of the Clover Imperial group consisted of popular songs and light classics, also suggesting that Sta, when she substituted for her brother, was fairly versatile in different musical styles. Lamb and the whole group must have been fluent in reading lead sheets and in performing arrangements for small ensembles, given the breadth of engagements that they played.

The Clover Imperial Orchestra performed together for the next few years, at least until 1909 and possibly even into the early part of 1911. By this time, various sized ensembles such as this were sought after all over — at gatherings and civic events as well as at cafes and restaurants. The extent of their repertoire reflected the public's wide-ranging musical interests at that time. The famed orchestra leader Maurice Levi once said that he always tried to honor requests from customers, and these requests could run the gamut from selections by Wagner to "Temptation Rag," a song that Levi was asked for nightly.[29]

At the time that this orchestra was really busy, the young men were also working at regular day jobs. The grueling schedule, though, particularly the night work in the orchestra, eventually took a toll on Van Gieson's health. His mother sent him to Pennsylvania for a while to rest and to regain his strength.[30]

In the meantime, however, the two young men commuted together from New Jersey. Van Gieson worked at the Hastings Clothing Company at 9 University Place, a clothing manufacturer for a San Francisco saleshouse[31] but walked with Lamb to *his* job at 2 Walker Street — not a short distance but a journey that they enjoyed. "Those were the days," Van Gieson said. "The walk from the ferry via the aromatic fruit and veg Commission brokers on Chambers St., and so on to your job," he later wrote to Lamb. "I must have liked your company or I would not walk that distance."[32] When they arrived at the Syndicate building, they passed the time with Teddy Gatlin, an individual with whom Lamb enjoyed discussing ragtime. Lamb developed a friendship with this musical fan who was the elevator operator in the Syndicate Trading building where he worked.

Theodore (Teddy) Gatlin was a congenial black man who loved ragtime. He and Lamb regularly conversed about their favorite musical form, dissecting its various phrases, rhythms, and melodies. They hummed motifs to each other. Those days were fondly remembered by both Lamb and Van Gieson. "You used to sing any new rag you intended to write," reminisced Van Gieson, "and he [Teddy Gatlin] would say if he liked it. You would hum the tune ... and I would do the double shuffle syncopation."[33]

Soon Gatlin admitted that he, too, had created a melody for a rag — "The

Lioneezer." The title of the piece was inspired by a man by the name of Lionel Whitner who also worked at Syndicate Trading. Gatlin sang his melody, and Lamb notated it in manuscript form, completing a full piano arrangement of the work at home. He then visited Gatlin's house to play the finished product for him. The man was thrilled but felt that the arrangement might be too difficult, and Lamb promised to write out a simpler one.[34]

According to the 1900 census, Theodore Gatlin lived on Blake Avenue in the East New York section of Brooklyn,[35] not an insignificant distance from Montclair. Lamb certainly valued his friendship as well as their musical bond enough to spend time creating a written version of "Lioneezer" as well as to make the trip to Brooklyn, most probably on a day off, to play and discuss ragtime with him.

Neither the original nor the revised version survived but Lamb's nephew later recalled his own father telling a story that would seem to have been about Teddy Gatlin. "Uncle Joe wrote a rag for this old black and handed it to him one day as he was changing jobs. There were tears in the old Black's eyes as they said goodbye."[36] It was never specified if this was the gift of a new rag or perhaps the original or revised piano arrangement of "Lioneezer." Teddy Gatlin would have been in his late thirties at the time (the 1900 census lists his birth year at 1870)[37] but to the young men, both around twenty years of age, this might have seemed relatively old. Nevertheless, the touching scene described illustrates the mutual respect and friendship between Joe Lamb and Teddy Gatlin and underlines their common bond of music.

Lamb also played (and hummed) some of his own compositions for his friend, as well. And it was Gatlin who suggested that one of them should be titled "Sensation."[38] This suggestion turned out to be lasting gift in itself. Both composition and title would ultimately make history, although neither man knew it at that point.

Lamb submitted "Sensation" and several other rags to John Stark to be considered for possible publication. This indicated that he must have felt somewhat confident in his work in the ragtime genre by this time and, of course, he was familiar with the process of submitting compositions from his association with the Harry Sparks firm.

Unfortunately, Stark sent a polite rejection note a few days later. Some individuals in Lamb's position might have lost heart after this or felt awkward about continuing to patronize the store. Far from taking the rejection personally, he continued to compose, visit the store, purchase sheet music, and chat genially with the Starks. And this rejection was far from the end of his ragtime story.

Joe Lamb would, just as John Stark had — and James Scott as well — reach a turning point in his life through an encounter with Scott Joplin, although the respective encounters of each were widely separated by time, geography, and circumstance. In Lamb's case it never would have happened if he had allowed rejection to discourage him from continuing to visit Stark's.

There are several versions of Stark's legendary meeting with Joplin. In one often quoted story, Stark dropped by the Maple Leaf Club — an exclusively black social organization in Sedalia — for a beer on a sweltering day. Supposedly it was there that he heard Joplin play his famous "Maple Leaf Rag." In another account, Joplin visited Stark in his Sedalia office to try and persuade him to publish this composition. (Joplin was either alone or enlisted the aid of a small boy who danced or played the piano as part of the sales pitch.) In yet another rendering, it was Stark's son, William, who actually struck the deal.[39]

What *is* known is that John Stark & Son published "Maple Leaf Rag" in 1899 in Sedalia, Missouri, agreeing to pay Joplin a penny royalty on every copy sold instead of insisting upon the customary outright purchase of the composition — an unusual practice at the time. History was made for both men with this contract and, of course, with the eternally popular rag that it represented.

Afterwards, Stark embraced good ragtime and was determined to publish the best piano rags that came his way. He coined the term "classic rag" and advertised accordingly, saying that the rags he published could be "lined ... up with Beethoven and Bach."[40] This was high class music with a well planned structure and artistic style, all shaped into a uniquely distinctive creation by an individual composer. Tin Pan Alley might have spawned thousands of poor imitations, but John Stark took the high road and endorsed the real art form with vigor, holding to exacting standards. It was his zeal to spread classic ragtime on a wider level that ultimately led him to New York where he felt that he could create a high respect for the form that he so deeply believed in and, at the same time, could help to build his business and boost sales of sheet music from his catalogue. These events had, indeed, been a turning point for Stark.

By the time that Scott Joplin had established himself in New York, he, too, was more determined than ever to prove that ragtime was a form of high artistic quality that should hold a recognized place in the world of serious music. Tin Pan Alley publisher, Edward Marks, observed that Joplin composed works that were "more and more intricate, until they were almost jazz Bach."[41] Aside from his rags and related instrumentals, he was intent upon composing an opera and other serious works grounded in classic ragtime idioms, sure that this would convince the world of the form's musical and cultural merits. He wanted to raise it to equal status with traditional classical music, believing that when well composed it shared the same quality as the music played on the venerated stages of major concert halls and opera houses.

While Stark believed this as well, he was a practical man. He knew that a ragtime opera or other serious work might have merit but it was not likely to attract mass interest or significant remuneration in the intensely commercial atmosphere of New York. Although he had gone out of his way to encourage Joplin in the past, both men had bills to pay, and Stark had a business to maintain. This situation would eventually cause a serious rift but, in the meantime, while the two men still maintained their business and personal relationship, Stark's office was destined to be the setting for Lamb's own turning point — and it was one that would definitely have a significant impact.

As Lamb later told the tale, he visited Stark's office one day[42] since, "I bought most of my rags there."[43] While browsing through the sheet music, he began telling Mrs. Stark that he liked the Joplin rags above all the others and wanted to purchase any that he didn't own.

While she chatted with Lamb, he saw a man sitting quietly nearby, his bandaged foot prominently noticeable. The foot ailment must have been somewhat incapacitating because there was a crutch near him. This man had been listening to their comments and then joined in the conversation. He offered some suggestions about potential sheet music selections to buy, and Lamb thanked him, taking his advice. That was almost the end of the episode.

However before getting ready to leave with his purchases, Lamb mentioned to Mrs. Stark that the one person he'd especially like to meet was Scott Joplin because he admired his music a great deal. "Really," she responded, gesturing to the gentleman with the bandage. "Well, here's your man."[44]

It was a stunning moment. (Years later, Joe Lamb's own children remembered him telling the story of meeting

Scott Joplin (shown in 1911) was a friend to Lamb, a champion of his work, and the catalyst for the publication of "Sensation" (Photographs and Prints Division, Schomburg Center for Research in Black Culture, The New York Public Library, Astor, Lenox and Tilden Foundations).

Scott Joplin over and over again at the dinner table so many times that they knew it by heart.) This was not only a personal thrill, being able to meet the famous composer whose works he greatly admired and had learned from, but it was also an opportunity on a professional level to discuss composing and to talk about the art of ragtime. At that moment, though, Lamb had no clue as to the serendipitous events that were soon to follow.

The two men began talking, obviously absorbed in their conversation. They eventually left the store together, and Joplin asked if Lamb would walk with him for a while. They strolled across 23rd Street to Madison Square Park where they sat on a bench and continued their discussion.

Madison Square Park was a six-plus acre pastoral oasis in the city. The second incarnation of Madison Square Garden was close by, a symbol of the gilded age, now all but drawn to a close. The edifice had achieved fame not only from past glittering spectacles but also from the incredible headlines that it generated after the murder of its fabled architect, Stanford White.[45]

Also in close proximity was the Flatiron Building, blazing a path towards New York's changing architectural skyline. The park had, in addition, once served as a temporary resting place for Lady Liberty's torch before the entire monument was completed and installed in its permanent place in the harbor. Madison Square Park was a blend of the old, the new, the evolving, and the American — similar to ragtime music itself. Both the park and the music were eclectic and unique. This was the perfect setting for these two men to become acquainted and to discuss their mutual admiration for ragtime's classic form.

Lamb confided to Joplin that he composed piano rags. Joplin, in turn, wanted to hear his assessment of them. Lamb responded honestly saying that he thought they were pretty good but he wasn't altogether sure, revealing that John Stark had recently rejected his submission of a few his ragtime compositions for consideration. At this point, Joplin may have realized that the rejection could have been for commercial and not artistic reasons, the name recognition issue a possible inhibiting factor. Although John Stark was sincere about publishing rags of quality, he also needed to think of the business side of things if he wished to remain solvent.

It was clear that Joplin had taken a liking to this affable young man almost half his own age — one who was so interested in the ragtime art form. He had to have admired his youthful enthusiasm for the music and his desire to compose. Beyond this, Joplin was intrigued enough to find out for certain just how good these compositions really were, and so he invited Lamb to come to his home to play for him.

Several nights later, Lamb arrived at Joplin's home. During this time period it is likely that Joplin lived in a rooming house in the Tin Pan Alley area, although exact confirmation of his address doesn't officially appear in records until 1910 when he boarded at 128 West 29th Street.[46] It is possible that this is where he resided when Lamb paid his first visit or else it was in a similar type of dwelling in the near vicinity. Given its probable location, it is no surprise that the home served as a gathering place for musicians and songwriters.

Lamb's visit might have been considered somewhat unusual for the time. A number of ragtime composers and performers then, classic and otherwise, were African Americans. Social mingling across racial boundaries was not always frequent in everyday life during that time period. While Lamb was growing up in Montclair, different ethnic and racial groups also congregated in separate neighborhoods, keeping to their own specific local schools and churches. Similar to John Stark, though, these barriers were something that Lamb never thought about. Years later, his nephew wrote that it was entirely possible that his uncle had established some connection with the black community in Montclair. "Uncle Joe liked Black people so he may well have cultivated some friends among them when he was young."[47] This would seem quite likely; therefore, he gave no thought to social boundaries of the times. Nor, would it seem, did Scott Joplin.

When Lamb arrived at Joplin's home, a large group of black men were scattered throughout the room, talking and socializing, when Joplin asked him to play. That comforting sound of voices, though, helped to calm Lamb's anxieties about playing for so famous an individual and also in the midst of a fairly large group of people. The fact that Lamb might have appeared unusual in this setting didn't seem to occur to anyone.

He started to play "Sensation," its lively, well crafted sound soon rendering the crowd silent. Once the conversation faded, Lamb became more nervous but knew that he must continue. There was no stopping now.

At the end, there was fervent applause. One of the men in the crowd asked if Lamb had been playing one of Joplin's rags. When Joplin immediately responded that the piece in question had been written by Joe Lamb, the guest commented that this was a "real Colored rag."[48] Lamb was thrilled. This was the best compliment that could have been offered because this was the type of music in which he wanted to excel, a style that he naturally gravitated towards. He then played several more of his compositions—"Dynamite Rag" and "Old Home Rag" among them, by now feeling more comfortable performing for the large group as well as for his famous host. It was a memorable evening for him and one that would open an intriguing new door.

Joplin only made one suggestion regarding the music that evening or, as far as it is known, at any time thereafter. In "Dynamite Rag," he suggested that Lamb consider re-working the octaves in the left hand in contrary, rather than parallel, motion to those in the right hand. Lamb tried it and liked it.

Lamb's first "classic" rag was published in 1908 by the Stark Music Company. Joplin's name was inserted as arranger in order to attract more sales (courtesy Charles H. Templeton Collection, Special Collections, Mississippi State University Libraries).

Otherwise, no record exists of any mentor or teacher type of relationship of this sort.

"Dynamite Rag" was published many years later as "Joe Lamb's Old Rag." The title was changed in 1959, and Lamb humorously commented that "in view of 'Scott Joplin's New Rag' why can't I call it 'Joe Lamb's Old Rag' for it certainly is old—it was written in 1907."[49] Joplin's suggestion of the contrary motion remained in the published edition.

Many years later, Lamb wrote that Joplin sat at the piano on the night of his visit and tried out his rags to gain "a real professional idea" of them.[50] Joplin was especially impressed with "Sensation" and suggested that they insert his name as "arranger" on the piece under Lamb's name as composer. Joplin felt that this might help to sell the work because of the public recognition of his name. This was not an uncommon practice of the day, and it was one that afforded an unknown composer some "name" endorsement and publicity—a definite boost to sales and future success. (Before the publication of "Maple Leaf Rag," Joplin's "Original Rags" had been published in a similar fashion with Charles N. Daniels listed on the cover as arranger.)

Joplin further offered to bring the rag back to John Stark for re-consideration. With Joplin's endorsement and offer to include his name on the cover for marketing purposes, Stark bought the rag immediately, offering Lamb $25 up front and another $25 after the first thousand copies were sold[51]—an amount that he received a short time after the rag was issued in 1908. Years later, Lamb's wife, Amelia, explained how proud he was that Joplin did not change even one note of "Sensation" before it was published.[52]

This was the beginning of a very cordial friendship between Joe Lamb and Scott Joplin that was to last for the next few years. It also inaugurated a professional relationship between Lamb and John Stark, while at the same time they continued their previous friendship. Now anything that he submitted, Stark bought, leading to an eleven-year publication record and sealing Lamb's ultimate fame as one of the "big three" classic ragtime composers— a fame that would be based upon the original group of twelve rags that was issued by Stark's music company. Since John Stark was the publisher of numerous works of this group—Scott Joplin, James Scott, and Joseph Lamb—as well as those of other fine composers, it made the firm, in Stark's own words, "the storm center of high-class instrumental rags."[53] With "Sensation," Joe Lamb officially entered this world of classic ragtime.

Five

A Real Ragtime Composer
(1908–1910)

"Ragtime was a fanfare for the 20th Century"—J. Russell Lynes

The year 1908 was "Welcomed with Wild Acclaim,"[1] observed *The New York Times* as it described the huge celebration that inaugurated a more than century-old New York tradition — the dropping of the ball in Times Square. The cheers could be heard for miles. It was a glittering introduction to a year brimming with fresh promise.

The final months of 1907 had been hard ones for the economy. The "Panic of 1907," remembered particularly for the crash of New York's estimable Knickerbocker Trust Company that fall season, was just one highlight of many financially ruinous occurrences in an economy where Wall Street was in chaos— tumbling stocks, runs on banks, and widespread public fear. With the dynamic intervention of J.P. Morgan and others, however, stability began to be restored.[2] Both private investors and independent businesses, though, were forced to take a hard, contemplative look at their financial situations.

The new year of 1908, though, showed some glimmers of optimism, and confidence started to be seen once more on a number of fronts. In the music world, always hard hit in any financial crisis, signs of resilience were especially evident. The opening editorial of the January issue of *The Music Trade Review* was filled with words of uplift. If the previous season had been difficult, it postulated, then piano manufacturers would only be more encouraged to re-examine their business practices and, as a result, outline plans of greater effectiveness and productivity.[3] This would all equal better business in the long run. This same philosophy of turning setback into success could be seen in other branches of the music world, too, especially in sheet music publishing.

In a poem entitled *1908*, Tin Pan Alley publisher Leo Feist wrote, "Although money is tight let our hearts be bright,"[4] as he wished everyone in the industry a prosperous New Year. Numerous firms took these sentiments to heart as they began confidently expanding their business plans in 1908. Publisher and music entrepreneur Sol Bloom, who had optimistically hired extra staff for the holiday season, now moved to a new office and store occupying four entire floors at 40 West 34th Street, the retail space boasting a total of eight sound-proof demonstrating booths.[5] This feature certainly indicated Bloom's abundant confidence that the economy, particularly the musical one, was on the upswing.

Bloom was not alone. Pease Piano Company installed a special booth of its own for demonstrating player pianos, which it felt had turned out to be "a paying investment."[6] Jerome H. Remick & Company moved to "spacious new quarters" on West 41st Street, and P. J. Howley took over a floor at 110 West 40th Street.[7] If optimism was the antidote to economic difficulties, then the music business embraced it with a whole heart.

Although 1907 had been a quiet year in terms of publications for Joe Lamb, 1908 was a banner one in contrast. "Sensation — A Rag," the composition that had so impressed Scott Joplin and the guests at his home, was officially published by the Stark Music Company, and Lamb received the payment for his work as promised. A rag of "boundless energy ... and jubilation,"[8] it reflected the vibrance of the age and the new turn-of-the-year optimism — a fresh era symbolized by the modernized Times Square New Year's celebration and the upbeat rallying of the music industry. "Sensation" was a joyous piece of music with a title to match, and it marked the beginning of Lamb's career in classic ragtime.

"Sensation" begins with a motif that was clearly influenced by the opening section of "Maple Leaf Rag," an obvious tribute to Lamb's favorite ragtime composer. After all, as he later confessed, he looked upon Scott Joplin as his "pattern in the ragtime game."[9] The composition quickly develops from this beginning with a good indication of Lamb's emerging, distinctive style — its harmonic choices and chord voicings quite thoughtful in comparison to so much of Tin Pan Alley's output. In the trio, some of the full chords in the treble are particularly challenging to play, as are the octaves in the left hand of the final section that, in itself, explores a wider range of the keyboard.

These were some of the musical components that Lamb would begin to explore on a more mature and complex level with subsequent compositions in the ragtime genre. "Sensation" was just the beginning, and it was an impressive one — a definite milestone for the young man. A half-century later Lamb recalled that aside from meeting Scott Joplin, one of his greatest ragtime thrills was "the day I first received published copies of *Sensation.*"[10] This composition was the earliest of what came to be known as his twelve classic rags. They would all be published by John Stark, and this entire collection would serve as the basis for Lamb's later recognition as one of classic ragtime's "big three" composers.

Not only was 1908 a memorable year for Lamb but it was also significant for other ragtime composers, too. George Botsford's enduring "Black and White Rag" was published, as well as Ted Snyder's "Wild Cherries" and May Aufderheide's "Dusty Rag." Scott Joplin released his "School of Ragtime," the exercises in it designed to instruct serious students in the proper techniques of playing the higher class version of the genre. Arthur Marshall, a young composer in Missouri, saw his "Ham And!" issued by John Stark this year, as well. This composition became a favorite in the literature of ragtime and one that Lamb also greatly admired. (More than half a century after both men were featured on Stark's list of 1908 compositions, Lamb wrote to Marshall in anticipation of an opportunity to finally meet him during a ceremonial occasion.[11])

And in 1908, even presidential candidates realized the value of ragtime as Adaline Shepherd's "Pickles and Peppers," a rag first published in 1906, would soar in popularity when a portion of it served as the campaign song for William Jennings Bryan. Lamb and his newly published "Sensation" were in good company during this year.

By now, classic ragtime had spread well beyond its Midwestern and, somewhat more specifically, Missouri centers. The public was attracted to its magnetic sound. However it was far from the only style eagerly sought out by a music-hungry public. Tin Pan Alley was still busy churning out a number of its perennially enduring hits during this year as well. Among them were "Shine On Harvest Moon," made famous in the *Ziegfeld Follies* that season, and "Take Me Out to the Ball Game," a song whose enterprising creators, Albert Von Tilzer and Jack Norworth, had never so much as witnessed an opening pitch at the ballpark.[12] Popular songs such as these, along with a mix of ragtime and other varied styles, were readily becoming hits with the public.

More active than ever, sheet music publishers were now densely clustered in mid-town New York neighborhoods, filling entire floors of individual buildings, and catching the attention of passers-by with elaborate displays. It seemed as if there were publishers on every block. F.B. Haviland was at 125 West 37th Street, with both Leo Feist and the Witmarks nearby at numbers 134 and 144–46 respectively.[13] Other firms, including Harry Von Tilzer and Jerome H. Remick, had already moved to the West 40s.[14] Most would follow within a few short years, continuing Tin Pan Alley's history of progressive moves northward over the previous two decades.

Sheet music was also still very much a part of the retail scene as were in-house concerts. Some frequently combined the two, such as the Henry Siegel store on 14th Street which proudly advertised an all-day concert in May of 1908 in conjunction with a sheet music sale on their busy third floor, where "Kerry Mills' latest" song was available.[15] Song slides, too, had risen in popularity. Such well known publishers as Charles K. Harris sold both the songs and the slides, and Jos. W. Stern advertised loans of slides in addition to his free professional copies of songs.[16] Music was on everyone's mind.

This was also a year in which many of Lamb's non-ragtime compositions appeared. This grouping consisted of eight poems that he had been asked to set to music for the Sparks publishing firm in Canada while still in school at St. Jerome's. Now they were being published.

Several of these poems were written by Llyn Wood, including "Dear Blue Eyes," which the Sparks advertisements referred to as "A dainty song above the average." The music is very nostalgic, with a musical accompaniment in the refrain that is reminiscent of the graceful parlor piano sound of the late nineteenth century.

"If Love Is a Dream Let Me Never Awake" is another work with lyrics by Wood. Here, Lamb's name is listed as "Josef" F. Lamb on the cover, an indication that it was written during his days in Berlin, Ontario, where the spelling would appeal to the German population in the vicinity. Advertised as a "pretty love ballad," this is another nostalgically sentimental song with music and arrangement to match.

Samuel A. White wrote the words for "Love's Ebb Tide," which Sparks called "one of the sweetest of ballads." The music was, once more, composed by "Josef" F. Lamb — at least on the cover. Inside, his name is spelled in the regular fashion, and a caption underneath it reads, "Composer of 'Celestine' Waltz." Evidently Lamb was known for this early piece within the Sparks sales territory. "Somewhere a Broken Heart," called "a song full of pathos," is another sentimental song with lyrics by White. Its music was composed by Earl West (another of Lamb's several pseudonyms) as was "In the Shade of the Maple by the Gate," a tearjerker of substantial proportions with words by Ruth Dingman.

In Margret Anger Cawthorpe's "The Lost Letter: She Tho't Him False, He Her Untrue," the sentimental words tell the story of a love letter that was lost for many years, reminiscent of the early 1890s mega-hit "After the Ball" and others like it. It is complemented by "Josef" F. Lamb's musical setting, the slow waltz of its chorus especially underlining the sadness of the tale.[17]

The music and arrangements for many of these songs were in keeping with the lyrical and sentimental styles of Victor Herbert, Charles K. Harris, and Reginald de Koven — composers whose work Lamb knew from his younger days through newspaper supplements, sheet music counters, and general popular culture. Although Lamb was asked to write these pieces while still at St. Jerome's, why Harry Sparks chose to publish these works in 1908 and not earlier is open to speculation. There could have been any number of considerations—financial and advertising among them. He would not have published these works at any given time, though, if he did not feel that there was a market for them. Whatever the reason, Lamb now had an impressive number of published compositions to his name. (He later stated that he had written "a couple dozen"[18] of these settings for Sparks, raising the question as to whether some additional works in the firm's catalogue might have been composed under yet another Lamb pseudonym that has yet to be identified.)

There is evidence that Lamb also experimented with other compositional forms, continuing to show his lively interest in all aspects of music. "Joseph Lamb's Medley Overture #1" (unpublished) is dated this year,[19] indicating an attempt to explore the possibilities of a longer work. This interest could have derived from his own exposure to a wide range of musical styles, coupled with his general dedication to composing or, possibly, from observing Joplin's immersion in his own more serious composing projects.

Another unpublished manuscript dated 1908 is titled "Samuel: Coon Song." This might have been a revised work from previous days since this style of song had already been popular for quite a while. The lyrics are written in the dialect intrinsic to this particular form, and the lively music even contains a catchy "vamp until ready" phrase commonly used in vaudeville and variety performances. "Coon" songs had been a staple of the popular stage and Tin Pan Alley, and, again, Lamb was experimenting with yet another style that was a pervasive part of the musical and theatrical culture of the day.

One of Lamb's most unusual pieces from 1908 was titled "Three Leaves of Shamrock on the Watermelon Vine." Published by Harry Sparks, the music was written under Lamb's own name and with words attributed to his pseudonym, Harry Moore. This composition was termed "historically unique"[20] by Lamb scholar Joseph R. Scotti because of its treatment of the subject matter — the courtship and marriage of an Irishman and a black woman. Its musical tone is upbeat with lyrics to match. The piano part in the verse has a repetitive fifth in the left hand, akin to the beat of a drum, and a melody that is reminiscent of an Irish tune. The refrain, on the other hand, is written in an upbeat cakewalk style. The cover art drawing of the couple, dressed in ethnically stereotypical fashion, depicts them doing a happy cakewalk together. To complete the eclectic nature of the piece, the music is attributed to "Josef" F. Lamb.

The subject of racially or even ethnically mixed unions of any variety was a sensitive one. Given Lamb's broad knowledge of songs prior to his arrival in Canada, though, it is possible that he was aware of some variations on this theme, including a Cole and Johnson song from the show *A Trip to*

Coontown in 1898 called "The Wedding of the Chinee and the Coon." The same publisher — Howley, Haviland — issued another song the same year, with lyrics by Tom Daley and music by Gus Edwards, entitled "Since Rachel Ran Away with a Coon." This time the story focused on a young Jewish woman and a black man who worked for her father, Mr. Cohen, in his clothing shop.

These songs and others like them were, of course, stereotypical on many levels and are a variation of the many ethnic satires that had long been popular on the stage. They reflected the cultural atmosphere of the time where immigrants from many groups blended together in their new country, all of them facing challenges as they adapted and struggled to survive. According to historians Rudi Blesh and Harriet Janis, these songs acknowledged the distinctive characteristics of each group while, at the same time, fostered an "intentional camaraderie,"[21] born of music and humor that is far from comprehensible in our contemporary times.[22]

Lamb approached this subject from his own unique perspective, one that was infused with humor and a good-natured message of love and happiness,

Joe Lamb (center) with two friends in 1908, the same year that "Sensation" was published (courtesy Patricia Lamb Conn).

which the couple seemed to find in his song. According to Harry Sparks' advertisement, the song was "New York's latest hit and a big seller."

Lamb's "Sparks" output from 1908 was certainly voluminous, not to mention eclectic. A number of other songs appeared with words and music written under the pseudonym "Harry Moore," including "I'm Jealous of You," "The Engineer's Last Good Bye," and "She Does'nt [sic] Flirt." The latter song, in particular, is a humorous one, its cover drawing depicting a beautiful, formally dressed woman wearing a crown. The lady in question gives "a shoulder good and cold" to amorous men, the explanation that she is a mannequin coming at the end of the chorus: "She's but a dummy and you see, Her smile is made of wax."[23] This was advertised as "The Feature of the American Whirl Winds Company." By this time, "Harry Moore" had achieved some degree of popularity since the cover of this work praises him as the "writer of the captivating song 'Sweet Nora Doone'"—a Sparks release from the previous year.

Socially, this was a happy time for everyone in Lamb's circle. By now, his sister, Sta, and his good friend, George Van Gieson, had become well acquainted through the Clover Imperial Orchestra. "During this time," wrote Van Gieson to his sons many years later, "your mother [Sta], Uncle Joe and I saw a great deal of each other. Took walks, went to dances, shows etc etc. Dad told me one day that he would give me a piece of property if I wished to get married, so that was a help."[24] The couple married in 1909 and moved to Great Notch, New Jersey. Van Gieson went to work for the L & N Railroad within weeks of their marriage.[25]

Lamb, himself, also had an enjoyable social life in 1908. Sometime during that year, he got back in touch with Adaline S. Bunten,[26] a friend from childhood in Montclair. Addie was an excellent pianist, having studied classical music for eight years. Beginning with Thanksgiving, the two began spending more time together,[27] sharing their mutual appreciation for music. Lamb enjoyed playing his completed compositions for Addie as well as those he was working on. He found an appreciative audience in this young woman, and she was an enthusiastic supporter of his work, saying that she "knew all of Joe's ragtime music."[28] Addie definitely encouraged his composing. In turn, he coached her in the art of playing ragtime.

Lamb was a busy young man. In addition to his job, his music store visits, his girlfriend, and his orchestra work, he still found time and energy to continue composing. He was hard at work creating more complex pieces within the ragtime form. Now that he had met Joplin and had begun in-depth explorations of his music and that of other ragtime composers, he embraced the form with vigor, discovering his own unique voice within the style. Some of Lamb's new rags possessed technical demands that could challenge many classical pianists, unlike so much of what was issued by Tin Pan Alley and called ragtime, which "could be played by almost any piano player,"[29] according to him.

These technical demands were especially evident in "Excelsior Rag" and "Ethiopia Rag"—both published in 1909 by John Stark and extremely difficult to play. Yet Lamb insisted that his compositions were not specifically created to present a daunting challenge. Instead, they "just came to me the way they were written [although] I might have revised or improved upon some parts of some rags after I played them a few times—maybe changes in harmony or construction of some phrases or chords."[30]

Given his eclectic background, working within the ragtime form now permitted him to synthesize a number of his musical influences and interests, and many of these comprised the basis for both the challenging as well as the unique aspects of his work. On the one hand, Lamb was a great admirer of Joplin's compositions, which contained elements of instrumental folk music, especially of the Midwest, as well as of European classics.[31] On the other, he drew upon the information that he gleaned from *The Etude* and other similar publications and from his sisters' classical repertoire, a style that he listened to continually and voraciously absorbed while growing up. In addition, there were influences from the German music in Canada, sentimental songs of the 1890s, the eclectic Sunday newspaper supplements, music publishers' house magazines, assorted live concerts, and the many miscellaneous printed works of Tin Pan Alley. It was the perfect time to compose classic rags but, more than this, it was a good opportunity to develop a signature approach within the style, and Lamb drew upon his many musical resources to do this.

After "Sensation," Lamb soon began to define his rags as either "light" or "heavy," and he consciously composed with these characteristics in mind. Compositions such as "Champagne Rag" and "Reindeer Rag," were written in the more popular ragtime style, leaning towards a cakewalk sound. They were among the "light" rags. The "heavy" rags—"Ethiopia" and "Excelsior" among them — were far more complex structurally, harmonically, and technically. They pushed the boundaries of the ragtime form and, as a result, they were more challenging to play.[32]

"Excelsior," in particular, is a demanding piece on many levels. Trebor Tichenor called it "a study in rhythm," with its syncopations "inextricably intertwined."[33] The composition begins in the key of Db, its five-flat key signature challenging enough, but when it ultimately moves to the key of Gb, the difficulty is further compounded by certain passages with double flats. The chord structures are more densely formed and, finally, there are passages that demand intense work on a fingering pattern that is both comfortable and navigable for the individual performer.

The use of difficult key signatures was seen in Lamb's very early work.

This classic rag, published in 1909, is one of Lamb's most technically demanding compositions (courtesy Charles H. Templeton Collection, Special Collections, Mississippi State University Libraries).

His brief, unpublished composition "Idle Dreams" of 1900 begins in six sharps, incorporating some double sharps within and demonstrating that he was already trying a more demanding setting — even as a very young man. He was able to create meaningfully within these keys if he felt that they were best suited to an individual composition, an approach that developed and matured over subsequent years in works such as "Excelsior Rag" and others.

John Stark asked Lamb to transpose "Excelsior" from the original key to something easier, feeling that it could be too daunting for the average pianist as it was composed. Lamb tried this but, in the end, both the beauty and impact were lost. Stark agreed, although he still maintained that it would present difficulties in amateur performance. Nevertheless, he published "Excelsior" in the original version anyway, artistic standards winning out. On the other hand, Lamb was eager to see "Excelsior" (and "Ethopia") published, although he acknowledged their technical difficulties. Therefore he would not accept payment for them from Stark, just pleased that the publisher favored art over commerce in keeping the original form intact.[34]

The title and cover of "Excelsior Rag" are intriguing and may have been influenced by Longfellow's poem of the same name,[35] which was written in 1841. This, in turn, had been inspired by the motto of the state of New York. The poem tells the story of a young man who holds a banner imprinted with this motto as he begins his quest to scale an alpine mountain. The word "excelsior" is often translated as "ever upwards" or "ever higher."

This poem also offered inspiration to others including the Irish composer Michael Balfe, who set Longfellow's words to music. Balfe was quite popular and should have been especially so in Lamb's family because of their mutual Irish heritage. Balfe's song was recorded as a duet in 1905 for an Edison cylinder (#8935) by Harry Anthony and Charles William Harrison.[36] Once more Lamb might have been influenced by the motto, poem, or song — or all three combined.

"Ethiopia Rag" was also a challenge, not only because of its key signatures (the key of Ab in the first three sections, and the key of Db in the final two) but also because of some of its technical demands. Lamb included octave scales in the left hand as well as complex chord progressions in the right hand, especially in the final sections of the piece. These are passages that require much dedicated effort to master, the type of effort that is usually required to learn traditional classical repertoire. (Lamb, himself, could span more than an octave when playing the piano, which may have been a factor when determining various chord structures and use of octave scales.)

Lamb began or completed a number of other rags during this time period but put them away for future review, perhaps because he felt that others were more suitable for immediate publication. Many of the neglected pieces remained unpublished for years, although he did eventually return to them much later on with an eye to revision.

As in the previous year, 1909 saw publications of some of Lamb's non-ragtime works. Sparks published "The Homestead Where the Suwanee River Flows." The song clearly alludes to Stephen Foster's well known "Old Folks at Home," both in title and in verse, again illustrating Lamb's interest in different types of music and his willingness to pay tribute to his favorite composers. Although Foster used "Swanee"—a shortened version of "Suwannee"[37]—Lamb used the actual name of the river (despite the misspelling in the sheet music itself). This piece quotes a phrase of Foster's well known music and words in the chorus. This practice of "quoting" was often used by both classical and popular composers and, in many cases, it was done to underscore a particular theme, inject humor, pay tribute to the original, or for any of a number of other reasons unique to the individual creator. Here, both Lamb's song and its "quote" emphasize the time-honored themes of home and mother that were prevalent in many late nineteenth and early twentieth century works. The cover attributes words and music to "Jos." F. Lamb (although inside, his first name is spelled out).

Julia Lamb had experienced a happy reunion in Montclair with a childhood friend from Ireland. They rediscovered each other quite by coincidence. Mary A. O'Reilly was a poetess who was delighted to learn about Julia's son and his compositional achievements. She subsequently asked Lamb to set one of her poems to music. The result was "Love in Absence," a song published in 1909 with a run of 500 copies that were printed for use in the Montclair area. The actual sheet music was issued by Gordon Hurst Music—another of Lamb's various pseudonyms—although Harry H. Sparks is listed beneath this imprint on the cover. Since Lamb mentioned arranging for the copies to be printed,[38] he probably approached Harry Sparks to facilitate the actual publication process. Julia Lamb and Mary O'Reilly were together active in the song's local distribution, and the work was included on the concert programs of one of Mrs. O'Reilly's sons, who was a professional singer.[39]

The cover of this music states that the "melody" was composed by Lamb, something that Joseph R. Scotti points out as unique,[40] particularly since the piano arrangement is far more "blandly harmonized"[41] than Lamb's usual work by this time. He also suggests that someone else may have arranged the music or participated in some aspect of its composition.[42] Another possibility to be considered is that Lamb created a more basic arrangement to complement the individual requirements of a specific accompanist, perhaps one who might have worked with Mrs. O'Reilly's son or another local singer.

Addie Bunten and Joe Lamb continued their friendship and, during the early part of 1909, they became engaged, music continuing as a strong bond between them. This same year he dedicated a song to her — "Gee, Kid! But I Like You." The song is built upon a variation of a current greeting of the time — "Hi Kid" — and it also reflected the couple's own variations on this phrase along with pieces of their conversation.[43] It was published by Maurice Shapiro, a Tin Pan Alley firm located at 1416 Broadway at 39th Street.

A photograph of Frank Rushworth is on the cover of the sheet music. Rushworth was a singer and actor who had appeared in the original production of Victor Herbert's *The Fortune Teller* (1898)[44] and, later, in other miscellaneous shows including *My Lady's Maid* (1906).[45] The cover of this work bears the signature of "Starmer," the logo of the famous brothers who were responsible for the design and artwork of a multitude of sheet music covers over several decades.

Lamb is again credited on the cover as "Jos. F. Lamb," just as he was on "The Homestead Where the Suwanee River Flows." The abbreviation of the first name was a style used by others in the music business. Charles K. Harris, of "After the Ball" fame, often abbreviated his first name to "Chas." on sheet music covers, and the Tin Pan Alley publisher Jos. W. Stern did the same. This abbreviation might have been Lamb's choice, given that it appears on works issued by two different publishers. He may have been trying to align himself with popular Tin Pan Alley customs, perhaps feeling that it would give him more cachet within this environment for his more popular works, while using his full, formal name on the classic rags.

"Gee, Kid!" in particular was a real Tin Pan Alley original for Lamb. Although Stark published the classic rags, and Harry Sparks issued many of the early nostalgic songs, Lamb must have also been interested in connecting with larger publishers for his work, something that was understandable for a variety of reasons — the most obvious being that the additional notoriety that a large publisher could attract meant a wider distribution of a given song. And Lamb, like anyone else in his position, would not have been sorry to see it become a major hit, although it may not have been his primary goal. Another and quite practical reason for approaching Shapiro was because his firm published this type of material and Stark did not.

Maurice Shapiro — the publisher of "Gee, Kid!" — was an enterprising veteran of the Alley who had previously been a part of a number of firms bearing his name — Shapiro, Bernstein & Von Tilzer and Shapiro, Remick & Company, among them. By the time that Lamb's song was released, he was publishing under the name of Shapiro Music Company. Shapiro died in 1911; however his name remained as part of the firm of Shapiro, Bernstein & Company.[46]

One of Lamb's unpublished compositions, titled "Dear Old Rose," is also dated 1909. Written in a fluid waltz style, its chorus echoed many love songs of the time: "It's plain to see that the girl who loves me is my Dear old Rose."[47] Roses were popular subjects for songs—love songs in particular. Also, it might have been more than just a coincidence that during the previous fall of 1908, Frank Rushworth had been featured in a production of *Marcelle* at the Casino Theatre, in which a song called "The Message of the Red, Red Rose" was among the most notable in the show.[48] Lamb perhaps thought that his own song, bearing the title of the same flower, would have been appropriate for this same singer/actor who was featured on the cover of "Gee, Kid!" For whatever reason, though, the song remained unpublished.

Despite Lamb's obvious interest in the popular song segment of Tin Pan Alley, he still continued quite seriously with his primary love—ragtime composing—and John Stark was always the publisher for these compositions. Lamb and Stark maintained their business association and friendship throughout many years, both in New York and at a geographic distance and, also, through many personal changes for both.

Now Lamb was at work on his next rag, something quite different in character from the challengingly complex "Excelsior" and "Ethiopia" compositions. This was one piece that Addie fondly remembered. Lamb "dreamed up" his new composition on her family's front porch one evening, she recalled, and subsequently put "the finishing touches to it in our living room."[49] "Champagne Rag" was the result.

"Champagne Rag" once more demonstrates Lamb's eagerness to experiment within the classic ragtime style by adding his own unique touches. The piece combines the elements of a cakewalk, a march, and a charming melody. It also incorporates an interlude, something that Lamb uses often in later works and a feature that is more unique to his style as opposed to that of Joplin or Scott.[50] "Champagne Rag" was published by John Stark in 1910.

At some point, Lamb changed regular jobs and possibly began working for the William Whitman Publishing Company. Addie remembers that he occasionally brought her complimentary books from the firm,[51] although there is no record of what type of job he held with Whitman or for how long. It is also possible that this position was somehow in connection with Syndicate Trading Company because a portion of their business concentrated on books.[52]

In the meantime, Lamb's friendship with Scott Joplin continued. Although the focus of some later commentary was on their famous encounters at Stark's music store and at Joplin's home, there is solid evidence of far more contact than that from the time of their initial meeting. In a letter written in 1959, Lamb mentioned that during the time that Joplin's "School of Ragtime" was issued (1908) that "we were close friends."[53] And when asked in a ques-

Addie Bunten remembered that Lamb "dreamed up" this lighthearted 1910 rag on her family's front porch one evening.

tionnaire that he later completed as to how many total hours he spent with Scott Joplin, Lamb's response was "innumerable, up to about 1910."[54]

During this time, Joplin played some of his opera, *Treemonisha* for Lamb.[55] This gesture indicates the respect that Joplin had for Lamb as well as for his musical understanding and abilities. Lamb also wrote in later years about having "heard him [Joplin] play Maple Leaf several times, as well as his others."[56] He even commented about Joplin's tempos while playing as well as the fact that Joplin "used to say that when a rag is played fast you lost the effectiveness of it."[57] All of this supports the continuing association and friendship between the two composers over a period of time. In addition, Lamb wanted Addie to meet Scott Joplin, and he took her to the composer's home, illustrating that the two men were close enough socially over the course of the previous years for Lamb to bring her to visit.[58]

Lamb also spoke of his collaboration with Joplin on a rag called "Scott Joplin's Dream," most probably written between 1909 and 1910. Joplin created the first two strains, and Lamb composed the last two. The entire piece blended together seamlessly, so compatible were their approaches.[59] Regrettably, John Stark would not publish the work, despite the fact that he thought it was a fine rag. He and Joplin had parted ways over a question of royalties as well as Joplin's opera, *Treemonisha,* which Stark said he did not have the resources or inclination to publish.[60] The two men had a definite falling out, and Joplin sought other outlets for the publication of his work. Lamb, however, managed to remain on good terms with both men, no doubt a delicate enterprise but one which Lamb addressed with his usual good-natured grace.

Nevertheless, since Stark would not issue anything with Joplin's name on it and Lamb was too honorable to remove it, the piece remained unpublished. In later years it was assumed that the manuscript was lost. There is an arranged version filed with the Library of Congress, but it does not reflect the style of either man and is not thought by scholars to have been derived from the original manuscript. Joplin's copy of the composition also went missing along with a group of his other works. It is a mystery that has not been solved.[61]

There were many changes for Lamb during 1910. Several of these were turning points that were to affect his professional and personal life, and they were, symbolically at least, as memorable as the return of Halley's Comet, an event that took place in May of that year — and one that was witnessed by Joe Lamb and Addie Bunten. The return of the Comet had prompted fear in those who believed it signified the end of the world and, as the appointed moment approached, many took cover, fearing the worst. Others, like Joe Lamb and Addie Bunten, sought higher ground to enjoy this spectacular natural phenomenon. They watched under the moon and stars, the serene beauty of the evening punctuated only by a brief, torrential rainstorm.[62]

The world did not end of course, but the spectacular arrival of the Comet marked a year during which there would also be some equally stunning events for Lamb. Changes were about to take place — some personal; others professional. Several were equivalent to that torrential rainstorm but Lamb did not take cover. Instead, he addressed events as they unfolded, all of them marking turning points in his life.

On the professional front, several of the music publishers who had figured prominently in Joe Lamb's life were about to be confronted with challenges that would directly affect them and, in turn, would impact him. In a poignant turn of events, John Stark left New York to return to St. Louis. The blatantly hardcore commercial approaches of Tin Pan Alley offered little room for the promotion of fine classic rags and had yielded less interest in the genre than the publisher had hoped for — artistically and financially. Decades later, Lamb commented that his rags and those of Joplin and Scott that were of the classic variety "were not well known around New York" because much of what was published there was just "the 'Tin Pan Alley' sort."[63]

John Stark was no stranger to marketing goods for a profit, but he refused to compromise his own personal and professional standards to do so. Tin Pan Alley was all about making money, artistic quality often falling far down on the list of priorities. For Stark, it came to a battle between the commercial and the artistic. Art won in terms of integrity but it didn't pay the bills. The atmosphere of Tin Pan Alley had disintegrated from one of exciting challenge to one of weariness and struggle for him. Stark knew that his days in New York were coming to a close. It was not his type of territory, and he was practical enough to know when to move on in a business venture.

The real overriding factor in Stark's decision to leave New York, however, was his deep concern for Sarah. Her health was failing. He wanted to bring her back to St. Louis where she would be comfortable, closer to family, and away from the pressures of life in New York. Sarah was more important to John Stark than any music publishing enterprise could ever be.

Sarah Ann Casey Stark had met her husband while a teenager in New Orleans during the Civil War as she accompanied her mother to sell homemade cookies to the soldiers in his company, the Indiana Volunteers. The two eventually married and lived a rustic farming life for many years, made especially magical each evening as Sarah enthralled their children by spinning wonderful fairy tales of her own imagining.[64] Sarah had been adaptable and adventurous during the many changes of people and places in her life, as well as a wonderful supporter of her husband's business enterprises. With her outgoing personality and creative gifts, she was a strong asset to the family's music firm. Above all, though, she and John Stark had a long-term, happy marriage and a close and vibrant connection with their three children.

For Lamb, the Starks had served as a role model of a solid marriage and family life. They were also true friends—not just a music publishing connection—a couple who had always treated him well and welcomed him into their lives.

In honor of the Stark's fiftieth wedding anniversary, Lamb wrote a rag, probably around 1909, entitled "Contentment." He presented it to them sometime before the couple returned to St. Louis in 1910, and Sarah was said to have been especially happy to receive this gift, given personally by Lamb to the pair.[65]

The cover of the piece was originally planned to depict a mature and contented couple. However, the rag sat unpublished for several years while life's events unfolded. Sarah's health continued to decline rapidly, and she passed away in November of 1910, soon after their return to St. Louis. Afterwards, John Stark came to New York briefly to close up the business there before returning to St. Louis permanently. When "Contentment" was finally published in 1915, the cover featured an older man alone, sitting in an easy chair by the fireplace and meditatively smoking a pipe. He appeared to be contemplating the framed portrait of a woman on the wall nearby.

Lamb always maintained fond memories of the Starks. They had both figured so significantly in his musical and personal life and had been the catalyst for his meeting with Scott Joplin as well as his entrée to being a published composer in the classical ragtime genre. Despite the geographical distance, he continued his association with Stark, who was to publish more of his rags over the next decade—all from his St. Louis headquarters. It still wasn't the same, though, as being able to drop by for a friendly chat about the musical scene and other happenings. Lamb would miss these friends.

This year also brought changes for Harry H. Sparks. Sparks and his wife were another couple, like John and Sarah Stark, who remained long in Lamb's memory. The Sparks firm went out of business in 1910[66] but not before Harry Sparks published several songs that Lamb had previously submitted to him. Among them were "Playmates," "I Love You Just the Same," and "My Fairy Iceberg Queen." All three of these songs are attributed on the cover to "Josef" F. Lamb, suggesting that Lamb had written them sometime during his Canadian days or, perhaps, if written later, the spelling was designed to appeal to an audience who still remembered his earlier Sparks publications. (However, as in some of his other Sparks works, the first page of the music contains the traditional spelling of his first name.)

"Playmates" was billed as a "beautiful waltz song," sung by "the peerless John Turton," a baritone whose photograph was featured on the cover. The lyrics of this waltz are about a young girl and boy and, by the second verse, the now grown young man tenderly reminisces about their school days as he asks his old playmate to be his sweetheart. This subject is in the same category as the Gus Edwards and Will D. Cobb hit, "School Days" of 1907, also a waltz.

"I Love You Just the Same" is a nostalgic song about a love that remained steadfast after the singer's journey "far across the ocean."[67] Its sentimentally composed and arranged style indicates that it was probably written during Lamb's school days and not later on.

The most curious of the three works is "My Fairy Iceberg Queen." According to the first page of its music, the lyrics were written by Murray Wood, who is assumed to have been one of the poets or lyricists employed by Sparks during Lamb's days at St. Jerome's. However the cover attributes both words and music to Lamb. In addition, Lamb said that this piece was originally intended to be a cowboy song but that Eskimos had gained in popularity by the time that the song was released[68]—all adding some confusion as to its history. There is the possibility that the final lyrics were Lamb's, perhaps after the song underwent its change from cowboys to Eskimos.

Unlike a number of other lyrics that Lamb set to music for Sparks that were in the nostalgic vein, this one is lighthearted. Its words contain direct references to a Tin Pan Alley song of the same year made popular by Blanche Ring—"I've Got Rings on My Fingers"[69] (by Weston & Barnes), whose chorus reads: "Come to your Nabob" and whose main character is one Jim O'Shea. Lamb's chorus goes: "Come to your Nabob; I'm no Jim O'Shea."[70] The twist on the Weston & Barnes song is in keeping with Lamb's humorous style and certainly shows a knowledge of current hit repertoire.

After these works were published, however, the Sparks firm closed and, with it, ended another chapter of Lamb's musical life. He did maintain contact with the publisher and his family over time.

Lamb had enjoyed some fine recognition in the music business during the previous few years. The solid list of published work to his credit was especially important to him and, at the top of this list, were the rags that had been published by John Stark, the connection that had been forged by Scott Joplin. By 1910, "Sensation" had been recorded on a piano roll and was featured in an advertisement in *The Brooklyn Daily Eagle* as being sold on the fourth floor of Loesser's Department Store, along with other rolls for everything from "Dreamland" and "Dusty Rag" to the *Cavalleria Rusticana* "Intermezzo" and "Play That Tandango Rag."[71]

With these credits to his name, being young and enthusiastic, and with the heart of the soaring publishing business a reasonable commute from his doorstep, the time now seemed perfect—Lamb decided to try the music business full time. He went to work as a song plugger on Tin Pan Alley, joining the firm of J. Fred Helf. This would be another turning point for Lamb as well as for Helf—the third publisher with whom he had an affiliation and a pleasant association.

Like John Stark, J. Fred Helf was a native of Kentucky. Unlike Stark, though, he came to New York as a relatively young man at age 31 to seek his fortune in the music business. He composed at least a hundred songs and collaborated with a number of lyricists. Early on, in 1900, Helf wrote a song called "The Fatal Rose of Red" in the sentimental style that was so popular during the day. It turned into a hit for his publisher, F.A. Mills—the firm owned by the famous Tin Pan Alley composer and Montclair resident Kerry Mills. Helf's other titles ranged from "If Money Talks, It Ain't on Speaking Terms with Me" (1902) and "Everybody Works But Father" (1905), to "Make a Noise Like a Hoop and Roll Away" (1908).

Helf was an enthusiast in general, and his name appeared frequently in conjunction with songs he had written, items about how his music was advertised, and news about his business (or businesses), personal, and musical life. He was a natural in the world of Tin Pan Alley. Helf wrote vaudeville songs with Will Heelan around the turn of the century and, later, maintained this interest in vaudeville, certainly from a musical perspective as well as a business one, by purchasing a "half interest from Joe Woods' vaudeville attractions" in 1907.[72]

Helf's name and advertisements frequently showed up in *The Music Trade Review* and other publications. He wrote for Sol Bloom's firm and was partner in a number of music enterprises that bore his name, including Helf & Falke, Helf & Haskins, and the popular company of Helf & Hager, called "a young firm of unusual energy and ability"[73] by Alley veteran Isidore Witmark. Helf's partner, Fred W. Hager, who also led the Hager Recording and Park Band, was an able teammate in the enterprise. Both men were "acknowledged hit-writers and hit-makers" ... with "some of that period's greatest successes."[74]

In popular advertisements the duo called their firm "Hitland." Their music and reputation were well known on Tin Pan Alley and, of course, to Lamb. In 1906, the firm was located at the heart of Tin Pan Alley on West 28th Street, which was not only near to other publishers but also to the offices of *The New York Clipper*, the publication geared to vaudeville, minstrel, burlesque, and dramatic arts in which many firms, including Helf & Hager, regularly advertised. Helf enjoyed being near the center of musical and theatrical action.

Helf & Hager also operated a retail music store at 1389 Broadway for a while, and this might have been one of many opportunities for Lamb to have come in contact with Helf. However by 1908, the partners decided that this retail enterprise took too much time away from their publishing activities and, therefore, turned it over to another manager.[75] In the same year the firm also joined other publishers who had already moved north, relocating to 1418 Broadway.[76]

In 1909, however, the two partners went their separate ways, and the firm of J. Fred Helf began. Lamb was hired by Helf as a song plugger around 1910,[77] probably securing the job after becoming acquainted with Helf in his musical explorations. By now Lamb was fluent in approaching publishers— years of experience behind him with Sparks in Canada, as well as with John Stark and even Maurice Shapiro in New York. Joe Lamb and J. Fred Helf also had to have been acquainted with many people in common by this time.

Helf's firm was located at Broadway and West 37th Street, just a few blocks from two of Lamb's favorite sheet music haunts— Macy's and Gimbel's. Maurice Shapiro, who had published Lamb's song "Gee, Kid! But I Like You" in 1909, was located two blocks away from Helf. It was a small world in music. (These two publishers were also linked by more than a neighborhood during this time. They settled an issue out of court in 1910 when Shapiro brought suit against Helf in an effort to prevent him from publishing a song called "When My Marie Sings Chilly-Billy-Bee."[78] Such disputes were not uncommon on the Alley and added to its continually expanding repertoire of colorful anecdotes and legends.)

It had been natural for Lamb to seek work in this exciting atmosphere. He was young, enthusiastic, and familiar with various styles of music. Later on he said that he thought it would help further his own music,

In 1910, Lamb worked as a song plugger and arranger for Tin Pan Alley songwriter/publisher J. Fred Helf (foreground, right), seen here in a rare depiction from 1900 with early collaborator, Will Heelan.

although New York really wasn't the optimum place for large sales within the classical ragtime form. Perhaps Lamb was referring more to a market for his own popular songs, since there was enormous emphasis on this at the time.

While working for Helf, Lamb met many people within the music industry — writers, pluggers, and performers among them. He said that he came in contact with a number of "names" through Helf, since this was such a closely knit industry. "I worked in a music publishing place in New York for about ten months back around 1910 to get the atmosphere and, naturally, met all the big songwriters of that era. Also the big vaudeville names. Everybody knew everybody else in the music game,"[79] he said. (He also particularly mentioned being "familiar with all the Sissle and Blake music because it originated mostly in New York,"[80] although he would have been referring to a time several years after he worked for Helf, when he observed the music business as a freelance arranger, not as a fulltime Tin Pan Alley employee.)

During the time that Lamb was employed by Helf, he noticed a visitor he thought resembled the famed Missouri composer and performer, William "Blind" Boone. This gentlemen "used to come into Helf's place back around 1910," although Lamb concluded that it probably wasn't him, but he couldn't be sure, though.[81] However, this underlined his acquaintance with this composer's music. Later, he mentioned Boone's work, comparing its essence to that of the music he used to hear and enjoy at the camp grounds near Baltimore.[82]

Exciting as it appeared on the surface, living the actual life of a song plugger on the Alley was another matter. Plugging songs was a time-consuming and abrasive art. Whether or not the plugger personally believed in the quality of the material at hand, his job was to ensure that the song became supremely popular. This was done by convincing performers and the public of a song's merits and doing anything to make it a hit — and a hit translated into sellable sheet music. And this led to sales of additional sheet music as the song was printed with a variety of different covers and arranged in vast numbers of different editions—for complete ensembles, pianos, organs, and even with special ukulele chordings.

Pluggers were aggressive sorts, spending each evening visiting theaters, movie houses, restaurants, clubs, retail outlets, and any other entertainment venues that looked promising — all in the name of pushing songs for their employers. They sang, talked, played, got others to perform, and used every tactic in the book to place their title on top. A good plugger could hit multiple venues on any given evening, and such an evening could last until shortly before dawn. Some of the more notable names in the lexicon of song plugging said that they could push a song up to fifty times a night — an exhausting enterprise. It was a grueling life, and it took a special kind of personality to continually market in this type of non-stop environment. It was definitely a profession that had to be embraced a hundred percent or not at all.

Some pluggers sang; others played piano. And the new motion picture industry, with short, silent films playing in nickelodeons and other small houses, relied on pianists. Publishers on the Alley loved it when pluggers could push their songs before or during the screen presentations. In this way, Lamb was especially valuable because he would have had a rapport with the house pianists and could certainly sit down anywhere and plug a song at the piano when the opportunity arose.

As much as he loved songs, sheet music, meeting new people, and everything about music, life on Tin Pan Alley was one that Lamb hated. It was not a creative job in the artistic sense, and it encompassed some of the more unsavory aspects of a carnival barker and high-pressure salesman. It was just not a part of his personality. Plugging was not destined to be for the long term, although he did apply himself fully to the job while he held it and covered all of the familiar routes of the plugger. His wife later commented that "he had said he played piano (when he worked for a publisher) in 5–10¢ stores plugging music."[83] This could have been at one of a number of establishments and was also around the time that Woolworth's had non-stop performances by pianists and singers at its larger stores. Full displays of sheet music and folios added to the backdrop. The success of this enterprise lasted for several years, and the store set a trend[84] for others in this category — all natural haunts for the song plugging fraternity.

Lamb did not want to remain in this job. But Fred Helf wasn't about to let go too quickly. He knew talent when he saw it, and he soon moved Lamb into a job making piano arrangements for the firm. This was something that the young man liked doing and an art at which he excelled. Both men couldn't have been more delighted.

Arrangers were key individuals in most Tin Pan Alley firms, although they did not always share the spotlight. They had the ability to listen to a songwriter sing his newest melody and immediately write it down (something songwriters often could not do). Then the arranger would add fine harmonies and create something both practical and appealing for the public to play. It was the same thing that Lamb had done for Teddy Gatlin out of friendship in previous years with his "Lioneezer Rag" as well as for the Sparks composer Charles Wellinger with his "Twilight Dreams: Reverie." In Lamb's own words: "I made the piano arrangements for the songs my firm put out as well as for several of the writers who, for some reason or other, liked my arrangements better than those of the firms who published their songs."[85]

Helf knew that Lamb was especially gifted in creating beautifully distinctive harmonies for each piece. He eventually became well recognized for this. When he composed his own works, he said that harmonies came to him at the same time as ideas for a new work. This held true when he arranged for others, the appropriate harmonies coming to him fluently as he listened to composers sing their melodies. Lamb was far happier in this job, and it prepared the way for future work that he was able to do as a freelance arranger for Helf and other firms as well as for individual songwriters,[86] both at this time as well as later on, as a sideline, after he returned to the business world full time. He must have done a significant amount of work during these and subsequent years, though, since his wife later commented: "I have a lot of songs and parts that he wrote and arranged for people."[87] Since the work of many arrangers is uncredited, though, it is impossible to trace Lamb's full accomplishments in this area, which would appear to be significant.[88]

Changes were on the horizon for Fred Helf that year, which would also have an impact on Lamb. In the fall of 1910, Fred Helf had a major hit — and a major problem — on his hands. Ballard MacDonald had written some lyrics for a song called "Play That Barbershop Chord," set to the music of Lewis Muir (who went on to write the hit song "Waiting for the Robert E. Lee"). For some reason, MacDonald abandoned these lyrics in favor of other pursuits.

The lyrics were subsequently finished by William Tracey, who received full credit on the cover when Helf published the song. There was no problem, at least not until Muir introduced the song to Bert Williams who turned it into a runaway success in the *Follies of 1910*. MacDonald was furious that his name was left off the cover of the music, despite his earlier lack of interest — at least when that song was just an ordinary one. A Bert Williams hit at the *Follies* was another matter altogether. MacDonald sued Helf for $37,000 and won. Helf went bankrupt and eventually lost his business.[89]

Fred Helf seemed like a decent individual and must have liked and respected Joe Lamb because, in spite of his own considerable problems, he offered to take the time to help him find another job on the Alley — again as a plugger. He also wanted Lamb to play in theaters.[90] By this time, though, Lamb had realized that this life was not for him. However he had already established himself as a fine arranger with a good reputation, and he continued to do this type of work at home on a freelance basis for years to come. He later said that he "made more money making arrangements for writers than my combined salary and arrangement jobs while I was there [with Helf]."[91] And, of course, he still continued composing. Whether he worked full time on Tin Pan Alley or not, music was still very much a part of his life.

Around this time, Lamb contacted the Head Music Company. "Head Has Hits," or so their advertisements said. He brought them some of his rags, perhaps because John Stark, now in St. Louis, was still dealing with Sarah's passing, or perhaps because these were rags of the more popular variety. Lamb's contact at Head was the manager and part owner, Clarence Engel, who agreed to publish the works. Unfortunately, Engel died before these compositions went to press, and his partner was uneasy about publishing ragtime. (He, instead, decided to stick with such tried and true hits as "The Old Man's Getting Younger Every Day.") The partner returned most of the rags to Lamb, although "Honeymoon Rag" was still in the possession of Engel's widow who couldn't locate it later on.[92] Years later, Lamb said that he remembered the music but not the words. (However, a very old typewritten copy of lyrics to "That Honeymoon Rag" was found among Lamb's papers years later — perhaps the words to this missing piece of music or an attempt to re-create it, although no verifying details could be traced.)

Finally, after all of these events had transpired, Lamb decided to re-enter the business world with its regular hours and paycheck and, also, with its less turbulent environment. He had tried Tin Pan Alley and felt that he was not suited for the life that it offered. He could still compose and arrange while keeping a lifestyle that seemed more normal and, away from the strictures of the music world itself, he had more artistic freedom — and available time — to compose in the way he wanted.

Lamb probably began seeking new employment sometime in late 1910 or early 1911. He mentioned having worked for Helf for about ten months, and Helf's business problems surfaced in October — a natural time to begin job hunting.

Before year's end, there was one other change that was to impact his life as well. This time it was on a personal level. Although fond memories would remain, Addie Bunten and Joe Lamb parted ways.[93]

Six

Classic Rags and Brooklyn Days
(1911–1920)

"When it is by Lamb it is good"— John Stillwell Stark

Although Tin Pan Alley was not the type of life that Lamb wanted, or even liked, the experience did provide some positive benefits, not the least of which was the definite knowledge that the commercial side of music — with its consuming hours, aggressive philosophy, and brash creative atmosphere — was not for him. He had experienced the inner workings of the music publishing world first hand, having had the good fortune to come in contact with a number of songwriters, performers, and publishers while, at the same time, gaining even more knowledge of the latest trends and styles of sheet music on the market.

Along the way, Lamb had also garnered a significant amount of respect within the industry for his superb talents as an arranger. It was this reputation that would help him to maintain his contacts on the Alley without having to be a part of it full time. This was a good balance, and one that would define his subsequent approach to music and to life.

Lamb had also acquired more fluency in creating appealing harmonic structures, one of the signature elements of his style. Not only had J. Fred Helf recognized this immediately but so had others, Harry Sparks and John Stark among them. Songwriters who were associated with publishing houses other than Helf's approached him on the side, asking if he could develop piano arrangements for them, realizing that his abilities were superior to their assigned in-house arrangers. It didn't take long for word to spread, and Lamb was hired to do freelance arranging in addition to the work that he did for Helf.[1] In turn, the richness and depth of his own compositions were enhanced by this intense concentration on harmonic and structural matters. Above all, arranging was something that he enjoyed.

Around the same time that J. Fred Helf was regrouping in the aftermath

106

of bankruptcy proceedings, Lamb took a job as a book-keeper and clerk, possibly once more with the Syndicate Trading Company.[2] Returning to a regular job such as this in the "real world" turned out to be a good move in a number of ways. Without the grueling hours demanded by Tin Pan Alley, Lamb had more time — time to compose and to enjoy his music in a more objective manner. And, free from the daily exposure to the commercial side of the Alley, with its songwriting formulas and intense sales methods designed to increase revenue, he had more latitude to develop his own unique methods of composing, as well as the independent ability to try out new ideas and styles in a more objec-

One of the only remaining photographs of Lamb and his first wife, Henrietta Schultz, who died in 1920 during the flu epidemic (courtesy Patricia Lamb Conn).

tive atmosphere. The further that Lamb moved from the center of Tin Pan Alley, the more artistic control he possessed.

Now he had stable working hours and financial security, allowing him to compose and to enjoy some free time. He still kept his contacts on Tin Pan Alley and, monetarily, his freelance arranging was lucrative. Lamb could build a secure, regular home life. As a single man, this would not have risen to such importance but Lamb was about to create a new home and family of his own.

On June 7, 1911, Lamb married Henrietta Schultz, a young woman who was from Brooklyn, not Montclair as had been originally surmised. Later on, his nephew stated that the couple had also met each other in Brooklyn, as well.[3] Perhaps the meeting took place through mutual friends or co-workers, although the circumstances are not known.

A petite young woman,[4] she is shown in rare portraits as attractive and with a serene expression, her brown hair softly upswept in the style of the day. She was called "Ettie" or "Etta" by family and friends.[5] Henrietta lived with her family at 60 Reeve Place and, according to the 1910 census, both she, then twenty years old, along with her sister Elizabeth, younger by five years, worked as stenographers for an insurance company.[6] After the couple married, they moved to Henrietta's home borough of Brooklyn, another new locale for Lamb and an easier commute to his job in Manhattan.

Brooklyn had been a separate entity until 1898 when it was incorporated into the City of New York as one of its boroughs. By the time of Joe Lamb and Henrietta Schultz's marriage in 1911, it was a growing community that had attracted thousands of new residents because it offered a better quality of life than that in the crowded old buildings of Manhattan. Yet Brooklyn had close access to jobs as well as to the friends and relatives left behind.

The borough's population had already grown to over a million people by the turn of the century, and industries were beginning to thrive in greater numbers, with more than 100,000 factory workers already employed there only a few short years before Lamb's marriage.[7] A subway link was now in place as were bridges—including the venerable Brooklyn Bridge—that connected the borough to Manhattan. Transportation was continually expanding.

New libraries, theaters, and cultural offerings were always being added. Beautiful parks were among the borough's most attractive features—particularly the stunning Prospect Park, a creation of Frederick Law Olmsted and Calvert Vaux. This appealing oasis invited picnicking, sailing, and strolling, and its musical events attracted an increasing number of visitors during their leisure hours. The Lambs did not live far away.[8] It was a fine locale for beginning their new life together.

Although Lamb was settling into married life, a new home, and a new job, he still continued to complete freelance arrangements, having by now amassed a number of contacts for this work. He was quite humble about this pursuit, however, and did not "name drop" as to his clients. Also, arranging had become such a regular part of life that it did not warrant special attention by then. Lamb was content to be professionally involved by completing the arrangements while observing the music business itself from afar—a more desirable point of view for him.

He was, of course, continuing to compose. By now, his work in the classic ragtime form was deepening and maturing. He still wrote popular songs and instrumentals, though, unafraid to experiment with different forms in whatever category appealed to him. Lamb just truly enjoyed composing. Ragtime, though, was still his primary musical love.

Although it was understandable that Lamb had nothing formally published in 1911—certainly a busy year between getting married and moving to

Brooklyn — there are several unpublished works listed for the following year of 1912, including the song "Let's Do It Again," as well as the piano intermezzo, "Spanish Fly," a vibrant work that is an intriguing study in sixteenth-note groupings in the opening portion and in triplets within the closing one.[9] His next major ragtime work, though, would not appear until 1913. By this time, the Lambs were comfortable in their new lives and routines.

During these years, John Stark had settled permanently back in St. Louis, where he remained for the rest of his life. He and Lamb kept in contact, though, maintaining their good relationship, although now separated by a great distance. Stark had resumed a regular schedule of publishing once more, after becoming more adjusted to the changes in his own life without Sarah.

Stark set up a second publishing firm called Syndicate Music, designed to accommodate more popular types of works. He also purchased a new building for his combined publishing enterprises in 1915 at the cost of $20,000,[10] an amazing sum of money for its day. Stark was as perseverant and resilient as he always had been. He would continue to publish Lamb's rags through his main imprint until 1919 when the ragtime era drew to a quiet close. This event was still in the future, though, and by the time that the Lambs were married, ragtime was enjoying yet another fresh burst of enthusiasm.

Irving Berlin's hit of 1911, "Alexander's Ragtime Band," proved that the public was still buying and enjoying any music related to the ragtime sound — and the ragtime name. Frank Woolworth, the music-loving chain store entrepreneur, made sure that Berlin's hit was regularly performed on the pipe organ at his Fifth Avenue store, as well as by a roster of pianists and singers throughout his chain who delighted customers with their renditions of this and other tunes.[11]

Berlin made the most of the renewed passion for ragtime and followed "Alexander's Ragtime Band" with "Ragtime Violin" (1911), "That Mysterious Rag" (1911), "Ragtime Jockey Man" (1912), and "Ragtime Soldier Man" (1912). He produced a seemingly inexhaustible supply of titles that contributed to the public's enthusiasm for the sound.

By the mid teens, even the prolific Sigmund Romberg, later known for his operetta works, was composing rag-type music for shows. "The Ragtime Pipe of Pan" of 1915 (lyrics by Harold Atteridge) was featured in *A World of Pleasure.* "Ragtime Calisthenics" (co-written with Otto Motzan, lyrics by Harold Atteridge) was from the *Passing Show of 1916.* These were not in the classic mode that John Stark endorsed but they were, again, another reflection of the popularity of ragtime in its many varieties. It was a banner era for ragtime once more, and both the positive and negative aspects of its musical implications and accompanying culture were again being discussed.

On one hand, ragtime was commended for having some positive aspects, even being credited with helping to alleviate panic as the Titanic was sinking. One survivor told of how the musicians switched from classical to ragtime repertoire after the initial crash. Some were said to have danced a cheerful waltz that was "one of the popular ragtime affairs."[12] However not all reports spoke so highly of its noble benefits.

By the early teens, ragtime had taken hold of more than just the listening public; it had also become inextricably linked with the world of dance. Dancing gave the ragtime craze another infusion of energy but one that only supplied its critics with increasingly negative eloquence. Now they could further denounce this musical style, whose evils had multiplied to an even greater extent with the devil gainfully employed on the dance floor.

The wicked excitement was catching on fast. Dancing became so diverse that it was, like ragtime itself, hard to define, with routines by now embracing everything from the tango and the two-step, to the Turkey Trot and the Grizzly Bear. Vernon and Irene Castle, elegant and popular as entertainment icons, helped to spread the dancing craze, performing with the well-known ragtime composer and band leader, James Reese Europe. Europe wrote a number of ragtime pieces with the Castles in mind — among them the "Castle House Rag," the "Castle Maxixe," and the "Castle Innovation Tango" — all published by Joseph W. Stern & Company.[13]

They even hired Henry Lodge to play the piano at Castle House in New York, a club where the team provided able dance instruction and thrilled their students with dancing exhibitions.[14] Lodge was a well known pianist and composer, whose 1909 work "Temptation Rag" was a hit, particularly on the vaudeville stage.[15] The Castles were shrewd to align themselves with such well known musicians while, at the same time, they made the most of every opportunity to popularize their art — and themselves. "Everybody's Doing It," or so went Irving Berlin's popular song, and it seemed as if everyone — rich or poor, awkward or graceful — was doing a dance.

Ragtime and its dances spread not only across America but also caught on like wildfire in Europe where additional critics emerged in harmony with their counterparts across the ocean. Now both the music as well as the dancing loomed large as a well-teamed foe of those who regarded themselves as the gatekeepers of public decency. There were some in London who were "deeply shocked at the suggestiveness"[16] of dances associated with this type of music. There was even talk of organizing an Anti-Ragtime League.

At home in the United States, social reformers and religious leaders decried dancing to ragtime as vulgar, suggestive, and evil. By 1913, even New York City's Mayor Gaynor was pressured to crack down on the music and the dancing, a thankless task that drew much humor from contemporary observers and certainly didn't accomplish its goal.[17] People still wanted to dance to the happy music and, observed a sly song from the *Ziegfeld Follies of 1913*, if restrictions prohibited this in public places, then an individual would just "have to go home.... And do the Grizzly with my wife!"[18] The classical music establishment made their disdain known as well, as did the medical profession that suggested both the music and its associated dancing could be a possible cause for insanity.[19]

If ragtime was frowned upon, and dancing along with it, the rapidly growing film industry was not much better off, especially when ragtime music joined in with it. Pianists were an important part of the nickelodeon film experience, accompanying the onscreen action and providing background music at other times. Ragtime was popular for all of it, and it was no surprise that there was a general outcry from its critics. Not only did ragtime often seem inappropriate for the particular scene being played, it was still not considered to be of a style that was "respectable ... for the middle class."[20]

Both Patricia Lamb Conn and Robert Lamb remember their father saying that he had played piano for silent films, although the specific details are not known. It is certainly probable that Lamb played during various junctures at nickelodeons while he was employed as a song plugger for J. Fred Helf. This activity would have focused on pushing Helf's current list of songs. However, Lamb also spoke to his children about matching the music to the action onscreen, indicating that he played as a regular silent film pianist, not just as a plugger. This might have occurred at any time and in a variety of circumstances. However it is most probable that he performed for one of the Brooklyn silent movie venues after he married and moved there.

Interest in film was locally high due to the fact that Vitagraph had studios at Avenue M and East 14th Street in the Midwood section for a while. Also, there were a number of new theaters being built in the borough to accommodate its growing population. It would have been natural for Lamb to act as pianist, even occasionally, at one of these theaters, large or small. There were also several potential contacts who might have been a catalyst for this activity.

The Music Trade Review reported that in 1914, Lamb's old employer, J. Fred Helf, gave up music publishing, which had been a rocky road for him after the 1910 lawsuit, and decided to go into motion pictures,[21] although it did not say in what capacity. At one point, he had wanted Lamb to play for films and might have once again urged him to pursue this as a sideline. Also, Henrietta's family (and, eventually, Joe and Henrietta Lamb, themselves) lived in close proximity to the Collins family with whom they would become friendly. These were musically inclined individuals, and the father of the family worked in theatrical management in Brooklyn for a number of years. He, too, may have paved the way for Lamb to work occasionally as a pianist for films, an activity that Lamb would have pursued both for his own enjoyment as well as for some extra money to supplement his income as a young married man. It would be impossible to imagine that Lamb did not somehow incorporate ragtime into his repertoire under these circumstances, thus putting himself in the critical spotlight for anyone who may not have approved of either the music or the surroundings.

On a personal level, Lamb's new family was divided on the issue of ragtime. Henrietta's brothers were enamored of the music and really enjoyed Lamb's piano playing. Their mother, however, did not seem to totally appreciate the form. This was certainly not unusual for the time, but it was awkward since her son-in-law was a composer in the style — albeit in the classic style — a distinction that Lamb, himself, might have been quick to underline, even though he enjoyed and experimented with composing in all forms. "Ragtime was considered *sinful* in those years!"[22] commented his nephew later on, no doubt after hearing the widespread debates on the subject early on.

Nevertheless, it would have been hard to imagine anyone objecting to a beautiful piece of music written in the pure classic ragtime format and titled after the name of a lovely flower: the rose. This was the focus of Lamb's composition published by Stark in 1913, the next of Lamb's classic rags to be issued after a hiatus of several years. In this same year, Ellen Wilson, wife of President Woodrow Wilson, directed the creation of the White House Rose Garden.[23] Roses were especially well liked flowers.

The American Beauty variety of rose — a hybrid, with a lovely fragrant scent rising from its medium bright petals — was a popular cut flower in the United States in the late nineteenth and early twentieth centuries.[24] This flower even figured significantly in literature, and Edith Wharton used it as a key symbol in *House of Mirth*, her novel of 1905.

This variety of rose was also the subject of a brief film created by the Edison Company in its studios in West Orange, New Jersey, back in 1906 — the same year that Lamb returned from California. The film was entitled "Three American Beauties." The opening of the film presents a lovely rose that is soon transformed into a beautiful young woman who, ultimately, fades into the final scene — a depiction of the American flag.[25] This work was shown in nicolodeons and would have been known in the Montclair locale where Lamb grew up, not only because of general public curiosity at that time about this relatively new entertainment form but also because of the area's proximity to the Edison studios.

American Beauty roses had been the topic of previous musical compositions, as well. Harry H. Zickel seemed especially taken by the subject as seen in his "American Beauty March & Two-Step" of 1908 and his 1910 ballad, "My American Beauty Rose." Both covers displayed roses as well as cameos

Published in 1913, this is one of Lamb's most beloved and frequently recorded rags. It was also arranged for large ensemble performance (courtesy Charles H. Templeton Collection, Special Collections, Mississippi State University Libraries).

of beautiful young women, a pairing reminiscent of the theme of Edison's film. These compositions were issued as advertisements for the Kalamazoo Corset Company of Michigan,[26] a business that would have realized the power of music, flowers, and beauty as a marketing device. These were far from the only compositions, though, with roses as a major part of the focus.

Although, Lamb had written two previous compositions about roses, both unpublished — "A Rose and You," of 1905, and "Dear Old Rose," of 1909 — "American Beauty Rag" of 1913 not only saw formal publication but also became one of his best known compositions. Beneath its title are the words "a rag of class." The original cover displays two beautiful full roses on a stem in a delicately stunning rendering by Henry Reichard, an artist who lived in St. Louis and created many covers for the Stark firm.[27]

The music itself possesses well shaped phrases and delicate beauty in its opening sections, all in proportionate contrast to the buoyant final sections which make increasingly expansive use of a wide range of the keyboard. The composition is a marvel of distinctive harmony and well planned structure, an outstanding example of Lamb's signature style.

Lamb admitted that he picked the title himself for this classic rag, as opposed to some of his other titles which were selected by John Stark. He later said that he considered it "a nice title and other rags had flowers for names so why not one of mine."[28] Ironically, the popularity of the American Beauty variety of rose waned somewhat after World War I, along with the decline in popularity of ragtime music.

Max Kortlander recorded "American Beauty" on Q.R.S. roll 100299 in 1914,[29] early in his career. Kortlander was a prolific artist within this medium and eventually became president of the Q.R.S. company. A number of other piano rolls of this work were made by various performers. "American Beauty" reveals, in the words of Trebor Tichenor, Lamb's "splendid bold originality,"[30] and it continued to be a favorite among recording artists into the next century.

"American Beauty" was so popular that John Stark had arrangements of it made for large ensembles. In 1914, an Army band played the work at the Union Square recruiting station, much to Lamb's delight — and surprise. A friend had insisted that Lamb eat lunch with him one day at a restaurant that was farther away than usual, thus enabling them to walk past the band. Upon a pre-arranged signal from the friend, the ensemble began the familiar strains of "American Beauty." Afterwards, performers and composer alike were honored with enthusiastic applause.[31]

The popularity of both this composition and its ensemble arrangements spread. Orchestras from as far away as Australia included "American Beauty" in their repertoires. J.V. Malling, leader of The Peerless Orchestra in Sydney, enthusiastically wrote to John Stark to tell him that he publicly presented this piece along with the additional ragtime arrangements of Etilmon Stark's "Billiken" and James Scott's "Grace and Beauty" during a week-long series of concerts. He called them "an oasis in a dreary desert of 'piffle.'"[32] And ragtime pianist Gene Hawkes toured the same country, featuring "American Beauty"[33] on his own programs. (Gene Hawkes also performed in Wellington, New Zealand, as part of a duo that brought "the latest in ragtine [sic]"[34] to audiences there.)

Several other Lamb rags were arranged for band by the Stark Music Company. "Champagne Rag" was one of these, sensitively orchestrated by R. (Rocco) Venuto—who not only completed band and instrumental arrangements but also, as an individual as versatile as Lamb himself, composed such pieces as "Meeneowha Intermezzo & Two-Step" and "Girliana Waltzes" in his earlier days.[35]

Lamb specifically commented on hearing this arrangement of "Champagne Rag" during the World War I years. It must have had a spectacular sound as performed by the 250-piece Army band directed by Charles Bollar, a group that was stationed at Union Square but played each day during the lunch hour at the Twenty-Third Street Recruiting Station, in the vicinity of Lamb's workplace. According to Lamb, Bollar wanted to meet one of the women in Lamb's office, so he was particularly glad to have his band play in that locale. Lamb happily gave Bollar three of Stark's band arrangements of his rags, which the group evidently performed. "They sure made those three arrangements talk," Lamb remembered.[36]

Aside from the publication of "American Beauty," 1913 was turning into another prolific year for Lamb. In keeping with his penchant for variety, he also composed some other types of works during this time. Two of them were lighthearted songs for which he wrote the music; however the lyrics were by "G. Satterlee." The firm of Satterlee Music Company published both compositions. Since there appears to be no record of a firm by that name, it is possible that this was a friend's short-lived imprint or else both the lyricist and publishing firm were pseudonyms for Lamb, although contemporary listings and directories indicate that there were real people by the name of Satterlee who were likely involved somehow.

The 1912 Brooklyn City Directory lists Joseph Satterlee, an accountant, at 315 Seventh Avenue,[37] the same address printed on the sheet music under the music company's name. Could a relative with the first initial "G" have been the lyricist? There was also a George J. Satterlee, listed in the 1920 census along with his wife and several children (one of whom was George J. Satterlee, Jr., age 18), living at 519 Eighth Street in Brooklyn.[38]

A *Mrs.* G. Satterlee (perhaps the wife of the family on Eighth Street)

wrote the words for a song called "The Bower of Love," also published by the
Satterlee firm in 1913. Page One of this song is advertised inside the sheet
music to Lamb's composition "I'll Follow the Crowd to Coney." Music for
"The Bower of Love" was written by Eugene Platzmann, an individual whose
work shows up elsewhere, as both a composer and, particularly, as an arranger
for dance folios and instrumentals of the era.[39]

Platzmann was surely known to Joe Lamb. They were both published by
the elusive Satterlee music firm, each with lyrics written by someone with the
last name of Satterlee. In another interesting coincidence, several issues of
The New York Clipper, a popular entertainment publication of the day, contained advertisements for Platzmann, who enthusiastically offered his services
to the public as an arranger, stating that he had arranged "HUNDREDS of
BIG HITS!"[40] At the bottom of his ad was not only his name but also an invitation to call him during a three-hour time segment on weekday afternoons
at the Shapiro music publishing firm located at 1416 Broadway. This was the
same firm (although Shapiro himself had since passed away), and at the same
address, that had published Lamb's 1909 song, "Gee, Kid! But I Like You."
Since Lamb was still active as an arranger and had previous contacts within
Tin Pan Alley as well with the Shapiro firm (as obviously so did Platzmann),
it is probable that the men knew each other.

Details about any other composers who may have been associated with
the Satterlee firm are not known, still raising questions as to the entire background of the enterprise. However both Lamb and Platzmann were fine rep-
resentatives of the imprint and further underline Lamb's continuing
association with professional arrangers and composers within the music business during this time.

One of Lamb's songs issued under the Satterlee imprint, "I'll Follow the
Crowd to Coney," is a lilting waltz, with words to match, about the popular
amusement area in Brooklyn which had seen so many developments in the
years since he wrote the unpublished "Meet Me at the Chutes." Coney Island
continued to draw large crowds for its amusements, its entertainment, and
its famous boardwalk. Plus, now that the Lambs were living in Brooklyn, the
area was much closer to them and, given its popularity with the public in
general, it was a natural subject for a song. G. Satterlee's lyrics convey the fun
of Coney Island, where "You can 'Tang-go' and 'Trot,' eat frankfurters hot."[41]
Lamb's carefree waltz tune and arrangement are reminiscent of some of the
earlier styles of Tin Pan Alley, such as the 1906 "Waltz Me Around Again,
Willie," and others like it.

Lamb's other Satterlee publication was "I Want to Be a Bird-Man," an
upbeat song with a vaudeville style sound. Presumably it is the little boy
depicted on the cover who, enthralled with aviation — one of the world's latest

fascinations—begs the "Bird-Man" in verse one to teach him how to fly. Lyrics were, again, by "G. Satterlee."

Each of these pieces of sheet music displays a whimsical line drawing on the cover. Lamb enjoyed drawing and, as his sketch inspired by the Tennyson poem in his youth as well as others could attest, he had some degree of talent

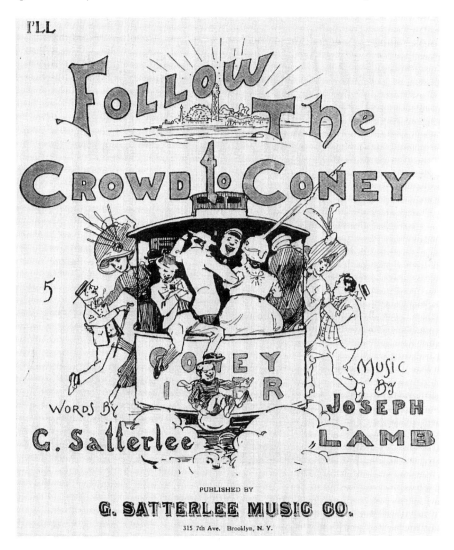

One of two 1913 compositions published by the Brooklyn firm G. Satterlee Music, this was a Lamb family favorite and was later republished and recorded in 2005 (courtesy Patricia Lamb Conn).

at it. Although there is no evidence, it is interesting to speculate that Lamb, himself, might have been the cover artist (or might have drafted a cover), especially since these works were not issued by a major Tin Pan Alley publisher but, rather, by one of a grassroots variety.

The same year as the Satterlee publications appeared, another song was issued that also contains some puzzling aspects concerning both the publisher itself as well as its sheet music cover. The piece was titled "The Ladies' Aid Song." Both words and music were attributed to Harry Moore, one of Lamb's Canadian pseudonyms from the days of Harry Sparks, a company now out of business. This particular song, however, was published by the Canadian firm of Musgrave Bros. & Davies in Toronto.

During the time that Lamb was going to school at St. Jerome's, Charles E. Musgrave was listed in the Toronto City Directory as a pianist and accompanist with the T. Eaton Company on Yonge Street.[42] With these piano skills, Musgrave would have been an asset to the firm both in musical instrument sales as well as in sheet music demonstrating and would have been a reasonably visible figure to the public. Later, he became manager of Dominion Music and soon afterwards opened a business with his brother, subsequently forming the short-lived firm of Musgrave Bros. & Davies.[43] It is possible that Lamb met Musgrave at some point in Canada on a trip to Toronto music stores and, in turn, Musgrave might have been familiar with Lamb's output as a composer for Harry Sparks.

Canadian music researcher Ted Tjaden discovered the existence of "The Ladies' Aid Song" and concluded that it might have been something that was awaiting publication at the Sparks firm when it went out of business.[44] Harry Sparks or someone else on his staff may have approached Musgrave with a request to publish his remaining outstanding manuscripts. The Sparks and Musgrave firms would certainly have known each other through the local Canadian music industry as well as through their geographic proximity in the Yonge Street area of Toronto over the preceding years.

The sheet music for this song reads "published for the author" on the cover and, by this time, Lamb had not lived in Canada for a number of years. This would support the theory that the publication might have been a gesture of friendship by Harry Sparks in some way. (Both Canadian and U.S. copyrights are held by Harry Moore, not the publishing firm.) Supporting Tjaden's theory that this was, indeed, a composition written by Lamb, the cover lists two of his other known Harry Moore songs—"Sweet Nora Doone" and "The Engineer's Last Good Bye." A third, "That's What the Little Girl Said," has yet to be found. The lyrics of the "Ladies' Aid Song" song reflect the sort of wry humor that Lamb favored.

One of the song's puzzling features, though, is the cameo photograph on the cover. It is not that of Joe Lamb, and there is no explanation as to the identity of this individual. However it is not unusual for photographs to appear on sheet music covers with no name or caption. "I'm Jealous of You," published by Sparks in 1908, contains the photo of a well-dressed man with no clue as to his identity. The photograph may have been that of a performer whose name and face were locally familiar at the time or it is also possible that this was an error.

In the meantime, Lamb turned to other musical possibilities including operetta, its songs popular both on the stage as well as in sheet music. Audiences enjoyed these tales of love with their lyrical music and convoluted plotlines. Victor Herbert had been a forerunner in the field for a while, and lighthearted romance was one of his specialties. His work titled *The Enchantress* of 1911 contained the hit song "To the Land of My Own Romance." Although unpublished, Lamb wrote a song called "Romance Land," dated 1913, its sound consistent with that of the operetta style. Given his eclectic interests, Lamb might have drawn inspiration from Herbert's works and those of others, and may have even considered operetta themes as a future possibility. Whether or not he began this composition earlier and returned to it in 1913 is not known.

Around this same time, Lamb also wrote "The 22nd Regiment March." Both Patrick Gilmore and Victor Herbert had at one time been conductors of this group. Both had written marches in its honor, and Herbert's was composed in 1898. The band toured extensively and played frequently in local areas, being a crowd favorite in Brooklyn. Given Lamb's previous exposure to band music in Canada as well as his knowledge of all types of American repertoire, it is not surprising that he, too, composed a march in honor of this famous group and in the tradition of two great conductors and composers of band music. Lamb's work could have been written earlier and just attributed to this year or, since he was now a Brooklyn resident and the bands had performed there frequently in the past, he might have developed a particularly strong interest in the subject that was prompted from a geographical standpoint. The work was not published.

There are several other compositions attributed to this period, which appeared to be both an eclectic and prolific time. One, from 1914, is particularly interesting because Lamb wrote the music and "Mrs. Joseph F. Lamb" (Henrietta) wrote the lyrics. The song was entitled "Wal-Yo" and refers to a greeting sometimes used within the Italian community. The text is obviously intended to be humorous and the song is similar to many others that depicted various different ethnic groups on the stage. Ethnic humor had never completely gone out of fashion, and every group had been the focus of songs, their stereotypical nature, although comic, a universal element of the style.

However, by this time, Lamb could have been uncomfortable with the subject matter and decided not to seek publication.

Lamb wrote some rags prior to this time, beginning as early as when "Sensation" first appeared, and revised this group through approximately 1914. However this was a continual process, and these may have also undergone some changes right through his mature life. They remained unpublished until after his death and include such titles as "The Bee-Hive," "Greased Lightning Rag," "Rapid Transit Rag," and "The Jersey Rag." The "Toad Stool Rag" was dedicated to Joplin, and "The Ragtime Special — A Slow Drag Two Step" (one that indicates revision over a longer period of time) contained the inscription "Respectfully dedicated to my Friend Scott Joplin." Years later Lamb referred to this rag in particular, saying, "It is dedicated to his [Joplin's] memory, which, I might add, will never be erased."[45]

According to most accounts, Lamb began to lose touch with Joplin after 1914. By the time that Lamb had moved to Brooklyn, Joplin was in the process of relocating to an apartment at 252 West 47th Street where he and his wife Lottie lived and ran the Scott Joplin Music Publishing Company.[46] He and Lamb were still in contact during this time, as supported by Lamb's later reference to the quality of Joplin's piano playing. "Personally," he wrote, "I don't think there was any difference between the Joplin of 1914 and the Joplin of 1908 ... and that was about the period that I heard him the most."[47] This established at least a six-year frame of contact in total between the two men. Lamb also continued: "To my recollection, he played his rags the way he wrote them. That's the way I always did."[48]

Geographical distance and life's changes had to have resulted in less contact between the two over time after 1914. Scott and Lottie Joplin eventually moved fur-

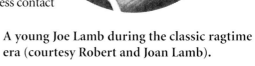

A young Joe Lamb during the classic ragtime era (courtesy Robert and Joan Lamb).

ther away to Harlem, where Joplin became increasingly occupied with his opera, *Treemonisha*, withdrawing from many of his former friends and associates. He was also coping with his continually declining health on a number of levels. Lamb's nephew said that his uncle "mentioned S.J. [Scott Joplin] was a very sad man. He was in NY trying to get a play he wrote on the stage but having no luck. S. Joplin was a sick man at that time."[49]

By 1914, there were other changes for Lamb as well. In the spring of that year, he answered a job advertisement for the firm of Dommerich & Company. As a result, he secured a position working in the import division of this firm as a customs house clerk at a salary of $25 a week.[50] The job was a responsible one that included "financing accounts of manufacturers, guaranteeing their sales and checking their credits,"[51] a process known as factoring. This was the company that he stayed with for the remainder of his working career. The job paid a higher salary than his previous one and allowed the Lambs more monetary latitude to move to a larger apartment and to enjoy a more comfortable lifestyle. It also paved the way for them to start a family under more secure financial circumstances. And, of course, Lamb was still doing arranging jobs on a freelance basis, another good source of income.

In 1915, four Lamb rags were published by John Stark. "Contentment," the gift rag that Lamb had presented to the Starks in 1910, finally appeared. Its cover depicted an older man sitting alone, smoking his pipe quietly in front of the fireplace and contemplating the portrait of a woman nearby. John Stark would always miss his beloved Sarah.

"Reindeer — Ragtime Two-Step" also appeared during this year. It is one of Lamb's lighter rags,[52] yet it has an appeal that bears the composer's definitive individual style.

Stark also published "Cleopatra Rag" in 1915. The design on the front cover depicts the Queen of the Nile in an exotic setting, the colors in a dramatic gold and black mixture. Lamb admitted that he did not name this rag. Its cover appears to be one that was already on hand at Stark's firm — the exact same cover was also used for James Scott's "Sunburst Rag" as well as for the posthumously published "Reflection Rag" by Joplin.[53] One theory is that it was designed by the renowned Starmer brothers but that Stark covered up the defining signature because it had been used before.[54] If nothing else, Stark always made thrifty use of his resources.

Published during the days of the silent film era, it was said that the style of the cover for "Cleopatra Rag" evokes the dramatic world of the cinema with its emerging stars such as Theda Bara and Rudolph Valentino. Whether or not this was actually the intent of either the artist or the publisher (or of Lamb, himself) is open to dispute, although it was suggested by Rudi Blesh years later.[55] However the work was published during an exciting era in the

One of Lamb's "lighter" compositions from 1915. Its exotic cover was also used by the thrifty John Stark for works by Scott Joplin and James Scott, the other two members of ragtime's "big three" (courtesy Charles H. Templeton Collection, Special Collections, Mississippi State University Libraries).

development of the film industry and, perhaps because of the time period in which it was written as well as its cover's power of suggestion, it is not hard to imagine the syncopated melody of the piece easily complementing the action of a silent film plot.

For the Lambs personally, this was an especially joyous year, marked by an exciting event: the birth of their son, Joseph Lamb, Jr., on July 23, 1915. This was a happy time for the couple. Lamb was now settled both in his new job and in his role as a family man, all of which he thoroughly enjoyed. He had also achieved musical success with the publication of more of his classic rags.

One of Lamb's most famous works was published in 1915 — "The Ragtime Nightingale" or "Nightingale Rag." "It is impossible for me to explain," he said, "just what caused the writing of any of my rags with maybe one exception — Ragtime Nightingale."[56] Its opening left-hand runs recall Chopin's "Revolutionary Etude," a work that he was familiar with from the days of listening to his sisters practice the classics. Lamb also confessed that he drew inspiration for his "bird sound" from a phrase in Ethelbert Nevin's "Nightingale Song" as published in *The Etude* magazine, as well as from parts of James Scott's "Ragtime Oriole," something he used in the final section of his own work. "I probably had in mind Ragtime Oriole when I gave it the name but the nightingale gave me ideas of bird sounds which I tried to incorporate in the first strain and then in the intorduction [sic] to the last strain," he wrote years later. "I haven't the slightest idea of how a nightingale sings but if you have ever played Ethelbert Nevins' [sic] Nightingale Song you will find that I got an idea for the latter example from that song. The other harmonies and melodies just came to me — that's all."[57]

The success of this rag was fairly immediate. It was published in 1915 and recorded on several piano rolls during the same year. A few issues of *The Music Trade Review* carried advertisements for these rolls. Ernest Stevens made an Artempo roll that was issued in July by Bennett & White Inc., in Newark, New Jersey. In addition, "Nightingale Rag" was listed with other rolls, both classical and popular, which the firm said "should find a place in the library of player pianists who discriminate in their selections."[58] In October of the same year, the Angelus Melodant Artistyle released rolls that included this piece in their lists of offerings as sold by The Wilcox & White Co.[59] More rolls were to appear.

Lamb continued with his ragtime works. John Stark published two more of his rags in 1916 — "Top Liner Rag" and "Patricia Rag." The first theme of "Patricia Rag" was based on a portion of "Hyacinth, A Rag" that was never published. (It was not, as often thought, named for his daughter, Patricia, who was born years later, nor was she named after the rag. According to her,

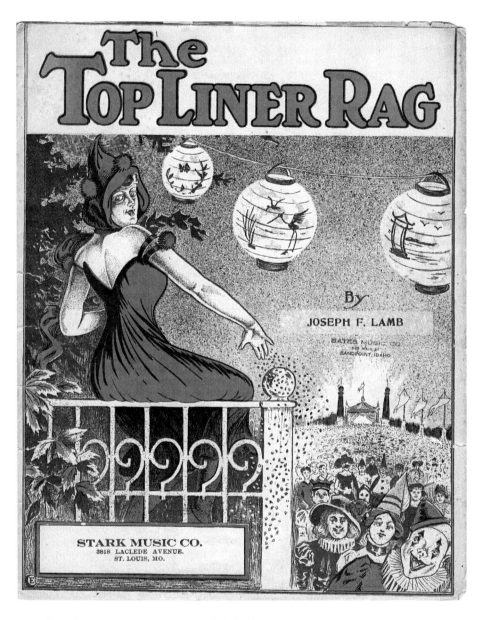

This classic composition was published in 1916 and also appeared in the popular *Christensen's Ragtime Review*, prompting one reader to confess that it transformed him from an opponent of ragtime into an enthusiast (courtesy Charles H. Templeton Collection, Special Collections, Mississippi State University Libraries).

Lamb had more trouble naming the rags than writing them, and he admitted that "not all the titles of my rags were mine."[60] Stark most probably named "Patricia Rag" himself but there is no explanation as to why. He might have just had a spare cover ready for use.)

"Top Liner" was originally titled "Cottontail" but since the ever practical and thrifty John Stark did have a cover handy, this time with a drawing of a circus performer, he renamed it. It was reported that Clarence St. John's piece, "The Carnival," was the source of this cover.[61] Lamb felt that "TOP LINER deserved a better name but maybe Stark thought that was better than COTTONTAIL."[62] The popular composer and performer, Felix Arndt made a piano roll of "Top Liner."[63] Years later, Lamb composed another "Cottontail," an updated and more mature version of this early work.

During the mid teens, Lamb gained additional notoriety for his rags beyond regular sheet music sales and piano rolls through the pages of *Axel Christensen's Ragtime Review*.[64] This publication might have been considered a ragtime version of *The Etude* — each issue containing articles, technical instruction, advertisements, and fully reproduced ragtime compositions. Its publisher, Axel Christensen, was a ragtime enthusiast who opened schools of ragtime instruction across the country. The magazine reinforced his principles concerning the art of playing ragtime well and provided detailed articles on many aspects of the subject. John Stark advertised there regularly.

Some of Lamb's classic rags appeared in *Christensen's Ragtime Review*, including "Ragtime Nightingale" (August 1915 issue), "Reindeer Rag" (September 1915 issue), and "Top Liner Rag" (March 1916 issue), thereby increasing the popularity of his music on a wider scale. There was no doubt now that Lamb was a recognized name in the ragtime world. One classical pianist wrote to John Stark after discovering "Top Liner" in the *Ragtime Review*, saying that although he had previously "tabooed ragtime," this piece "made me a convert."[65]

World War I had already cast a gloomy shadow over Europe, and Americans were following developing events with a wary eye. Like other composers of the time, Lamb was patriotically minded. In 1916 he composed "The Cause of Liberty" in which he refers to those "who stand for all that's right and true."[66] Another with no date but possibly from the same era is called "The Dying Hero."

Themes such as these were at the forefront on Tin Pan Alley, and songs were an integral part of getting the country into a patriotic mindset for its inevitable entrance into the war. Obviously Lamb felt strongly on the subject. Although these and other songs from this time were not published, this was due to the fact that Lamb was so involved with his job and family that he didn't have time to make the rounds of various music publishing houses that issued this type of work.

The sound of ragtime was already beginning to fade with the country's potential entry into the war becoming more of a reality. The naïve and light-hearted days when this music enjoyed its highest popularity seemed out of step with serious global issues on the horizon. Scott Joplin, still the leading name associated with ragtime, died in 1917, his illness having emaciated him and his dream of seeing his ragtime opera, *Treemonisha,* fully produced and artistically recognized long shattered. Within days of his death, the United States formally entered into World War I. This signaled the end of an era and the beginning of a new and more serious one.

Lamb wanted to volunteer for active duty but decided against this since he had a family to care for. According to his draft registration card, he was the sole provider for his wife and son. However he wanted to do something for the cause so he joined the New York State Home Guard's Cavalry unit at this time,[67] later joking that he never actually did get on a horse.

In the meantime, Lamb's family life occupied much of his time. Joe Jr. was still a toddler and keeping the couple busy. Plus there was Lamb's family to visit in New Jersey as well as Henrietta's nearby in Brooklyn. And their neighborhood was active socially.

The Lambs were located in an area which was a hospitable one — everyone was acquainted, and many developed friendships with those who lived nearby. (On Lamb's Draft Registration Card, they were listed as living at 615 Avenue C,[68] although they were shown as residing at 15 Reeve Place[69] by the time of the 1920 census.)

The Lambs were in close proximity to the Schultzes, and Henrietta's two teenaged brothers— Herman (Hermie) and William — had become quite friendly with Lamb and really enjoyed his piano playing as did their friends. Hermie Schultz continually praised Lamb's talents to everyone in this group and beyond.

The Collins family also lived close by, and these and other families all knew each other and were often a part of get-togethers. One of the local weekly gatherings was called the "Light Up"— a friendly event where teenagers and young people in the neighborhood could socialize, eat snacks, and listen to some music. Lamb was included in these and was popular there since everyone looked forward to hearing him play the piano.[70] Given the growing seriousness of the world at large, this type of happy, casual event was a welcome one.

One night Hermie Schultz invited his young neighbor, Amelia Collins, to hear Lamb perform. Hermie was also good friends with Amelia's brothers and had been insistent that she join the group. Her brother, Jack, also urged her to come along and participate in the event since he, too, enjoyed music and appreciated Lamb's talents. Amelia preferred to get together separately with her own friends, though. Nevertheless, since one of the gatherings was being held at her brother Dorrie's house, she finally agreed to attend one evening with her sister, although it was with reluctance.[71]

Joe Lamb was playing the piano, always welcome entertainment for anyone there who loved music. Amelia carefully listened to Lamb at the keyboard and then asked "Mr. Lamb" if he would play "Daisy"— possibly the popular old favorite "Daisy Bell"— as well as a few other songs. He refused. She asked once more and, again, he refused. Finally, and with his wry sense of humor, he said that it was because she called him "Mr. Lamb" and not "Joe."[72]

Amelia was furious. Because of the marked difference of their ages, she was not comfortable calling him by his first name. It was not the custom of the time. Lamb was being humorous and perhaps did not want to be considered old by the substantial number of younger people there. Amelia was quite angry and vowed never to have any contact with him again.

Despite this incident, though, she did become friendly with Henrietta Lamb and even babysat for Joe Jr. once a week while Etta played cards with friends. The two women would also occasionally have ice cream together. However Amelia continually refused to have any more to do with Joe Lamb after the evening of the infamous social gathering.[73] The weekly "light-ups" continued without further incident— and without Amelia.

The ragtime era was now drawing to a close. Stark was to publish the last of Lamb's classic rags in 1919—"Bohemia Rag"— which may or may not have been named in recognition of Balfe's popular operetta *The Bohemian Girl,* as observed later by Rudi Blesh[74] and implied by its cover. A strong possibility exists that Stark had the cover and paired rag with artwork but, in this case, it may have been a closer match of the two than usual since, as Trebor Tichenor points out, the piece does offer a lovely suggestion "of Slavic rustic dances."[75] "Bohemia" marked the final publication of Lamb's classic rags by Stark. The ragtime era was over.

The lighthearted young people who had played and sang and danced to ragtime were world weary now, unable to maintain the innocent sparkle that was once theirs. Ragtime's vehement detractors had other worries, many soon to wish for the days when the only threat to their youth and their nation was a syncopated rhythm and a joyous dance step. The United States was now embroiled in a war to end all wars. More than a hundred thousand of its soldiers would die on foreign soil, causing heartbreak for a generation that had once been so happy.

Life was changing for the Lambs and their extended families, too. Julia Lamb had remained in Montclair, not far from Anastasia and George Van Gieson in Great Notch. The Van Gieson children were young and must have seen her enough to have had a fond nickname for her. Paul Van Gieson remembered, "We called her 'Ababa' (broad 'A' as in Rabbit) but aren't sure why. I guess that was Buckie's [George Jr.] way of saying Grandmother."[76]

Julia Lamb, however, would not have the privilege of seeing her young grandchildren grow up. In 1919, she passed away from a stroke. Joe Lamb's mother, to whom he had long ago dedicated the beautiful waltz, "Mignonne," was now gone. Additional sorrow would follow.

Apart from the war, there was another enemy, one that was now attacking the world with a vengeance. It hit on home soil as well as abroad, affecting everyone in all parts of the globe — the flu.

The flu epidemic began in 1918 and lasted for approximately two years, sickening hundreds of thousands around the world. Otherwise healthy young people were not immune to its ravages and complications. It hit every age, locale, and social group — rich and poor alike. In Brooklyn, Joe, Henrietta, Joe Jr., and their numerous relatives, friends, and neighbors all became ill.[77]

Doctors could find no vaccine to cope with this strain. It was too virulent and moved far too quickly. There really was no cure. Millions died — a larger number than were lost in the war. Sixteen million were casualties of World War I; however, fifty million died of the flu in the entire world. More than a quarter of the population in the United States alone was afflicted in some way by the illness.[78]

The famous composer and pianist Felix Arndt, known for his enduring novelty work, "Nola," and who had also recorded a piano roll of Lamb's "American Beauty" and others, passed away from the flu. So did Rose Cleveland, sister of former President Grover Cleveland. And so did millions more.

And on February 6, 1920 — towards the very end of this horrible epidemic — it also took Henrietta Lamb.[79] She was just thirty years old.

Henrietta's death was a horrific blow for the entire family, a scene that was repeated over and over again in thousands of other homes across the country. Now, a devastated Joe Lamb was left to raise five-year-old Joe Jr. alone.

Seven

A Time of Transition (1920–1922)

"The type of guy that everyone liked"— Paul Van Gieson

Early 1920 was bleak for both father and son. For a while, they stayed with Henrietta's family in their Brooklyn home[1] on Reeve Place, the same street on which the Lambs had resided.[2] Complications, however, soon arose. Music, which had always been Lamb's joy, and now his consolation, was giving rise to some difficulties.

Unfortunately, his mother-in-law, Mrs. Schultz, was among those who viewed ragtime in a negative light. Despite the fact that the popularity of the style had waned by this time, her antipathy was evident. It was still not an uncommon view that ragtime music and its associated culture were not suitable in proper circles.

The issue of music was not a new one. Mrs. Schultz had never approved of Lamb's piano playing,[3] and now its sounds were resonating under her roof.

There were others factors that added to the general discomfort. Cultural, ethnic, and other considerations— religion being one of them — all with their unique frames of reference, certainly complicated the situation. Henrietta grew up in the Lutheran religious tradition but converted to Catholicism when she married Lamb, a situation that troubled Mrs. Schultz at the outset and intensified after Henrietta's death.[4]

Without Henrietta, the magnitude of any issues were bound to grow, musical ones included. Henrietta had enjoyed her husband's compositions and, even before their marriage, had owned copies of the sheet music to some of the Sparks songs—"Etta Schultz" written on the covers to such compositions as "The Lost Letter," "Dear Blue Eyes," and "In the Shade of the Maple by the Gate."[5] She also wrote lyrics to one of Lamb's unpublished songs, "Wal-Yo"[6] and was certainly familiar with the classic rags and other works, especially since Lamb wrote a number of them during their marriage.

Henrietta's brothers had been enthralled with Lamb's compositions as well as with his piano playing, particularly the younger of the two, Herman Schultz ("Hermie").[7] The two men were good friends. This may have exacerbated Mrs. Schultz's feelings over the years as well.

As time progressed, however, it was natural that Herman Schultz would become more occupied with his own life as well as with his job responsibilities which, according to the 1920 census records, were as a clerk at a wholesale paper company.[8] His older brother, William, was in the army at this time.[9] Both of the Schultz brothers were also dealing with losing their sister. In addition, since Herman Schultz and Joe Lamb were friends, this placed each one in an awkward position with regard to the family situation.

Although there is little information about the senior Mr. Schultz, the 1920 census indicates a change of employment[10] after many years as a lumber inspector, his profession as cited in both the 1900[11] and 1910[12] census records. This shift from a long-term career by the later age of 51, combined with grief over Henrietta's death, and worries about a son in the army, constituted a potent enough mix to raise stress levels within this or any family. Also, there is no apparent record of Henrietta's sister after the 1910[13] census, and no mention is made of her in subsequent research materials—indicating another possible concern for the family.

Now, Lamb and his son had joined the Schultz household, both also stricken by the loss of someone dear to them. Although the differing musical philosophies paled in comparison to larger issues, they only intensified under the circumstances, and this could have provided a vent for all of the underlying worries, tensions, and heartache that were of a more complex variety. The total situation, coupled with the stress of close proximity in the aftermath of a tragedy, became uncomfortable.

Despite their differences, one thing that Joe Lamb and his mother-in-law did share is certain—their deep sorrow over Henrietta's death. Living under the same roof, however, did not offer any mutual solace. It was time for a change.

Lamb and his son left the Schultz house within several months of arriving there. In the process, much of the sheet music that he had accumulated over the years was lost, something that he later referred to as having come about through "unpleasant and unfortunate circumstances."[14] He did not offer clarification, except to remark years later that the rags were irreplaceable.[15]

Father and son returned to New Jersey, this time to live with Anastasia and her family. The same understanding sister, who had once helped her small brother with his little round notes at the piano so many years before, again came to his aid, this time providing a home and a haven for him and his son. They were to remain there for the next two years while trying to put their lives back together.

Anastasia was now married to George Van Gieson, Lamb's boyhood friend, commuting companion, and fellow performer from the Clover Imperial Orchestra days. The couple lived in Great Notch, a rural area adjacent to Montclair. Kate Lamb, who had remained single, also lived with the family, giving piano lessons to the Van Gieson boys.[16] (Later, when the Van Giesons moved out of state, she went to work as a housekeeper for an executive in New Jersey.[17])

The Van Giesons had two sons—George Jr. ("Bucky"), who was born in 1910, and Paul, who was born in 1914, both just a little older than their cousin.[18] For Joe Jr. this was a wonderful diversion and adventure to be able to share the company of his two cousins and experience a new area that was worth exploring, its country-like atmosphere a sharp contrast to the city environment he had known in Brooklyn. It was a welcome change for the boy during a difficult and confusing time.

By now, Joe Lamb had been promoted to Bank Office Manager at Dommerich,[19] his responsibilities having increased since first joining the firm in 1914. His association with the company promised to continue being a substantial one, and he would establish a life's career with this firm. Again, he commuted by train to New York, just as he had when a young man in Montclair. This time, though, he departed from the Great Notch station, a small yet active place that served the nearby communities well. It had a hometown atmosphere, and its station house was a friendly place, known to local residents. Although traveling from Great Notch was not a short commute and the station was a substantially long walk from the house, the peace and comfort that Lamb and his son found at the Van Gieson home made it more than worthwhile.

The three children loved the adventure of trekking a mile from their house to meet Lamb at the Great Notch station where the Erie Railroad-Greenwood Lake Branch stopped. Together they would all return to the house, nestled in its woodsy surroundings, where Lamb would play the piano for the family in the evenings.[20]

By this time, the novelty piano style had blossomed in popularity, its flashy technical demands and happy dash of syncopation holding tremendous appeal for audiences as well as for pianists of all levels. It wasn't ragtime but it was one of several relatives of the style. The late Felix Arndt had been among the first to attract marked interest in the novelty form with his 1916 composition, "Nola." Now, Zez Confrey had become one of its leading figures, and his 1921 work, "Kitten on the Keys" was a hit — so much so that Confrey, himself, eventually performed it on Paul Whiteman's famous 1924 Aeolian Hall concert program, "An Experiment in Modern Music."[21] Confrey, an active pianist and arranger for a number of piano roll firms, was busy popularizing the novelty form in the early 1920s. His work was eventually issued in a folio of novelty solos published by Jack Mills, Inc., in 1923, underlining the continuing demand for his compositions.[22]

Lamb immediately learned "Kitten" and delighted the family as well as the neighborhood children with his repeated performances of this novelty number. It was one of their favorites. "I can still hear him," confessed his nephew, George Van Gieson, Jr., years later.[23] He recalled his uncle playing them "with the interlocking finger technique typical of the style,"[24] demonstrating that Lamb was familiar with the performance practices of this form, one that combined elements of both classical music and syncopation and was technically demanding. He also played his own compositions for them, but the children felt that they were not fast enough.[25]

"Uncle Joe," as he was known to all of the local children, played "Maple Leaf Rag," too—a composition that he returned to throughout his life. He never forgot his friend Scott Joplin and his magnificent music from the old ragtime days. Although he enjoyed playing the currently popular novelty numbers, he continually stressed his belief that they were not in the same class as ragtime compositions.[26]

There were also the frequent sounds of Lamb creating a new piece of music. "He would compose ... on a Saturday or Sunday," wrote one of his nephews, "because he would ask my Father & Mother to listen to a bar or two to get their opinion."[27] Lamb was already experimenting with the new novelty style.

Aside from the sounds of Lamb at the piano with his renditions of varied repertoire, the children were used to hearing other music in the house. George and Sta Van Gieson often played duets together—semi-classical music in particular. Paul Van Gieson remembers his father playing the violin quite well. "He played Paganinis Moto Perfectuo among other things."[28]

Joe Jr. was happy in these new surroundings, sharing adventures with his cousins and enjoying the relaxed atmosphere with the Van Giesons. He and his father maintained a close relationship, and he remembered how Lamb came home from work and brought him O'Henry candy bars a few times each week, the boy's favorite treat.[29] Lamb consistently paid attention to this and other such small details that would make his son feel special and happy.

The three children flew kites with their fathers and, occasionally, these fathers would enjoy this same pastime themselves. "After we were in bed," reminisced Joe Jr., years later, "he [Joe Lamb] and Uncle George would fly them [the kites] and sometimes even lose them in the trees."[30] Perhaps this reminded the men of their own carefree boyhood days in Montclair.

The young boys were mischievous, too, sometimes engaging in pranks. However, Lamb always tried to make sure that Joe Jr. was treated well, being the youngest of the group. Lamb would caution them to be sure that Joe Jr. did not get lost during the boys' hiking or fishing excursions during the day, although Paul Van Gieson confessed that they once left him in Indian Cave as a practical joke but came back for him.[31] His brother later recalled the aftermath of a prank of his own saying that he felt that he owed "Uncle Joe some respect. He was chasing me one day to box my ears because I was teasing Joe Jr. I jumped over a brook & he jumped in it."[32] Despite the childhood teasing, the Van Giesons and Joe Jr. remained close for life.

The 1920s—the Roaring Twenties—were now ushering in a new age, one that was far removed from boyhood adventures with kites and was more of a reaction to the sorrows and heartache that had played out on both the world stage and on personal levels.

In contrast to the age of ragtime with its spirit of buoyant happiness, the war as well as the flu pandemic had given the nation and, especially, its youth a jaded sophistication born out of hard times. Now they met life full force in a desperate effort to have fun and to eradicate memories of recent horrors. And this fun, and the changes that came with it, lacked the more innocent simplicity of the ragtime age.

There were major social changes that had been taking place. Prohibition had just been mandated. This did not eradicate alcohol; it just enhanced its glamour, giving rise to speakeasies, bootleg liquor, and a whole new brand of crime. New musical styles, as always, accompanied and reflected these changes. There was, of course, jazz—a freer and more sophisticated style that had been around for a while but now took a more prominent place in the spotlight.

There were other important changes, as well. Women were now being granted the right to vote and were treated as equals at the polls after a long battle to win this right. The era of the flapper had also begun. Women cut their hair, wore short dresses to match, and smoked in public. F. Scott Fitzgerald, the glamorous writer whose work reflected the times, was busy penning his novels and short stories—from "Bernice Bobs Her Hair" to *The Great Gatsby*, works that observed changes in the contemporary culture.

Automobiles were commonplace now. Many were flashy and sophisticated, a sign that the age of the horse-drawn carriage was coming to a close. Money was easy and spent freely. Airplanes were coming into vogue. Radio was an increasingly appealing innovation, and even though silent films were still the rage, "talking" pictures were waiting in the wings to make their grand entrance on the entertainment scene. Life was definitely moving faster.

Music was changing, too. Jazz, blues, and more up-to-date Broadway songs captured the public's attention. In 1920, popular titles included "Dardanella," "Whispering," "Avalon," and "St. Louis Blues." Subsequent years featured such hits as "Ain't We Got Fun," "The Sheik of Araby," "Basin Street Blues," and "Runnin' Wild." The word "rag" was rarely seen. Although the days of "Maple Leaf Rag" and "Sensation" were a memory, some things never really did change. Jazz, a freer form with its own unique sound, was the favored style. Now former critics of the evils of ragtime music had a vast new frontier open on their collective horizon with the advent of jazz, prompting Ann Shaw Faulkner to ask in a 1921 edition of *The Ladies' Home Journal*: "Does Jazz Put the Sin in Syncopation?"[33] Judging by the article, it apparently went beyond sin to downright evil. Of course the fact that jazz was often played in speakeasy clubs where liquor was served further fueled its sinful reputation, but even when performed in legitimate venues, it was considered to be at the root of a moral downturn. This, of course, made the ragtime of years gone by seem harmless in comparison. The same distaste that critics had once held for the one-step and the Grizzly Bear was soon transferred to the Charleston, the Black Bottom, and other emerging dances.

For the most part, the Lambs and the Van Giesons were removed from all of this, living their daily lives in the peaceful setting of Great Notch and going about normal activities as usual — jobs, commuting, home music, and flying kites amply filling their time. However Lamb still pursued music in some of his spare time, aside from the daily ritual of playing the piano each evening for the family. Once he brought home a clarinet and a flute, explaining that he was taking lessons.[34] It is possible that he wanted to delve into jazz, since instruments such as these were favored over the piano in the small bands and ensembles that were now performing in the popular style. He might have also thought of forming an ensemble of his own once again. Whatever the case, these short-lived woodwinds mysteriously vanished one day.[35] It is probable that the improvisation inherent in the jazz genre, particularly as performed on non-keyboard instruments, was not for Lamb and, beyond this, the piano was still his first love.

When not spending time with the family or playing the piano, Lamb could now be found working on his automobile, a lovely yellow Kissel.[36] These beautifully crafted cars were made in Hartford, Wisconsin, and, although the company did not have a long life, it had an illustrious one while still in business. It was an especially popular vehicle among celebrities. Amelia Earhart owned a Kissel as did Sennett actor/comedian Fatty Arbuckle and pianist, Eddy Duchin. And actress Anita King — known as "The Paramount Girl" — had done much to enhance the cachet of this automobile by being the first woman to drive cross-country totally alone in 1915 in one of them. Yellow, in particular, was a favored color of the manufacturer, so much so that it named one of its models "The Goldbug."[37]

This was the color car that Lamb owned. He had purchased the Kissel

Amelia Collins, circa 1922 (courtesy Patricia Lamb Conn).

from a neighbor in Great Notch, Walter Yahn.[38] Aside from being the previous owner of this car, Yahn would soon be a helpful part of Lamb's life in another way in the near future. For the moment, though, the Kissel represented a happy diversion and welcome transportation. With its cheerful color and key to the open road, it was a joy to own and drive — a definite lift to the spirits, holding the promise of happier things to come.

On weekends, Lamb worked on his beautiful car, putting his technical know-how and love of precision to good use, ensuring that the vehicle was efficient, reliable, and presentable. All of this was quite important because he began making trips in his car back to Brooklyn. He still had many friends in his former neighborhood but soon there was an even more distinct purpose to those trips. He was now regularly visiting the young woman who swore that she never wanted to see him again — Amelia Collins.[39]

Eight

A Happy Family (1922–1948)

*"We will have a wonderful time"— from the Dorrie Collins
and Joe Lamb minstrel show song "Here We Are Again"*

Amelia Collins ("Melie," as she was called) was a petite, pretty young woman with dark hair, a sweetly expressive face, and a lively personality. She was the youngest of five children, closest in age to her sister Genevieve. Their father, Augustus (Gus) was in the theatrical business, holding jobs as a treasurer[1] and, eventually, a manager.[2] He was remembered to have worked locally and, since credit was given to Fred DeLappe at Werba's Brooklyn Theatre for the loan of props to a Lamb-Collins 1929 minstrel show production, it is likely that Collins was associated with this or one of Werba's other many venues over the years. Given his career within the industry, Collins may have also been a connection for some early silent film piano jobs for Lamb, since they had known each other as neighbors on Reeve Place during the previous decade.[3]

The entire Collins family enjoyed music a great deal, and Augustus Collins, along with his three sons— Augustus (Gus Jr.), Dorrington (Dorrie), and John (Jack)— sang in barbershop quartet harmony at family gatherings. A couple of them played instruments as well, including the banjo and saxophone,[4] and Lamb enjoyed their musical companionship.

Joe Lamb and Jack Collins were particularly good friends. Now they were to become brothers-in-law. After a courtship during which Lamb regularly drove his distinctive yellow Kissel from Great Notch to Brooklyn, he and Amelia Collins were married on November 12, 1922, at St. Mark's Roman Catholic Church there.[5] This was the beginning of a long and happy family life, one in which music played an important but balanced part.

At first, Lamb, Melie, and Joe Jr. lived with the Collins family. Lamb had purchased some property in the Sheepshead Bay section of Brooklyn and planned construction on a house there at #2229 East 21st Street. This was to be his and Melie's permanent home, and it was just across the street from the Collins family. The actual construction of their new house was completed by George Van Gieson's brother and uncle, along with builder, Walter Yahn, a neighbor from Great Notch. (It was Yahn who had sold his Kissel car to Lamb, a vehicle upon which Melie eventually learned to drive).[6]

Sheepshead Bay was experiencing a housing boom at this time. It was close to Avenue U and its local shops as well as to good transportation. The community, located in the southern portion of Brooklyn, rimmed the local waterways. By the time the Lambs settled there in the early 1920s, the commute to work in bustling Manhattan was attractive, yet families could also live a quiet life in this little residential haven. It hadn't always been so.

In its early days, Sheepshead Bay was dotted with serene farms, and fishing was both a pastime and a local industry. But in 1880, it became home to a racetrack, appealing to the rich and famous for their entertainment and the sporting life. Everyone from W. K. Vanderbilt to Diamond Jim Brady could be seen in its environs.[7] Also, the area was near to Brighton Beach as well as to the popular Manhattan Beach section of the borough where there were lovely hotels and the frequent performances of bands under the direction of John Philip Sousa, Victor Herbert, and others — all legendary to local history. And, of course, Sheepshead Bay was just a short distance from Coney Island with its acclaimed amusements. There were many opportunities to enjoy the area's beaches and to sample the food from the popular hotels and restaurants. This whole portion of Brooklyn was alive with activity.

When the racetrack closed in 1915, an automobile speedway soon took its place. After a brief and spectacular flourish it, too, was demolished. Within a short time, the land was divided and sold in the early 1920s for housing.[8] From 1922 through 1923, the borough itself was reportedly at the forefront nationwide in building new homes,[9] and Sheepshead Bay was certainly among the most popular of areas in this regard, with a public eager to get in on the ground floor of the post-speedway real estate opportunities there. After the flurry of building and influx of new residents subsided, Sheepshead Bay returned once again to a semblance of the quiet life it had once known before its several decades of glittering fame. It would mature into a lovely middle-class neighborhood of tree-lined streets and daily family life.

The Lambs awaited the completion of their new house with eager anticipation but that was far from the only exciting event on the horizon. On February 6, 1924, their daughter Patricia was born[10] and when she was six months old, the growing family finally moved into their new home.

Patricia was not, as some have speculated, named after Lamb's 1916 rag. And the composition, as the family would humorously comment on in time to come, was not named after her (as was also sometimes thought), since she was born a number of years after it was composed. Her birth year, though, was filled with a number of enduring new songs—"It Had to Be You," "Fascinating Rhythm," and "Goodbye, My Coney Island Baby," among them — just not ragtime works. By now, ragtime as Lamb had known it had faded, with new forms and variations on the rise — among them stride, novelty, and jazz (often as difficult to define as ragtime had been).

Joe Lamb had little leisure, though, to ponder this shift in musical tastes. He and Melie were occupied with their new home and their growing family. Three more children were to join Joe Jr. and Patricia over the next few years: Richard, on March 19, 1926; Robert on November 20, 1927; and Donald on July 18, 1930.[11] The Lambs would lead a vibrant family life, with extended relatives nearby adding richness to the mix. Music would always be a part of this home for the children as they grew.

Lamb was certainly aware of the latest hits in the music world and would occasionally bring home professional copies of sheet music, indicating that he did maintain some contacts within the industry. He added these copies to a piano bench already bursting with all types of sheet music — rags, songs, instrumentals, and manuscripts.

What Lamb especially enjoyed as the children were growing up was the evening family ritual. Each night he would come home from his job at Dommerich, change into an old flannel shirt, and have one

Joe Lamb and Amelia Collins around the time of their marriage in late 1922 (courtesy Patricia Lamb Conn).

One of the twelve classic rags that was published in 1916, this was not named for the Lambs' daughter, Patricia, nor was she named after the composition (courtesy Charles H. Templeton Collection, Special Collections, Mississippi State University Libraries).

glass of sweet white wine before dinner; "white port is my favorite,"[12] he later said. After the meal, he would help Melie clean up the dishes, and then he'd head for the piano. There Lamb immersed himself in his music, often rocking a new baby to sleep—his foot on the "old, ivory wicker bassinet"[13]—while playing the piano at the same time. Then he would experiment with a new composition, pencil in mouth, keeping time by nodding his head.[14] Spending these precious hours with his family and his music together was something special, and he often mentioned this to his friends and business associates.

Lamb didn't completely abandon his outside musical pursuits but, with an active family life, they were less time-consuming than before. According to Melie, he continued to create arrangements for various publishers on a freelance basis, though.[15] However, it is not known which publishers in particular he contracted with—or perhaps which independent songwriters—or for how many years this activity lasted.

Early in the 1920s, Lamb still occasionally approached a publisher with his own work for potential consideration. He was knowledgeable enough of the contemporary trends in music publishing to have been aware of the fact that Jack Mills of Mills Music occasionally bought rags, although many were now leaning in the direction of the novelty variety. An innovative businessman, Mills became one of the top publishers of novelties, and he was certainly unafraid to publish what he liked. He was savvy enough to recognize the talents of Zez Confrey, having published his "Kitten on the Keys" in 1921,[16] a composition that the world loved—pianistic difficulty notwithstanding. This was one of Lamb's favorites, too, and he had played it since it was first published, during the time he lived in Great Notch.

Perhaps one of Mills' most captivating moves for those who still favored ragtime was to issue Joplin's "Magnetic Rag" in a 1923 folio of piano novelties.[17] This might have been a reason behind Lamb's approach to Mills during the 1920s with one of his own works—a piece called "Chasin' the Chippies—Two-Step." However, according to Lamb, Jack Mills "said he didn't go in for rags,"[18] and he suggested that Lamb send it to John Stark instead, even though both of them knew that Stark was planning on going out of the publishing business in the not-too-distant future. Lamb, who was still in touch with his old friend and publisher from ragtime days, followed Mills' suggestion.

John Stark was now living in St. Louis with his son, Etilmon and his family. The elder Stark still rose early and went to his office on a daily basis, despite the paucity of sales within the ragtime sector. When not working, he enjoyed spending time with his granddaughter, Margaret Eleanor, discussing philosophy, religion, and myth—subjects of long-term interest to him and to her as well. The two had a good rapport.[19]

Stark was interested in Lamb's composition and bought the piece, keeping it for future publication at an appropriate time. Unfortunately, this plan never materialized. Stark passed away in 1927. His death diminished any lingering hope that classic ragtime still had a place in the contemporary music world.

This was obviously a turning point for Lamb. He felt that ragtime died with Stark. "No other publisher could do with ragtime what John Stark did,"[20] he later admitted. Stark had been a friend as well as a special connection to the ragtime world, just as Joplin had been. Now, they were both gone.

"Chasin' the Chippies" was never published, even though the Stark firm continued to stay in business for several more years. The composition was believed to have been among the items destroyed when the company's St. Louis printing plant burned in 1929.[21] A composition with the same title, dated 1914, was included in *A Little Lost Lamb*, the 2005 folio containing some of Lamb's previously unpublished works. (Lamb was known to re-use a title of which he was particularly fond if the original title was changed or if the music was lost.)

In the meantime, though, Jack Mills was still in contact with Lamb. He was adamant that Lamb provide him with other compositions, particularly novelties— or "novelettes"— similar to the late Felix Arndt's "Nola," written in 1916. During his short life, Arndt had an eclectic musical career, something that would have caught Lamb's attention early on and even if not, "Nola's" popularity would have been enough to draw his interest. Arndt wrote songs for vaudeville and also served as a church organist.[22] He was a friend to and inspiration for George Gershwin, possibly for his "Rialto Ripples," and also turned out a record number of piano rolls,[23] including a rendition of Lamb's "American Beauty." His famous composition "Nola" was considered to be a forerunner of the novelty style and achieved wide popularity in sheet music and also in piano rolls and recordings. Mills felt that these types of compositions were increasingly well received by the buying and listening public and, of course, he now published the work of novelty music's current rising star, Zez Confrey.

Lamb complied with Mills' request, producing a total of fifteen works. The first was titled "Waffles." A set of four additional works were to follow and, eventually, ten more novelettes. Among the entire group were such intriguing titles as "Banana Oil," "Apple Sauce," and "The Berries."[24] It is interesting to note that one of Felix Arndt's published compositions from 1914 was titled "From Soup to Nuts." The title might have offered inspiration to Lamb and, in any event, he certainly focused on what seemed to be the theme of food in this set of novelties. However, some of these titles had double meanings or were, in effect, slang expressions. Arndt's "from soup to nuts" also meant "from beginning to end." And Lamb's pieces also had slang equivalents—"banana oil" denoted "nonsense," "applesauce" was a substitute for the old expletive "horsefeathers," and "the berries" meant "pleasing," and so forth.

Regrettably, these works were never published because while waiting to be issued, they were lost when Mills moved its offices to a new location. The compositions were not recovered. "Where are they now?" Lamb mused later on, referring to these lost works. "I wish I knew."[25] Both Lamb and Mills had been anxious to see them in print but there were no copies, and Lamb couldn't recreate them — only a few phrases lingered. He said that he usually didn't remember the works that he sold because he felt that, "I would have the [printed] music before long and I could use that."[26]

In the meantime, the bulk of Lamb's professional energies were devoted to his full-time job. He was still employed at L. F. Dommerich and Company, which had moved from 254 Fourth Avenue to 271 Madison Avenue at East 43rd Street in Manhattan. Lamb joined the firm in 1914 and remained with them until his retirement. He enjoyed his work and was a loyal member of the staff. According to Melie, they were "factors for all kinds of business materials—rugs—lace I guess everything that was domestic or imported. He had charge of the Foreign Works."[27]

Lamb thrived in this corporate environment and was not only good at his job but also made a positive impression on all of his business associates. Marjorie Freilich-Den discovered much valuable information about Lamb's business career during her research.[28] She had the opportunity to speak as well as correspond with several individuals who had been associated with Lamb over the years. One of them, Frank Stayskal, spoke of how conscientious Lamb was in his capacity as head of the Import-Export portion of Dommerich's business in the 1930s, functioning as "financial adviser to the textile finishers and importers."[29] He clearly remembered Lamb discussing his family with great affection and as coming first in his life and, then, subsequently, would speak of his music and how he composed. The man was thrilled to eventually receive a gift from Lamb of seven autographed copies of his classic rag compositions.[30]

Other individuals shared reminiscences from various time periods during the 1940s. One woman remembered that Lamb preferred working at an old-style, roll top desk and when he made a phone call, he spelled out his name, further explaining that it was as "in lamb chops or lamb stew."[31] Another individual found Lamb to be "inventive" in his job as well as quite "influential and helpful" to the firm's officials.[32] Lamb had been in charge of the entire billing department for Dommerich in the 1950s, and his secretary during this time praised him as "a wonderful man."[33]

Lamb enjoyed the international aspects of his work and had even taken a course in Spanish because in his "job as Foreign Traffic Manager ... all the documents required by Cuba and most South American countries had to be in Spanish."[34] It is possible that he first developed an interest in and a knowledge of the global business world back in his Syndicate Trading days, since they had interests both domestically and abroad.

Lamb spoke highly of the company's staff and also remembered the firm's lovely annual Christmas party at the Waldorf Astoria Hotel. No one overindulged, he recalled, and he relished being a part of the festive atmosphere. There was a dinner, a band, and dancing, and they always announced the Christmas bonus at this event.[35] He appreciated the company and its respectful treatment of its employees. The Dommerich firm, well known within the financial industry, eventually merged with Chemical Bank, becoming its own separate division. This merger took place, though, after Lamb retired in 1957.

Lamb often went to mass during his lunch hour at a church nearby to his workplace. His religious commitment was strong and something that meant a great deal to him. He carried on the traditions of his boyhood years and became involved, along with his family, in the life of their local parish in Brooklyn, as well.

The family now attended St. Edmund's Church on Ocean Avenue at Avenue T, nearby to their home. This parish was a fairly new addition to both the Brooklyn diocese and the neighborhood, and the Lambs as well as the Collins family participated in church events there. The Lamb children attended its associated grammar school after spending their beginning year at the local public elementary school, P.S. 206.

It was here at St. Edmund's that Lamb used his musical talents during the Great Depression. His efforts were especially remembered for his work on the popular minstrel shows that were produced by the Holy Name Society there. These were professionally presented, well supported by church members and the surrounding community, and served a definite philanthropic purpose during a challenging time for many families from 1929 on.

Minstrel shows had not really waned in popularity with the public but some changes had taken place. Historically, these shows had been performed on the stage or in local venues. By the 1920s and '30s, portions of the standard format and content had also worked their way into radio and film. Variations on the jokes and banter that were a regular portion of the shows were now included in such radio favorites as *Amos 'n' Andy* as well as the *Blue Coal Minstrels*. And since films had expanded from silents into "talkies," minstrel themes were woven into the plots, dialogue, and music in such historically significant works as Al Jolson's 1930 movie, *Mammy*, whose story focused on the world of a traveling minstrel show.

These shows, however, were more frequently seen on amateur stages, their performances produced by members of local religious and civic groups for entertainment and, particularly, for fundraising purposes. As the Great Depression descended upon the country, they offered a happy diversion at a time when people needed an uplift in spirits.

Lamb was familiar with the minstrel show form. He had grown up during the time when these entertainments were popular on the stage and when the songs used in the shows were in print, both in regular sheet music form and occasionally in newspaper supplements. Also, this format was popular with local groups across the country, and Montclair had been no exception. Churches, civic associations, and other organizations with amateur performers favored the minstrel show as lighthearted entertainment, something that provided a creative outlet and built a sense of community. It also offered an opportunity for a large number of individuals with varied talents to participate — in musical, acting, dancing, comedy, backstage, administrative, and other capacities. With so many people involved, a good sized audience of family and friends was always assured.

The amateur minstrel show market had long been recognized for its lucrative potential by the Witmarks as far back as the time when Lamb was working at Syndicate Trading and visiting sheet music stores and counters. The ever-enterprising trio of brothers did a large business, particularly by mail order, in providing a full line of products—from books of minstrel show overtures, and instructions on playing bones and tambos, to costume supplies, and even magic paraphernalia — all through their Crest Trading Company. They issued such titles as *Minstrel Shows By Mail,* so that groups could get personalized assistance in planning their shows, as well as the *Witmark Amateur Minstrel Guide and Burnt Cork Encyclopedia,* through which a group could plan each element of the show for itself.[36] Lamb was well acquainted with the tradition and its music from his youth as well as with the Witmarks and their line of products, since they were major names on Tin Pan Alley from its earlier days. Now he would have the chance to build a production of his own.

In 1929, St. Edmund's Holy Name Society launched a series of minstrel shows[37] that may have been originally conceived just for the entertainment of its parishioners and local residents. However they immediately assumed another important purpose — a proven method of raising funds to help local individuals and families who were in economic need due to the Depression.

The first of these shows premiered in November of 1929, a mere few weeks after the stock market crash. There were to be six annual minstrel shows in all, between 1929 and 1935, produced during the most severe economically deprived years. In a short poem in the introduction to the program

Tuesday and Wednesday Evenings, November 19, 20, 1929

ST. EDMUND'S HOLY NAME SOCIETY

presents

"BLACKBERRIES *of* 1929"

A distinctive and unique entertainment, featuring

NELSON, ARUNDELL AND DAVITT
HANLON AND COLLINS
DON FINERTY WITH
JIMMY MAYO AND HIS ORCHESTRA
AND A GALAXY OF THE PEPPIEST MINSTRELS IN THE DIOCESE
Lyrics and Music of the theme song "Barbecue" by Joe Lamb and Gus Collins
Musical Direction by Joe Lamb
Orchestral arrangement of "Barbecue" by Merle T. Kendrick
Settings designed by Gus Collins and executed by Louis Banks
Credit is given Fred DeLappe of Werba's Brooklyn Theatre
for the loan of part of the properties
Draperies Donated by I. M. Friedman & Co., Inc.
Entire production conceived, directed and produced
by Gus Collins and Joe Lamb
Stage Crew—I. Fairbrother, R. Carberry, W. Weber, W. Smith, J. Flood, N. Tesauro
Electrical Effects—W. Farrell, R. Russell

PART ONE — THE MINSTREL CIRCLE

INTERLOCUTOR—Ed. Burns

On Your Left	*On Your Right*
Second Row	
Paul Fallon	Lawrence Flanagan
John McGrath	Ray Shea
John Tracy	Jack Barbieri
First Row	
Joe Arundell	Ray Nelson
Marty Davitt	Joe Manning
Mike Honan	Tom Toomey
Vin Macrone	Gene McKenna
Charlie Smith	Arthur Murnane
Chappie Hueston	James Shea
Carroll O'Rourke	Vinnie Carberry
END MEN	
Pete Hanlon—*Steve*	Jerry Collins—*Sam*

On the Band Platform

Jimmy Mayo .... *Trumpet*
Peter Corrella .... *Trombone*
Vincent Lucadano .... *Drums*
Donald Finerty .... *Banjo*
Mario Egrine .... *Saxaphone*
Peter San Severa .... *Saxaphone*
Joseph Ulliano .... *Saxaphone*
Leon Tinelli .... *Piano*

(Program continued on second page following)

Program page from the first St. Edmund's minstrel show, "Blackberries of 1929" (courtesy Patricia Lamb Conn).

from the 1931 edition of this series, it was made quite clear that a goal of these shows was to elevate everyone's spirits in order to "conquer the devil defying Depression!"[38] The shows not only boosted spirits but they also, through their fundraising efforts, assisted families who had real financial needs. Local businesses, many of which were struggling themselves, came forward to help, particularly by buying advertising in the extensive program booklets that were given to the audiences.

"The Blackberries of 1929" was presented on two consecutive evenings in November. Joe Lamb was integrally involved — producing, directing, composing, writing, and conducting rehearsals. Yet, he did not perform in any capacity for the actual shows; instead, he preferred to remain out of the spotlight.

The productions followed traditional minstrel show formats with such standard components as the minstrel circle, the olio, original and interpolated songs, and a comic play. Simple jokes also helped keep the mood of the shows buoyant. ("Q: Can a leopard change his spots? A: Yes; when he's tired sitting on one spot he changes to another.") Performances were initially presented by a cast of men in blackface. Women only joined the shows in the later years.

Music was an important part of this and of all minstrel shows, and it was only natural that Lamb composed some new songs to be included in the productions. He also acted as rehearsal pianist as well as co-produced and co-directed the shows with Melie's father and brothers, who assumed various other capacities themselves. Dorrie Collins always acted as the end man in the shows and also wrote some lyrics one year as did his brother, Gus, who also designed the innovative sets. Other family members and friends performed.[39] It was a chance for many individuals to get involved in an enjoyable and beneficial project.

Rehearsals were held in the living room at Lamb's house. Young Patricia's bedroom was directly above this area, and the lyrics and music of the songs came through loud and clear as she was trying to go to sleep. She heard them so many times that she remembered them all in years to come.[40]

Since Lamb played the piano at rehearsals only, other musicians were used in the public productions. A seven-piece band, led by trumpeter Jimmy Mayo, played in the 1929 and 1930 shows, with arrangements for this ensemble completed by Merle T. Kendrick.[41] It is possible that Kendrick was a friend or acquaintance of Lamb's from the music business because his name is listed as arranger on many published works of popular music throughout the years. These included an orchestral arrangement of "All Through the Night," "With the Help of the Moon," and other popular works.[42] Kendrick and his orchestra were also the subject of a Vitaphone musical short in 1938.[43] "Al White and His Melody Makers," believed to be a local group, served as the orchestra with the 1931 show.[44] The use of these ensembles as well as of outside arrangers all indicates the professional level of the productions as well as the extensive network of contacts that were available to Lamb and Collins.

The songs that Lamb composed for the shows continue to demonstrate his practice of drawing upon a variety of musical resources, many of them culled from different time periods. In 1930, the song "So Here We Are" employs some vaudeville exit music as well as the "villain music" used by pianists during the silent film era.[45] The lyrics of this and of all the opening songs are definitely upbeat and were designed to lift the audiences up from the worries of the Depression. "So here we are all set and ready for fun.... Minstrel shows are good for the heart."[46]

"Purple Moon," a special favorite of the Lamb children, was also from 1930. It has an upbeat march quality, with a fanfare type interlude that contains the essence of turn-of-the-century ragtime and cakewalk compositions, according to Galen Wilkes, who also indicates fine parallels between this piece and both "Bohemia Rag" and "Champagne Rag."[47] The composition is also reminiscent of the lively marches of comic operettas from bygone days as might have been heard in the works of Herbert and Romberg. In addition, the introduction to this piece could even be a tip of the hat to Scott Joplin's "Antoinette— March & Two-Step" (1906), which opens with a similar musical pattern.

During the six years that these minstrel shows were produced, changes were transpiring in music and in entertainment in general. Movie and show sets and costumes were more elaborate and lavish, with big production numbers and more sophisticated songs to accompany them. These types of productions served as a good diversion for audiences from the somber atmosphere of the Depression, an escape into a more glamorous world. Such changes were all reflected in the "Blackberries" series, which exhibited many modifications over time — in music, sets, costumes, make-up, and even in the increasing size of the cast.

Wilkes mentions that "Hi, Everybody," used in the 1935 show, is in the cut time style of Irving Berlin, found in such songs as the 1929 hit, "Puttin' on the Ritz."[48] It is more modern in style than some previous compositions, and it has the sound of a glittering production number (and the look of it, with the glamorous costumes used for the show)— the theme based on the newly popular greeting, "Hi."[49] As usual, Lamb was attuned to trends in language as well as in music.

Whether composed in the old style or the new, all of the lyrics emphasized having fun and forgetting problems. As Dorrie Collins wrote in his 1933 lyrics to "Here We Are Again": "Throw away your cares."[50] And Lamb, himself, who penned the words to "Hi, Everybody" in 1935, wrote: "Chase all your troubles, give 'em the air."[51]

A fragment of the piano score for "Hi, Everybody," a Joe Lamb song from the 1935 production of the minstrel show (courtesy Patricia Lamb Conn).

Lamb's children thoroughly enjoyed these shows, and they knew all of the songs, often singing them at home, especially "Purple Moon." Although they were too young to stay up for the evening shows, they came to the dress rehearsals on the Sunday afternoon before the public performances, where they had the opportunity to see Joe Lamb in action, exuberantly directing and rehearsing the cast for the show.[52]

There were some especially amusing moments for them, as well. A vivid memory stood out from one of the later years. Around this time, the Disney cartoon, *The Three Little Pigs* (1933) was a huge hit. Its featured song, "Who's Afraid of the Big Bad Wolf," achieved independent success. This was the first cartoon theme song and the beginning of a successful run for this Disney movie. The song also went on to become a theme song of the times— casting the Depression itself in the guise of the Wolf, a creature not to be feared.[53]

One of the later "Blackberries" shows included a humorous rendition on this theme. Joe Jr. appeared in the show during the wolf's song dressed as one of the three little pigs, much to the merriment of all and to the equal dismay of Joe Jr. The story became a family classic, and Joe Jr., of course, never quite heard the end of it.[54]

By 1935, some visible changes had occurred. Only the end men were in blackface as a result of growing discomfort in general about the negative stereotypical images portrayed in minstrel shows. Women were included in the cast by then as well. And this final production had sixty performers, a much larger number than before, all clad in lavish costumes that were influenced by the popular movie musicals of the time.[55] Much had changed in the six years since the show had first been produced.

Word spread of the popularity of the St. Edmund's minstrel shows and, subsequently, a few synagogues approached Lamb to adapt the material and present it to these congregations. He revised the original scripts, including the jokes, making them appropriate for these audiences. The result was a huge success. All of Lamb's time and energies were donated, whether it was for his church or for a neighborhood or other synagogue.

Although the minstrel shows came to a close in 1935 at St. Edmund's, music still sounded in the Lamb household—just not the sounds of show rehearsals in the living room. The three Collins brothers and their father continued to gather at the Lamb house and sing. Singing was not one of Lamb's specialties but he, of course, contributed his superior piano accompaniments to the group as needed. Some of the Collins men also played instruments, and this led to tuneful get-togethers and jam sessions that were memorable. Singing barbershop type harmony was one of the Collins family specialties, and[56] they had also performed together as a quartet on occasion at the minstrel

shows. Music was definitely a joy for them, whether performed in public or in the confines of the family living room.

Although quartets and related forms of small singing groups had been around for a long time, the male, four-voice barbershop-type groups had gained in popularity during the days of vaudeville when they also added a comedic element. Ironically, the first supposed printed use of the word "barbershop" in conjunction with music was in "Play That Barbershop Chord,"[57] the infamous song that caused J. Fred Helf's legal troubles in 1910. Tin Pan Alley helped to spread the popularity of this form of singing even further by making it readily available in user-friendly sheet music, and the sound industry raised the bar on this appeal by issuing the recordings of numerous professional groups. There was plenty of opportunity for members of the public to listen to the style and to try and emulate it in their spare time. Singing barbershop and group harmony became a favored entertainment at social and home gatherings across the country, something that lasted well into the twentieth century. And the Collins men had their own ready-made family group.

Lamb still played his own rags and those of Scott Joplin and James Scott and, of course he never tired of telling the story of how he met Joplin, so much so that his children knew it by heart. He repeated it often at the dinner table.

Now that the children were older, he didn't need to rock them to sleep in their wicker bassinets while playing his music but would, instead, provide a piano background while they were doing their homework after dinner. He interspersed the rags with popular ballads, some of which he still obtained as professional copies from publishers. Melie and the children would sit and listen as he performed these new songs, and then they would vote on their favorites.

There were always the sounds of many voices as the whole family gathered around the piano after dinner and sang old favorites, including songs written by Lamb himself. A much-loved choice was "I'll Follow the Crowd to Coney." Years later, Robert Lamb mentioned how he especially enjoyed these after-dinner singalongs and, also, how important he felt this was to keeping them close as a family. This was a custom reminiscent of the old gathering around the parlor piano that had been so popular at the turn of the century.

Opposite: **The cast of "Blackberries of 1935." Changes had taken place over the previous six years, with more elaborate costumes, women included in the cast, and only a few performers appearing in blackface. Joe Lamb is to the left on the floor (courtesy Patricia Lamb Conn).**

Lamb played other old songs, too, and also incorporated some forgotten works into the family's repertoire, occasionally trying to sing, although he was notorious for his lack of singing skills. One particularly intriguing piece that he enjoyed singing to his children was the 1907 "Brother Noah Gave Out Checks for Rain" by Arthur Longbrake, a baseball song with religious imagery drawn from black culture.[58] Lamb's daughter, Patricia, remembers her father singing the chorus of the song that began: "Eve stole first, and Adam second."[59]

Lamb's lighthearted introduction of this work into everyday family life demonstrates the continued importance of music for him, even in the smallest of ways. The indelible imprint of his early musical exposure was evident. In the case of "Brother Noah," he was harkening back to the days of Tin Pan Alley as well as to his interest in the black musical/religious traditions that he had referred to in his youth, when he listened to the music at the camp meetings when visiting Baltimore.[60]

Although Joe Jr. studied violin for a while and Dick took the saxophone, Patricia was the only one of the Lamb children who seriously studied the piano. She took lessons from the church organist at St. Edmund's, a woman with a high regard for the classics and an aversion to ragtime that must have carried over from years previous. Joe and Melie Lamb respected this teacher and even purchased a new grand piano at her suggestion. The teacher felt that this was a necessary move in order for Patricia to progress at the keyboard. It replaced a Steinway upright that was originally in the family parlor. However the grand was a piano that Lamb never felt quite comfortable with himself. He eventually purchased a Knabe upright that became a permanent fixture in their home.[61]

Patricia enthusiastically shared with the piano teacher that her father composed ragtime. She was quite proud of his accomplishments, as were all of the Lamb children. The teacher, however, immediately told her never to play that sort of music. According to Patricia, "I played it anyway."[62] She still remembers performing piano duets with her father, often doubling the melody of one of his compositions at the very top of the scale, and she loved to turn the pages of the sheet music for him while he played. He always used the music because he felt that this ensured that it would sound just the way that any given composer intended it to. Lamb carefully listened to his daughter's practicing sessions. If she strayed from assigned pieces for her lessons and into ragtime, he would call out for her to count or to adjust a tempo.[63]

Melie Lamb enjoyed her husband's compositions as well but found some of them too difficult. The piece that she played the most on the piano was "I Love You Truly," a turn-of-the-century work by Carrie Jacobs Bond and one that capsulized the close marriage of the Lambs.

Melie was an energetic and vivacious individual. She always seemed to be running at top speed and laughing with good humor. Devoted to her family, she enjoyed cooking and sewing for them. Melie also helped her husband with some of the lyrics for his songs and loved to sing while working around the house.[64] Lamb joked later on that he and Melie came from different backgrounds—he, Irish, and she with some English heritage in her mother's family. He once quipped: "I eat English muffins and she eats Irish stew."[65] There was always music and humor and togetherness in the household. Said one young girl in the neighborhood, "When I get married I want to be like Mr. and Mrs. Lamb."[66]

In his spare time, Lamb still continued to revise some of his old work as well as compose new rags—such as the 1936 "Chimes of Dixie." However public interest in the rag style seemed non-existent by this time. Lamb created for his own enjoyment, though, and the neighbors and the children's friends were unaware that he was a published composer, so great was his modesty.

When asked if he had written down the notes to a composition or perhaps the name of its title, he would sometimes say, why bother? No one is interested in this kind of music anymore. Yet he still continued to compose and it was still in a version of the ragtime style, but as he described his efforts: "ragtime came to the fore but it seemed in a more modern version. But my particular style could be read in them."[67]

The Lambs enjoyed being at home together;

Amelia and Joe Lamb (circa 1930s) (courtesy Robert and Joan Lamb).

they did not seek a busy social life. Aside from the piano, Lamb enjoyed other leisure pastimes, particularly reading and listening to the radio. He could often be seen studying the pages of *National Geographic*, too. Later, he admitted that he also read the *Saturday Evening Post* and frequently clipped poems from this publication to send along with letters, especially to his sister Sta and her husband, George Van Gieson. Both Lamb and Van Gieson were avid correspondents, particularly now that they were geographically far removed from each other and, in addition to exchanging news of family and friends, they would include jokes, humorous asides, and fond reminiscences. Patricia says that she remembers her father reading Van Gieson's letters and laughing until the tears ran down his face.

Radio programs were a special delight for Lamb, *The Shadow* and, especially, *The Lone Ranger* being among his favorites. He also had a great respect for Pauline Alpert, a multi-talented, conservatory educated pianist, composer, and arranger who performed frequently on radio programs in New York for many years, including one that she shared with acclaimed harmonica performer, Larry Adler. Alpert made hundreds of piano rolls of ragtime and novelty compositions and was well known for her technical capabilities, even capturing raves from George Gershwin, and when she performed "Kitten on the Keys," she received high praise from the composer, Zez Confrey, himself.[68] Lamb enjoyed listening to her superb radio repertoire, which also included the still popular "Nola."

To his daughter's recollection, Lamb only went to the movies once, and that was to see *Trail of the Lonesome Pine* in 1936 — a film of great interest to him.[69] There might have been a nostalgic connection to this work for several reasons. On the more positive side, the music to the title song itself was written by Harry Carroll, a composer who, like Lamb, had long been an arranger on Tin Pan Alley. They might have once crossed paths. In an ironic coincidence, Carroll's hit song of 1917, "I'm Always Chasing Rainbows," was based upon a Chopin melody,[70] just as the opening of Lamb's "Ragtime Nightingale" of 1915 was influenced by a strain from a work by the same composer.

On the other hand, the words to the film's title song were by Ballard MacDonald, the individual who was responsible for J. Fred Helf's difficulties in 1910. Lamb could have been curious to hear the work of this lyricist whom he certainly would have remembered.

One further coincidence might have been that this title song was arranged as a "turkey trot" in 1913 by Eugene Platzmann, Lamb's fellow composer at the Satterlee Music firm.[71] (This was the same year that both of Lamb's Satterlee compositions were published.)

The sheet music for "The Trail of the Lonesome Pine" was originally issued by Shapiro and Bernstein in 1913, and Lamb's early work, "Gee, Kid!

But I Like You" of 1909 was published by Shapiro, another interesting coincidence. Finally, the 1936 film itself was a remake of an earlier version that had first been directed by the famed Cecile B. DeMille in 1916, and Lamb might have seen the original. Whatever the reason, this was one film that intrigued him enough to attend.

Lamb still enjoyed his carpentry projects, just as he had when he was young, and now he had the opportunity to engage in them for the benefit of the whole family. He also spent time drawing house plans in his spare time, again a remnant of his youth, having been influenced by both his father and his brother in their chosen line of work. Now he had an opportunity to put some of this training to good use in the family summer homes.

When one of his sons was diagnosed with asthma, it was decided that some clean mountain air, particularly in the summertime, would be good for him. Therefore, the Lambs purchased a summer home in West Townsend, Vermont. Melie and the children spent summers there, and Lamb would join them on weekends. He entirely renovated this house, finishing off the second floor. As Robert Lamb commented, any building project that his father completed was of the highest quality. He worked with great care and craftsmanship and always did a really professional job.[72]

The second home that Lamb truly enjoyed, though, was in Packanack Lake, New Jersey. The Lambs had owned property in the vicinity since 1932 and bought their house in 1937.[73] Only about an hour's drive from Brooklyn, this was an easier retreat from city life as time went on and one that Lamb particularly relished. He always referred to it as their "country estate."[74] Here was a quiet community with a beautiful lake nearby to enjoy. And the area had many wonderful trees, something that he loved. Lamb preferred the country atmosphere, although Melie was a city girl. The country reminded Lamb of his boyhood in Montclair, a place for which he held a lifelong affection.

Lamb also renovated the Packanack Lake home, adding an extra room. This was another form of creativity that he really enjoyed. Patricia remembers commuting there with her father from the city on weekends when she was still single, and all of the Lamb children visited frequently with their own families as time progressed. It was a serene and welcome getaway.

Lamb described the home vividly in his letters—from its white façade to its asphalt roof shingles, even noting such small details as the blending of their reds, browns, and blues. The house faced north, getting the summer sun only in the afternoons; otherwise, its shady surroundings provided a pleasant temperature. A silhouette of a lamb could be seen on a blue shutter, and a sign inscribed "The Lambs" was framed by illustrations of the species.[75]

Joe Lamb had purchased many pieces of property over the years, something that he enjoyed doing and often with the idea of building on it.[75] Both his father and his brother had done the same. However the Packanack Lake location was his favorite of all.

By this time it seemed as if ragtime had been totally forgotten. Although music was always a daily activity in the Lamb household, it had become a bit quieter. As for Joe Lamb, playing some old rags and working out an occasional new theme seemed just a pleasant pastime. The old days of classic rags and talks with Scott Joplin and John Stark were a distant memory. Even the excitement of working on the minstrel shows was fading with the passage of time. And as the extended families grew older and became involved with their own lives, the musical jam sessions and gatherings were, naturally, fewer.

After its joyous years of popularity, ragtime had long before yielded to jazz and then to swing. The era of the big bands had arrived, and Lamb's sons all admitted to having a fondness for this type of music.[77] It was the music of their generation. In the meantime, many of ragtime's composers and performers had either passed away or faded into obscurity.

Sometime in the late 1930s and early 1940s, though, little changes were taking place. An occasional sound of something akin to ragtime began surfacing once more in various corners of the country. It was soon embraced by a few talented admirers. This was a low-keyed phenomenon and far from a widespread revival at that point, with just a relative few who ventured into this arena.

Lu Watters, a trumpeter, created a band on the west coast — the Yerba Buena Jass Band. The group performed a wide variety of styles, not content to solely concentrate on the big band sound which was so popular at the time. Watters wanted to explore something beyond the currently accepted repertoire and provide his audiences with an eclectic sound, one that would generate some real enthusiasm in his listeners— a style different from what they had by now come to expect. Subsequently, he began injecting a few rags into their performances.[78]

According to Wally Rose, the pianist for the band, these ragtime compositions worked especially well as piano solos with banjo and percussion accompaniments. Even better, they seemed to elicit a real response from the listeners. Soon the group decided to make a recording of "Black and White Rag." This turned into an enormous success and was a breakthrough of sorts because it was continually heard on the radio, something that had not been expected. This was one of the clear indicators that ragtime was no longer totally relegated to the past. More interest was to follow.[79]

A few new magazines were beginning to appear around this time, and they began to incorporate ragtime information into their articles and news items. This helped to stimulate further interest in the form. *The Record Changer* and *Jazz Journal* discussed and reviewed records and offered signifi-

A rare photograph from the 1940s of the entire Lamb family. Bottom row, left to right: Donald, Richard. Middle row: Robert, Amelia, Joseph, Jr. Top row: Joseph, Sr., Patricia (courtesy Robert and Joan Lamb).

cant background details. These publications helped to authenticate ragtime and to clarify the history and performance styles of the old days.[80] It was an indication that the sleeping interest in ragtime was starting to reawaken on a larger scale.

Then, around 1945, Johnny Wittwer recorded "Ragtime Nightingale." Soon there were others who joined him in regularly making recordings in the ragtime style. Of course there was Wally Rose, who had been a part of the Lu

Watters group, who was continuing to take an active role in playing and recording the repertoire, but there were also other performers who began embracing ragtime from own perspectives. Suddenly, what was old had started to become new and exciting once more.[81]

Pianist Ralph Sutton was earning a reputation as a ragtime player, and was eventually introduced as such on a radio show called *This Is Jazz*, hosted by Rudi Blesh, a jazz aficionado who had written on music for newspapers and magazines.[82] Although Sutton and other figures were associated with jazz, they now incorporated ragtime into their performance and recording repertoire, continuing to build renewed interest in the form.

In the meantime, Joe Lamb was busy with his job and family, music taking its regularly enjoyable spot in the household after dinner. He was basically unaware that ragtime was gradually moving full circle into the spotlight towards serious recognition once again. This was about to change.

Nine

Ragtime Revival (1949–1960)

"Suddenly, he was viewed as a celebrity"— Marjorie Freilich-Den

Rudi Blesh began writing his book on a dare.[1] He was skeptical at first, believing that the subject had already been covered several times over. This skepticism, however, soon faded — quickly replaced by surprise at the scarcity of existing works on the topic. Soon Blesh was thoroughly committed to the project, convinced early on of the historical importance, and even the necessity, of completing this work. By the time that he marched down East 21st Street in Sheepshead Bay, Brooklyn, one autumn day in 1949, it had become his consuming passion. His subject was ragtime.

Blesh insisted that Harriet Janis, his coauthor of several other works, join him once more. She agreed. They were determined to tell the story of this great music and, for the better part of a year, the two traveled —from the Library of Congress archives to a mortuary in Kansas City, from Harlem to St. Louis, and beyond.[2] And all the while, they realized that they were working against time in an effort to find the lost people and places of a shining bygone era before they all vanished. Towards the end of this quest, they faced one of their greatest challenges— locating, and perhaps even verifying the actual identity of, one of classic ragtime's "big three" composers.

Now Blesh reached his destination: a modest white frame house set in an orderly row of similar structures and tucked into a peaceful corner of Brooklyn. There was no answer, however, at the door of number 2229.

East 21st Street was quiet, as quiet as a residential street in Brooklyn could get at midday. Men were at work, their wives indoors tending to children and the dozens of responsibilities of family life. Sounds from the traffic on a nearby avenue murmured faintly in the distance.

This street had a strong sense of community, though, as did much of Sheepshead Bay, and a neighbor had already spied this stranger as well as his companion, who now waited in their parked car. By the time Blesh realized

159

that no one was at home to answer the door, the neighbor was already directing his attention to another home just down the block.

The neighbor surely continued watching as this well-dressed man made his way along the street. If others hadn't at first noticed the unfamiliar car with its two passengers pull up to the curb, they were by now totally aware of Blesh striding up East 21st Street, his sense of purpose more obvious with each step. He was determined to find out if this place held the answer to the one remaining, but elusive, link to ragtime history. And Rudi Blesh was nothing if not perseverant.

Harriet Janis remained in the car as Blesh approached the second house. All she could see down the block was the young woman who answered the door upon his arrival. Their exchange was brief, inaudible to Harriet Janis despite the gentle hush on the street. It was possible that this trip to Sheepshead Bay would be fruitless, this street the end of their quest with all possibilities exhausted.

Suddenly, Blesh turned. His shout punctuated the quiet atmosphere. "We found him!"[3]

And with this, a new chapter in the continuing story of ragtime began.

Rudi Blesh (1899–1985) was ardently enthusiastic about a number of topics— art, film, and jazz among them. He had already penned a biography of Buster Keaton as well as a book on modern art. He had also written columns and reviews for the *San Francisco Chronicle* and the *New York Herald Tribune* and hosted a radio show — all focusing on jazz. His book on the subject, *Shining Trumpets: A History of Jazz*, became a classic of its time.[4] An astute observer of the music scene in general, Blesh was aware of the growing revival of interest in ragtime but hadn't delved into a serious study of the form just yet. That changed with the prompting of his friend and colleague, Harriet Janis. It was, in reality, more than just a gentle prompting; Blesh referred to it as a friendly sort of a dare. And Blesh always enjoyed a challenge.

Harriet (nicknamed "Hansi") Janis (1898–1963) was an artist and art connoisseur. She and her husband were particularly well versed in many facets of modern art and, together, they ran the Sidney Janis Gallery on West 57th Street in New York. She enjoyed painting and exhibiting her own abstract pastel works and wrote extensively about the art world, co-authoring a book on Picasso with her husband and another on DeKooning with Rudi Blesh.[5] However Harriet Janis also loved music and, not content to be just a bystander, she became actively involved in several projects related to the subject.

Blesh and Janis were good friends and business associates and, in addition to co-authoring several books together, they also eventually founded a jazz recording label, Circle Records. So it was not unusual on any given day that their topic of conversation turned to music.

It was on one such occasion that Janis asked Blesh if it might be time for him to write another book, quickly following up her question with the suggestion of ragtime as a specific focus. His response was immediate: there must be many books already in circulation on the subject. Harriet Janis was adamant in her disagreement, saying that she would "like to bet ... that there're none."[6]

This was the beginning of *They All Played Ragtime*, the groundbreaking book by this team that unfolded the almost lost story of this American music — its people, places, and traditions— as a social history. Not only did they do an intense amount of archival research but they also traveled from city to city, seeking out and interviewing surviving composers and performers from ragtime's glory days. It was a journey during which the adventurous pair tracked down names that were all but forgotten, except on yellowed pieces of sheet music or in fireside reminiscences.

Yet of the hundred or so individuals whom they sought, Joe Lamb was by far the most difficult to find. Less dedicated researchers would have given up and accepted a common theory that Joseph F. Lamb was just a pseudonym for Scott Joplin or someone else.

But Rudi Blesh just couldn't accept any of it. Some instinct haunted him; he was convinced that there was more to the story than this. Ragtime compositions had their own personalities, and Lamb's were unique.[7] So he and Harriet Janis continued to dig for information as to Lamb's whereabouts, seeking whatever details that they could find in various cities and checking addresses on old copyrighted material in the Library of Congress. From there, it was a process of more trial-and-error — talking with people, looking in phone books, making calls, and focusing on more specific geographic areas.

They finally narrowed their search to Sheepshead Bay in Brooklyn. One fall afternoon they decided to drive out to their destination, feeling that a personal visit would be better than a phone call. After all of their research, they needed to actually see for themselves if they had found their elusive composer.

When they arrived at 2229 East 21st Street, it was only to discover that no one was at home. Lamb was at work, and Melie was out for the afternoon.

The neighbor who spoke with Blesh directed them to the Lambs' married daughter, Patricia Conn, who lived with her husband and their young family up the street.

When Patricia answered her door, she of course told Rudi Blesh that Joe Lamb was her father. However, she said that she "didn't invite him in." Instead, she suggested that he return to her parents' home for a visit in the evening after work.[8]

A random visit from a pair of strangers—no matter how well dressed or mannerly—would have been enough to raise a skeptical eyebrow anywhere. However two strangers, appearing from out of nowhere to reveal that they were researching a book on ragtime and had gone to a great deal of trouble to find Joe Lamb, were enough to raise full-blown suspicion, particularly since ragtime was still out of the general public spotlight. And despite the fact that neighbors and friends knew that Lamb played the piano at home, no one associated him with any sort of past musical fame—certainly not in ragtime, a music that was just a distant memory. So Blesh and Janis raised more than just curiosity—they sparked wariness and concern.

But there was even more cause for suspicion. Even though East 21st Street was a safe, family-centered block, the Lambs had been recent victims of a random break-in and robbery. Several valuable items had been stolen, and now the family and the neighbors, too, were more on edge, sensitive to the possibility of a repeat crime of any sort and alert to anything or anyone that was out of the ordinary.[9] Enter the team of Blesh and Janis.

The afternoon wore on and, as Patricia suggested, the two returned that evening to meet Lamb after he returned home from work.

Although Joe and Melie Lamb were gracious and welcomed the duo into their home, they had their reservations about the unusual story that their visitors told. Lamb was astounded that the pair wanted to write about ragtime. He believed that no one cared about this music anymore, and he wasn't really aware that any type of revival had begun in earnest. Despite their pleasant chatting, Lamb was still skeptical, feeling that although Blesh and Janis might indeed be writing a book, that there was probably an ulterior motive in their herculean efforts to contact him. He took Blesh aside at one point to ask him a question. "Mr. Blesh, how much is it going to cost me to get into your book?"[10]

It was now Rudi Blesh's turn to be amazed. He assured Lamb that there was nothing like that on his mind and that he and Harriet Janis were genuinely thrilled to have found the last surviving member of the "big three" ragtime composers. Then they revealed even more about their research and the people they had previously discovered.

After the initial suspicion began to fade, Lamb offered his recollections about Joplin, Stark, and the long forgotten heyday of the ragtime era. He shared anecdotes, sheet music, and photos for their book, his own fascinating story combining with those of the many others whom the authors had encountered. "Rudi and Harriet are tops,"[11] remarked Lamb later on in a letter to a friend, still thrilled to have been included in their history of the ragtime era's greats.

Blesh was so excited to have found Lamb that he asked him to make a recording for Circle Records, the label run by the indefatigable Blesh and Janis duo. Lamb initially declined, feeling that he was out of practice at the piano. Also, he was still adjusting to the surprise of this sudden interest in him and in his compositions. (Later on, when it seemed more plausible, he reconsidered. By this time, though, Blesh and Janis had sold their business to Ben Grauer of Riverside Records.[12])

The first edition of *They All Played Ragtime* was published by Alfred A. Knopf in 1950. The book exploded on the music scene, generating a widespread and enthusiastic response and intensifying the currently reawakening interest in the subject of ragtime. It was an unrivaled success. Blesh and Janis admitted that their timing in researching the work had been good because within a year of the book's publication, a substantial number of the individuals whom they had so tirelessly tracked down and interviewed had passed away. Three more editions of the work were to follow over the next twenty years.

According to Lamb, *They All Played Ragtime* was "what was actually responsible for the sudden resurgence of ragtime."[13] And, as a result of the

Joe Lamb (center) with two colleagues at Dommerich & Company, the firm where he spent an enjoyable working career from 1914 through 1957. After retiring, he devoted more time to composing and musical activities (courtesy Patricia Lamb Conn).

book, Lamb was receiving notoriety such as he hadn't known during his earlier composing years. Letters came pouring in from ragtime fans and those who had long admired his music but hadn't realized that he was still around or, to be more accurate, hadn't even known who he was, despite their familiarity with some of his music. Now Lamb "started to realize that he really was appreciated by people who knew ragtime. It made him very happy and proud."[14]

Blesh and Janis first contacted Lamb in 1949 and although he returned to composing and revising around this time, he was still employed fulltime at Dommerich & Company, having held a succession of positions there with increasing responsibility. In December of 1957, Lamb formally retired from the firm after forty-three years of service (although he did go back for a short time at the beginning of 1958 to assist when the individual who replaced him became ill).

By the time of his retirement, Lamb was in charge of the billing department at Dommerich, including all claims and accounts receivable.[15] It was a responsible position that demanded a great deal of energy, and it was one that he also enjoyed. Although he remembered his years at Dommerich as "the happy days," he also added, "I'm glad I have retired."[16] After retirement he had the flexibility to devote more time to composing, seriously motivated by the renewed interest in him and in his compositions sparked by *They All Played Ragtime.*

The book, the growing interest in ragtime, and the additional time that retirement provided all served to re-energize Lamb. Now, he not only began creating compositions again with heightened enthusiasm but he also started to seriously write down those melodies and arrangements. There were new rags and novelty numbers, and he also retrieved some old, unpublished rags that he had been keeping in the piano bench, reworking them to his satisfaction. It was a brand new era for Joe Lamb and one that turned highly prolific.

At the outset, his ragtime fame had been based upon the twelve classic rags published by John Stark — the fewest number of compositions produced by any one of the "big three." During the course of the ensuing decade, however, he became the most prolific of that number because of his new output. These additional compositions exhibited a mature perspective and a realization of Lamb's accumulated musical knowledge and creativity. He worked on expanding the boundaries of the form, demonstrating that ragtime was a fluid style and still had much to explore within its scope. Yet Joe Lamb never forgot all of the many musical inspirations from previous days, especially the classical influences gleaned from his sisters. ("Ragtime Bobolink," for one, begins with a tantalizingly brief turn of phrase that is reminiscent of the opening of Cecile

Chaminade's "Scarf Dance," a parallel that is mentioned by Milton Kaye, the performer who recorded many of Lamb's works in later years.[17] Lamb had to have remembered Chaminade's graceful composition being played by Kate or Sta during his youth; it appeared in the January 1897 edition of *The Etude* magazine when he was nine years old and became an enduring favorite of piano students for years.)

And now, too, just as he had always done, Lamb enjoyed experimenting with different styles and forms. His work entitled "Hot Cinders" (written for his granddaughter, Laura Cindy[18]) was composed in the novelty style. On the other hand, his "Alaskan Rag" explored the multiple possibilities within the ragtime form itself. As was pointed out in the notes for a historic 1959 recording of this piece, it is the only rag that has a rest in place of a downbeat[19]—a very creative innovation in a rag that was considered by many, Lamb included, to be among his best.

Now, too, Lamb was able to at last experience the thrill of well-deserved public recognition and could enjoy some unique musical and personal opportunities based upon his accomplishments. An inveterate letter writer, Joe Lamb responded to all correspondence that he received. According to his daughter, Patricia, if he received a letter in the morning, he would respond within the same day. He loved writing letters, blending news and nostalgic anecdotes into substantial pages of single-spaced prose—all completed on a manual typewriter with carbon copies retained for his own files. He also generously sent out copies of his music, enclosed news clippings of significance, and showed genuine interest in the lives and musical pursuits of those with whom he corresponded. "When I hear from anyone interested in the real old-time rags," he wrote, "I get wound up."[20]

It was the 1950s, when having an interest in old-time rags seemed incongruous with the contemporary world as well as with its musical trends. It was the era of Eisenhower, the Cold War, and the McCarthy hearings. By the end of the decade, the country was at the brink of space exploration and, on terra firma, it was about to add two new stars to its flag. In music, Chuck Berry, Little Richard, and groups such as Bill Haley and the Comets with their hit "Rock Around the Clock" had made significant names for themselves. Elvis Presley was continually topping the charts with renditions of "Don't Be Cruel" and "Heartbreak Hotel," while rocking national television on the *Ed Sullivan Show*. Was there any place for ragtime?

Although ragtime had seen a renewed interest in the 1940s, by the 1950s it was gaining attention with recordings and various televised performances in the popular honky tonk style. There were new rags written as well as older ones performed in this style. In 1955, "Crazy Otto Rag," as recorded by Johnny Maddox, was a hit single. (Maddox, a superb performer, historian, and collector was well versed in all facets of ragtime.) On television, Big Tiny Little was a fan favorite on *The Lawrence Welk Show*, performing honky-tonk style repertoire. In one of his letters, Lamb even mentioned hearing Little perform a honky-tonk rendition of "Maple Leaf Rag" on the show.[21] Albums by a number of performers, many using pseudonyms, sold well throughout the 1950s and into the early 1960s. And through all of it, there was still a marked interest in the original, classic style of ragtime — the traditional and the new sharing the stage in its own way with fans cutting across the generational spectrum. More was to come.

One young man who was interested in the traditional forms of ragtime was Mike Montgomery, who began writing to Lamb and subsequently visited one weekend when he was in New York in 1957. While on this brief trip, Montgomery's goal was to contact and talk with composers and performers within the ragtime and jazz world. He was an avid collector of piano rolls and had, of course, become acquainted with some of Lamb's compositions through these recordings. As a result, he became a fan of Lamb's.

Montgomery had one question that he particularly wanted to ask: Did Lamb ever make any piano rolls himself? Even though this question was answered (Lamb never did), Montgomery really wanted to have more than just this short conversation on the phone. He needn't have worried. Lamb was delighted by the call and offered the young man an invitation to dinner that same night. When Montgomery arrived in Brooklyn, the Lambs were sitting on the front stoop and waiting for him to arrive. They looked like an everyday neighborhood couple (which they were) — not a famous ragtime composer and his wife.[22] A wonderful evening of ragtime reminiscences followed.

Both men played the piano that night, although Lamb was at first reluctant, saying he was out of practice. After some coaxing by Melie, though, he finally sat down and played "Excelsior,"[23] one of the most difficult of his compositions. That evening led to a warm friendship between the two men and many letters exchanged on the subject of music.

Montgomery later sent Lamb some tape recordings containing several of his own performances of Lamb's compositions. Lamb was thrilled. "Your rendition of American Beauty," he wrote, "was like coming up for a breath of fresh air after a sojourn in a coal mine."[24] He felt that its interpretation and tempo "brought out whatever the rag contained."[25]

Although others, Montgomery included, had themselves recorded Lamb's works on rolls, records, and tapes, there were many who now expressed a real interest in recording the composer himself. As Lamb commented: "The St. Louis gang is hot on my trail to record a 12" LP ... of my published rags ... and also want one of my unpublished, and even my unwritten rags."[26] And of course, there had been Blesh and Janis who were among the first to request a recording. These particular projects never materialized. Aside from the fact that Lamb felt he was out of practice, he was also concerned about how his hearing problems would affect his playing.

For a number of his mature years, Lamb had experienced hearing difficulties. Even while still employed at Dommerich, the staff had recognized this problem, particularly since Lamb was not always able to hear the phone ring, and they subsequently devised a system to alert him.[27] Lamb was especially aware of how this challenge could impact his piano playing and, therefore, was quite hesitant to be recorded by anyone.

It was Mike Montgomery, though, who eventually persuaded Lamb to reconsider. He suggested making a tape recording in the familiar surroundings of Lamb's own home, feeling that this might alleviate some of these overriding concerns. In the meantime, Montgomery had purchased a fine reel-to-reel tape recorder while on Army duty and stationed in Germany and asked if he could send it to the Lamb home for safekeeping until he returned to New York. Of course Lamb agreed. The first steps towards a recording were now in the works.

"I suppose you could induce me to play something on your new recorder," Lamb joked, "but I'd hate to be responsible for spoiling the first tape you make."[28] This had never been a worry for Montgomery. When he visited Brooklyn once more in 1959, he taped Lamb playing a varied selection of his old and new rags, including most of the "classics" as well as some newer and revised works, ranging from "Dynamite Rag" to "Alaskan Rag" (his newest composition). There were two dozen works recorded. Later, a set of five works were added to these, drawn from a performance by Lamb in Toronto. Together, these tapes formed the basis for a recording entitled "Hot Cinders!" Montgomery seized this wonderful opportunity to preserve Lamb's performances of his own compositions for posterity, making an important contribution to the history of ragtime.

By this time, Lamb had been corresponding with a number of others who were eager to discuss music. One such individual was Russ Cassidy, who both exchanged letters with Lamb and also visited him at home. A music enthusiast, Cassidy was a writer and eventually co-editor of *The Jazz Report* and *The Ragtime Review* with Trebor Jay Tichenor. Cassidy wrote a series of articles about Lamb ("Joseph Lamb — Last of the Ragtime Composers"), based upon information from his letters and visits. These were published in *The Jazz Report* as a tribute after Lamb's death and were recognized as a fully comprehensive biographical portrait of the composer, being reprinted several times in different publications over subsequent years (most notably in *Jazz Monthly*).

Lamb with Russ Cassidy in the late 1950s. Cassidy was the author of a well-respected series of biographical articles on Lamb, which were published in 1961 after Lamb's death (courtesy Patricia Lamb Conn).

When Cassidy visited Brooklyn during the 1950s, Lamb played a number of the compositions that he had previously set aside as well as some new works. One in particular, drew Cassidy's notice, and he suggested that it be called "Blue Grass Rag." Lamb followed up on the idea, and it was eventually published with this title in the posthumous *Ragtime Treasures* collection.[29]

Cassidy later commented on the whole arc of Lamb's career, underlining how he helped to demonstrate that the ragtime form and its syncopated style did not have to be pigeonholed as a "dated composition."[30] Lamb developed his ideas and proved that the form was not only beautiful and workable, but "essentially timeless,"[31] according to Cassidy in his articles.

Trebor Jay Tichenor was another individual who corresponded with Lamb and appreciated the depth and variety of his work. As Cassidy's co-editor as well as a pianist, ragtime scholar, and collector — Tichenor wrote a fine series of companion articles to Cassidy's biographical pieces. Entitled

"The World of Joseph Lamb — An Exploration," they individually analyzed Lamb's twelve classic rags as well as a representative selection of others. Tichenor's writings offered fine technical and historical analyses as well as astute observations on the compositions as a whole. These also became a well respected resource on the composer, providing a wealth of useful insights.

In addition to those who were interested in recording Lamb or speaking with him about his life and his music, there were others who sought his opinion on ragtime subjects. One topic that came up frequently was that of the art and technique of arranging solo ragtime works for ensembles. Tony Hagert was one such individual who corresponded with Lamb in order to obtain some of his insights. Lamb had clear-cut ideas on the subject.

In a response to Hagert, he used his own "Reindeer Rag," "Cleopatra Rag," and "Bohemia Rag" as illustrative examples of adaptable types of compositions for ensemble arrangements. They were in the march and two-step category, forms that he felt were easier to work with. Their melodies "and harmonies ... can be used to good advantage,"[32] he said, adding that it was definitely a solid practice to pass phrases of melody from one instrument to another. However, he believed that some of his other classic rags were more difficult to score because of their more indefinable melodic lines, offering the arranger a substantial challenge.[33]

Lamb was also quite specific about certain existing orchestrations of his work, comparing the arrangements of "Sensation" as performed by Mutt Carey's band (which he thought was terrible) with that of a Swedish ensemble (better, but with specific issues), admitting that this was quite a difficult piece to arrange because of melodic line issues.[34] These observations demonstrate Lamb's awareness not only of the complexities of ragtime but also indicate that he had carefully pondered the technical and artistic issues of arranging on a number of levels.

Interest in Lamb and his compositions continued to build during the 1950s. After Montgomery's visit to tape record Lamb, more invitations of this sort were to follow. One of the most notable came in 1959 from ragtime scholar and researcher Sam Charters of Folkways, and it would lead to a memorably historic recording. According to Lamb, Charters "couldn't rest until he got me."[35] Lamb was again reluctant to take on this project for the same reasons that he had expressed before: he was out of practice and his increasing hearing difficulties could be challenging while playing the piano. Instead, he suggested that Charters' wife, Ann, an excellent pianist, be the one to perform.

Lamb admired Ann Charters' pianistic talents. "You should hear her play ragtime," he wrote to a friend. "She plays it the way it is written and in the proper tempo."[36] Sam Charters, however, realized the historical value of

Lamb performing himself, and he continued to persist until Lamb finally agreed, but only on the condition that the recording be made at his home and on his own piano. Lamb did not want to go to a recording studio.

Sam and Ann Charters visited East 21st Street on several occasions, setting up the necessary equipment and recording Lamb performing his own works. "They are a wonderful couple,"[37] Lamb commented. In turn, Ann and Sam Charters seemed to feel at home with the Lambs. Charters distinctly remembered the comfort of the surroundings and even having to stop taping occasionally so that Amelia could make noise in the kitchen while mashing the potatoes for dinner.[38] The sessions ran for about six hours with a dinner break to eat those potatoes along with the rest of Melie's wonderful meal.

Sam Charters' liner notes for the original recording provide a good overview of Lamb, his musical output, and his surroundings. "The story Sam wrote for that record didn't miss much of whatever we talked about,"[39] Lamb later commented. Although he didn't notice Ann Charters writing too much in the notebook that she brought, he observed that "she must have been"[40] because the account seemed so complete.

Joe Lamb at his home piano in the 1950s, the instrument on which he performed for the historic Folkways recording *Joseph Lamb: A Study in Classic Ragtime* (courtesy Robert and Joan Lamb).

Charters did reveal that Joe Lamb was adamant about playing every note as it was written.[41] Lamb felt strongly (as Joplin also had) that classic ragtime was to be played just the same as classical music — as written. (Years later, it was argued that since some classical cadenzas contained improvisatory elements, it was fine to do the same with classic ragtime.[42] However, those who knew Lamb stated that he would not have agreed with this premise.) Lamb believed that the melody should be primarily emphasized along with the rhythm.[43] Improvisation had the potential to detract from this focus.

And just as Joplin had

always stressed, Lamb felt, too, that rags should not be played fast and should hold to an even tempo. Again, later commentators have pointed out that these tempo considerations might have been necessary during the time that ragtime compositions were used as dance music.[44] Lamb never mentioned this, clearly stating that if a rag was played too fast or if the tempo was distorted, both the flow and the sound of the beautiful inner voices and creative harmonies could be lost. He shared his thoughts on these and other musical subjects with Charters during the course of their taping sessions.

Sam Charters' persistence paid off. The result was a beautiful recording: *Joseph Lamb: A Study in Classic Ragtime.* Personal reminiscences by Lamb himself were also included, featuring his retelling of the story of his meeting with Joplin. A true piece of history, this is still an available part of the Smithsonian Folkways recordings series.

Lamb was quite proud of the recording. He wrote a lovely thank you note to Moses Asch, the producer at Folkways, not only expressing his gratitude for the record but also praising Ann and Sam Charters as "a wonderful couple, one of many brought into my life since *They All Played Ragtime.*"[45] Everyone from his former employer, Alex Dommerich, to famed pianist, Johnny Maddox bought a copy. And Lamb gifted each of his children with a signed copy of the album, something that made all of them quite proud. He later confided in a letter: "I have recently made a recording of ten of my rags for Folkways Records and I certainly hope it helps towards the revival of Ragtime which seems to be in the making."[46]

It was also during the late 1950s that Lamb began receiving letters from a young man called Ragtime Bob Darch, an exuberant musical entertainer who traveled around the United States and Canada with his own "saloon" piano. The piano dated from around 1900 and was said to have been purchased by Darch in Alaska.[47] He somehow managed to travel between his performing jobs, pulling the piano from a contraption on the back of his car.[48] It seemed inevitable that the two men would meet, given Lamb's rediscovery and Darch's ragtime performing travels. Darch eventually visited the Lambs at their home.

Among Darch's many connections was a venue called Club 76 in Toronto, Canada. An active group of ragtime enthusiasts frequented this spot, and Darch performed there regularly. Based upon his association with the Club as well as his newly formed friendship with Lamb, Darch came up with a plan, based not only on the fact that Lamb was a famous ragtime composer but also upon the Canadian connection from his school days at St. Jerome's and his early publications with the Harry Sparks firm in Toronto.

Darch arranged for Lamb to come to Toronto from October 7 to 10, 1959, to play for the crowd at Club 76, a thrill that Lamb spoke of often.[49] By now, Lamb had been recorded and was also more accustomed to playing the

Among the most famous of his works and popularly known as "Ragtime Nightingale," Lamb both performed this 1915 rag and spoke about how he composed it on the Folkways recording (courtesy Charles H. Templeton Collection, Special Collections, Mississippi State University Libraries).

piano for visitors at his home, his initial reluctance to perform for others lessening. In addition, he had fond recollections of Canada, and here was a chance to re-visit the place where he first sold his music for publication. Bert Wilks, the owner of Club 76, issued the formal invitation.[50] "Being one of the three 'greats' of the old ragtime era," quipped Lamb, "Bob Darch made the most of it and had them invite us up there."[51] Always enterprising, Darch took up a collection from ragtime fans at the club in an antique whisky bottle to help make this trip a reality.

For Lamb, this was an experience of a lifetime. He and Melie were flown

Lamb performing at Club 76 in Toronto, Canada, in 1959, at the saloon piano owned by Ragtime Bob Darch (courtesy Patricia Lamb Conn).

to Toronto (the first airplane flight for both) and treated like royalty during their stay there. As soon as they arrived, Melie was presented with a huge bouquet of American Beauty roses.[52] A special lunch was hosted for them, along with a tour of Toronto and special press coverage. "The press," Lamb said, "escorted us everywhere we went."[53] And the couple was, in Lamb's words, even put up at a "swank hotel."[54]

Toronto was a homecoming of sorts for Lamb who had gone to school at St. Jerome's so many years previously, and who had also been published by the Harry Sparks music firm. During this current trip, Lamb had the welcome chance to re-visit St. Jerome's in Kitchener, Ontario (the town's name having been changed from Berlin as a result of World War I). One of his former teachers was still there and "showed him the old school desk, still *in situ*, with the initials, surreptitiously carved: J.F.L."[55] He also had the opportunity to reconnect with a few of his former classmates, several of whom had become priests, and he played the piano for them. Some Canadian radio and television stations broadcast portions of this trip.[56] Then there was, of course, a lunch at the now famous Walper House Hotel, the site from which Lamb drew inspiration for his first titled rag, "Walper House Rag."

Lamb performed for enthusiastic crowds at Club 76 — twice each night — and held them mesmerized. He played for a longer amount of time and performed more compositions than originally scheduled, so popular was he with the crowd.[57]

These were evenings of fine music, heartfelt tributes, and a bit of showmanship as well. During one of these performances, Bob Darch played "Cleopatra Rag." When it was his turn to perform, Lamb, with his famous flair for humor and to the great amusement of the crowd, joked: "Now I'm going to play it right."[58] Afterwards, he signed autographs and gratefully received a beautiful memento of the event — an engraved silver tray from the Ragtime Music Lovers of Toronto.[59] The audience, many of them young ragtime fans, "rose to cheer."[60] Lamb was also promised an album of photographs from the event. According to Melie, her husband "could not believe that so many people actually knew and played his music."[61] Their son Donald and his wife joined them for one of the performances, flying to Toronto just for the evening in order to be present for this event.[62]

While Lamb was in Canada, he also paid a visit to the gravesite of Harry Sparks at Park Lawn Cemetery in Toronto, placing flowers on his grave on a windy, rainy day. He remembered his friend and first publisher of so long before — "the man who discovered him,"[63] according to a contemporary newspaper account. Lamb's association with Harry Sparks held fond memories, and he was grateful to have had the opportunity to get to know him and to have had a substantial number of compositions published by his firm. Lamb evidently kept in touch with the Sparks family long after he left Canada in 1904. Harry Sparks' son, a Toronto doctor, and his wife were present at Club 76 during that week for one of the performances, a nice reunion in itself. Lamb commented that he hadn't seen him since 1933.[64]

The Toronto trip was one that Lamb continually spoke of. "Honestly, I can't get over it," he wrote, adding: "Boy, am I glad I am one of the big three of ragtime and still around to enjoy it."[65]

After the trip, Bob Darch was still in contact with Lamb. Also a composer, Darch sent one of his own pieces to Lamb for his review. In the tradition of both Charles Daniels and Scott Joplin before him, Lamb included his name as "arranger" on the cover of Darch's "Opera House Rag." The two corresponded on numerous occasions, and then Darch initiated the subject of issuing some of Lamb's previously unpublished rags.

In addition to his life as a composer and pianist, Darch also ran The Ragtime Publishing Company, his own business enterprise. He was anxious to be the one to issue some of Lamb's rags and promised to publish seven of them[66] (something that did not come to fruition as planned). Some of these were older compositions, including "Dynamite Rag" (eventually renamed "Joe Lamb's Old Rag")—the piece for which Joplin had made the one suggested change so many years before during Lamb's famous visit to his home. "Alaskan Rag," his newest composition, was among the ones also discussed—a piece that had been written much later on. According to Lamb: "He [Darch] liked it very much,"[67] and had wanted to introduce it at a July 4th celebration in its namesake state,[68] although there is no available record of this having happened. "Alaskan Rag" first appeared in the third edition of *They All Played Ragtime.* Darch did not publish any of Lamb's compositions. Some, such as "Joe Lamb's Old Rag," later appeared in a folio titled *A Little Lost Lamb.*

Aside from coordinating the trip to Toronto, Darch was also instrumental in making a connection between Lamb and folksinger/actor/writer, Burl Ives, another resident of Brooklyn. Darch urged Ives to sponsor Lamb's election to the American Society of Composers, Authors, and Publishers (ASCAP). The motion was approved,[69] and Lamb was accepted into the organization in 1960.

The accolades and increased attention continued. In 1960, Lamb was thrilled to be interviewed in his home by Whitney Balliett of *The New Yorker* magazine. This and other notoriety came as a result of the Folkways recording. The subsequent article provided a detailed narrative about Lamb—his past days in ragtime, his current life, his family, and his love of music—all in a concise space. Balliett even physically described Lamb—jovial, with a thin face, and generous nose—and Melie as short and pretty.[70] Lamb played the piano for Balliett during the interview—the classic "American Beauty" and the newer "Hot Cinders."[71] He was now thoroughly enjoying his long overdue fame.

During the same summer, Lamb was approached by NBC television for a Project 20 special. They were planning a program in the upcoming fall season about ragtime, and details about Lamb were to be included.[72] (Additional talk of a possible minstrel show for the sponsor, Chevrolet[73] was also in the air.) Things proceeded far enough for Lamb to loan some sheet music and photos for the program as well as to talk in person to a representative from the network. He was quite excited about this and looked forward to the show which was slated to be finished and aired that October. Lamb mentioned the project in a letter to ragtime composer, Arthur Marshall, calling it "a TV Spectacular on Ragtime which may also affect both of us. Here's hoping!"[74]

Since the experience of making the Folkways recording had been so successful, Lamb also talked of completing a similar project for Delmar Records (subsequently known as Delmark), and there had been some contact with the label to this end. He mentioned that one of the people there wanted "to come to Brooklyn later in the year to record him."[75] The fall and winter of 1960 were promising to be busier than ever.

Above all, though, Lamb was especially looking forward to traveling to Sedalia, Missouri, in October of 1960, to be a part of the second Scott Joplin Festival there. Even though it was more than four decades since Joplin had passed away, Lamb still spoke of him with fond remembrance and great admiration. Lamb's composition, "The Rag-Time Special" (dated 1959), was subtitled "a slow drag two-step" and "respectfully dedicated to the memory of my friend, Scott Joplin."[76] This memory, he stated, "will never be erased."[77]

Lamb had written to Arthur Marshall, and the two men would finally get a chance to meet each other and discuss ragtime, Scott Joplin, and their mutual publisher from the old days—John Stark. Lamb was quite fond of Marshall's music, especially the rag "Ham And."

Marshall had also known Joplin well. In his case, it was back during his days in Sedalia when Joplin had stayed with Marshall's family for several months while waiting to get settled in his own living quarters. During this time, he helped the young Marshall with piano and with composing.[78] The two collaborated on the cake walk, "Swipsey" in 1900 and, much later, on the 1907 "Lily Queen—A Ragtime Two-Step." He and Lamb would be able to personally reminisce about their friend and fellow composer of long ago, a wonderful and rare opportunity for both.

Tom Ireland, a clarinetist, was also slated to join them at the festival. A long-time Sedalia resident who was now in his nineties, Ireland had been a member of Joplin's famed Queen City Concert Band and, later, became a local newspaperman.[79] Lamb wrote to Marshall: "I had always felt ... that I knew all you fellows because, being fellow ragtime composers, it seems that there was a common bond among us."[80] He signed off by saying that he "would very much like to hear from you—for old times' sake."[81] Lamb was taking much pleasure in connecting with others in the musical world with backgrounds and interests in ragtime. "It's a great life," he said, "and it helps me to enjoy my retirement."[82]

Despite this new notoriety, though, Lamb never neglected his family and was always there for them. They now included a growing number of grandchildren, many of whom lived close by, and Lamb was always interested in their lives and activities. And they, too, were aware of how much music was a part of him and how it was always a part of their lives, even in little everyday ways. One of his grandsons remembered that when he roller skated on the street, he could hear the sound of Lamb playing the piano in the background.[83]

In addition to working on the new music, entertaining people in his home, and answering the many letters that he received, he still found time to enjoy traveling with Melie out to the family's "country estate" as he called it, at Packanack Lake in New Jersey. It was a nice place to get a change from all of the letters and calls, much as he looked forward to them. Lamb considered the Lake to be a reasonably short drive, and now they could make the trip in their new car. After many jokes about getting a red thunderbird car, he settled on a white Studebaker Hawk with a black top, a car he considered "sporty enough."[84]

Life had become an attractive balance of family, music, enjoyable correspondence and notoriety, trips to the country, and the promise of upcoming and exciting ragtime events. Through it all, Lamb was still composing songs as well as rags, just as he did in the old days. One that he wrote in 1959 particularly stands out, though. It

One of the last known photographs of Joe Lamb (circa 1959) (courtesy Robert and Joan Lamb).

was titled "It Breaks My Heart to Leave You Melie, Dear"—perhaps a premonition.

In August of 1960, Joe Lamb suffered a heart attack and was hospitalized. When he was released, he spoke of his joy on returning to East 21st Street where: "the old homestead looked good. And better still was when I sat down for supper."[85] At home, he avoided the stairs and rested in an effort to make a full recovery. He spoke fondly of the many cards he received and of the call from Alex Dommerich, Jr. Also, it pleased him enormously that new fans were writing to him all the time, and he spoke in particular of a young man by the name of Peter Lundberg from Sweden,[86] marveling at how far some of these letters had come.

On September 3, Lamb spent the day at his beloved piano, although when his sister-in-law, Genevieve Collins, came to visit, she told Melie that something didn't sound right about the way he played. Melie responded that he was probably just working through a new composition.[87]

It was a beautiful day. Melie washed her long hair and went out into the backyard to let it dry in the sunshine and to enjoy some of the late summer weather. Lamb had gone to his favorite place on the front porch to read some of the new letters that he had just received.

When Melie came inside, she found the letters and his glasses on the floor beside him.

He had quietly passed away from another heart attack.[88]

Joe Lamb left this world in the comfort of his home—a home that was always filled with everyone and everything that he cherished—Melie, his family, his friends and fans, his piano—and the sounds of his beautiful music.

Ten

Keeping the Music Alive (1960 and Beyond)

"A final legacy to ragtime tradition"— Joseph R. Scotti

Gravesend Neck Road at East 22nd Street is in the center of Sheepshead Bay, Brooklyn, its intersection bordering near orderly, tree-lined residential streets. At the beginning and end of the school day, the air is punctuated with the chatter of students from P.S. 206, the local elementary school located there.

At first look — with its brick façade and tall white columns surrounding the main entrance — the school appears no different from many of its counterparts in other sections of Brooklyn or anywhere else in the five boroughs of New York City. Since 1976, however, it has officially been called the Joseph F. Lamb School — a name that sets it apart, a significant distinction not only to the school itself and its neighborhood but also to ragtime history. Obviously Joe Lamb's story did not end on September 3, 1960.

P.S. 206 was officially renamed at a gala ceremony on May 27, 1976, commemorating the life and accomplishments of its honoree. The school is a short walk from the home where Joe and Amelia Lamb had lived for so many years, and their children attended kindergarten classes there. This personal connection, coupled with the family's longtime roots within the surrounding community, made this gesture all the more meaningful.

The celebratory event had been several years in the making. It all began when the school decided to choose a new official name in honor of its upcoming fiftieth anniversary — a name representing a notable and inspiring individual. The administration felt that involving the student body in this process would be a good idea and, therefore, established an essay contest as a means of suggesting potential candidates. Stella Laufer, a sixth grader at the school, pondered the choices for her own essay quite carefully.

At the end of each school day, Stella returned to her home and greeted

179

Amelia Lamb, who regularly babysat there for Stella's younger brother, Jeremy. Stella loved talking with Melie and often visited her at her own home, as well. Years later, she vividly recalled Melie as a "great lady" who could tell "wonderful stories"—and many of these stories were about her late husband, Joseph Lamb, and his music.[1]

The Lamb household was still overflowing with copies of old sheet music, further adding to the character and luster of Melie's tales. This bygone era, and the music and the people who were a part of it, now took on a fresh life as the young woman listened. Stella was enthralled and came away with a vivid impression of Lamb as a dedicated composer who had been a direct link to the historic ragtime music from the early part of the century, which was at that current time experiencing a strong revival.[2] Here was a man who had lived his daily life just like everyone else in one of the neat rows of houses in the neighborhood—except for his luminous musical reputation, one of the "big three" along with Scott Joplin.

Music was on everyone's mind. By the time that the essay contest was announced, the music of Joplin, and ragtime in general, was undergoing a fresh, new revival—the recordings of Joshua Rifkin and the popular film soundtrack to *The Sting*, in particular, capturing the public's attention. The assistant principal at P.S. 206 was also especially fond of music, although traditional classical repertoire was her preferred choice.[3] Whatever the style, however, the subject of music was definitely at the forefront.

It was more than the ragtime revival and the current emphasis on music, though, that fascinated Stella. Joseph Lamb had come to life through Melie's engaging tales of former days, stories that also put a personal face on a man who was now an eminent figure in American music history. Here was a talented and famous composer as well as a warm and devoted husband and father whose family held the highest priority in his life. Stella confided to her own family that she had decided upon a worthy candidate for her essay—Joseph F. Lamb. (According to Stella, Melie would never have suggested her husband as a topic for the essay, as reported in a contemporary newspaper account. She was far too humble for that.[4])

Drawing on what she had learned, Stella wrote that "many music critics believe that ragtime is an original American type of music and deserves an important place in American music history."[5] She then placed Lamb within this context as having been "among the best ragtime writers, which was the most popular music of the time,"[6] mentioning both his lapse into obscurity after the ragtime era as well as his subsequent rediscovery. It would be a "great tribute to Joseph F. Lamb," she concluded, and "a great honor for our school to be named for 'The Chopin of Ragtime,' who lived around the corner from P.S. 206, Brooklyn."[7]

Stella's essay won the contest, something that she later said came as a shock to her, albeit a positive one. She had already moved on to junior high school by the time the judging process had been completed and returned to P.S. 206 for the festivities. (In an intriguing coincidence, Stella was to return to the school once again after graduating college to work as a speech teacher there.[8])

The huge ceremony was held on the school premises and included many musical selections and special tributes. Stella Laufer, of course, read her winning essay. Then, Rudi Blesh, one half of the perseverant team who rediscovered Lamb in 1949, spoke on "Joseph F. Lamb's Place in American Music."

The school newsletter's announcement for the name change (courtesy Patricia Lamb Conn).

Pianists Milton Kaye, Max Morath, and Audrey Collins, as well as the school's own recorder group, performed a number of Lamb's compositions, ranging from the Stark classics such as "Ragtime Nightingale" to some of his later works including "Alaskan Rag." The school's Glee Club presented a set of Brooklyn and New York selections including Lamb's joyous "I'll Follow the Crowd to Coney."[9]

During a presentation made by John Nikas, an aide to Secretary of State, Mario Cuomo,[10] Amelia Lamb received flowers and an official Distinguished Service Award in honor of her husband, "whose reputation as one of the country's outstanding composers of ragtime songs persists 60 years after the height of that music's popularity."[11] Later, she wrote about the evening, both thrilled and moved by the tribute. "It was beautiful," she said. "They gave Joe a citation from the state and a beautiful bouquet and of course I couldn't speak. I just cried."[12]

On another evening, there was a special dinner for Melie, hosted in conjunction with the ceremonial occasion. "I was the 'Guest of Honor,'" she wrote, "can you imagine that?"[13]

Years before this landmark tribute, Amelia Lamb would definitely not have been able to imagine everything that was to transpire on her husband's behalf after he passed away. There would be heightened interest in his compositions and in his life as well as more honors of all types. New friends and ragtime enthusiasts would continue to enter the picture, including some who were a part of the special P.S. 206 celebration. And Amelia and her family were to be very much a part of it all.

Shortly after Lamb's death, Amelia had taken action to ensure that much of her husband's unpublished work would become available for music enthusiasts to perform and enjoy. She brought a group of thirteen of his unpublished rags to Mills Music. They consisted of some older rags which Lamb had revised over the years as well as those written after his rediscovery by Rudi Blesh and Harriet Janis. These compositions represented a mix of approaches from the more traditional "The Old Home Rag" to the novelty rag type piece "Hot Cinders."[14] The result was a comprehensive volume entitled *Ragtime Treasures*, a collection that was edited by the well respected Bernard Kalban, and published by Mills Music (Belwin Mills) in 1964. It also contained an introduction by Rudi Blesh, who called this group of Lamb's work "a priceless, unexpected legacy."[15]

By the time that *Ragtime Treasures* was published, the growing awareness of ragtime that had been evident in the 1950s spilled over into the new decade and was gaining more momentum, with interest in the classic rag becoming heightened. Audiences enjoyed the sound.

Within the year before Joe Lamb passed away, a landmark public television series debuted on station KRMA in Denver, Colorado, that would draw much attention to ragtime and help give Max Morath national recognition as an acknowledged authority on the subject.

Morath not only informed viewers about ragtime music, history, and culture, but he also did so in an entertaining and engaging manner, breaking ground for a whole new brand of educational television. Using a variety of props and vintage clothing, as well as singing and playing a wealth of ragtime repertoire, he genially yet informatively presented details about all facets of this form of music. According to David Stewart, this series—*The Ragtime Era*—was one "that would change noncommercial television forever."[16] Part Two, titled "Any Rags Today," devoted a segment to Joseph Lamb, during which Morath discussed the components and structure of the ragtime form, performing one of Lamb's most challenging works, "Excelsior Rag," as an example.[17]

The entire twelve-part program was subsequently rerun in other parts of the country and became an audience favorite, its innovative and educational format earning praise from viewers and critics alike. When it aired in New York in 1961, *The New York Times* referred to it as being among the "engaging little sleepers"[18] of the upcoming television offerings. This paved the way for a new perspective on educational television and, at the same time, helped to further popularize ragtime — and Joe Lamb along with it.

In 1961, station KRMA launched another series, *The Turn of the Century*, for national distribution. It consisted of fifteen half-hour segments, the fourth of which was entitled "Classic Ragtime." Here, Morath discussed the lives and music of the "big three," with portraits shown of each. He devoted a solid portion of the segment to Lamb, commenting on his life and unique musical gifts and, also, quoting Russ Cassidy. Morath performed both "Ragtime Nightingale" and "Top Liner Rag"[19] within this segment, offering viewers good examples of Lamb's style and sound. This program did much to heighten the public's awareness of the place of classic ragtime in American musical history.

Morath was established in New York in the same year that *Ragtime Treasures* was issued by Mills Music. It was 1964, and another "Max," namely Max Gordon, owner of the Village Vanguard in New York, took note of the growing interest in the ragtime form, particularly among a new generation. The Vanguard had been opened in 1935, and entrepreneur Gordon hosted poets and comics over the years there but, most of all, jazz musicians— its line-up reading like a who's who in the greats of jazz —from Thelonious Monk and Miles Davis to the Bill Evans Trio. Situated on a singular wedge of property in Greenwich Village, the place had become legendary.[20] The word "ragtime," however, was not usually associated with it. Changes were about to come.

Max Morath on the set of "Classic Ragtime," a segment of *Turn of the Century* (1961), the second of two groundbreaking educational television series that were aired nationwide. Part of this particular program was devoted to Lamb, during which Morath performed both "Ragtime Nightingale" and "Top Liner Rag" and talked about Lamb's life and achievements (Don Allen-KRMA Denver).

Max Morath, now a well known favorite with the public, had formed a group called the Original Rag Quartet. In 1964, when Max Gordon decided to spotlight ragtime in the Village Vanguard's summer line-up, he invited Morath and his group to be featured entertainers. Gordon enjoyed pleasing his audiences, and both ragtime and these performers had gained enough notoriety to be headlined at this jazz stronghold. It was a sure indicator of the continuing strong revival of the style. Gordon even decorated the establishment in keeping with the theme, its walls now lined with portraits of Scott Joplin, Tom Turpin, Harry Von Tilzer, Joe Howard, and — Joe Lamb.[21]

The members of the Original Rag Quartet were an eclectic group, something that Joe Lamb would have found intriguing, given his love of all types

The Original Rag Quartet, featured at New York's Village Vanguard in 1964, where portraits of Lamb and other ragtime composers served as a backdrop to the music. The group performed to rave reviews there and on tour, contributing to ragtime music's continuing rise in popularity. Left to right: Max Morath, Jim Tyler, Barry Kornfeld, Felix Pappalardi (courtesy Max Morath).

of music from Bach to Joplin. A classical lutenist, a conductor of a baroque ensemble, and a folk music performer — now entertaining on guitar, banjo, and *guitarron*—joined in with Morath at the piano[22] to play with verve their special instrumentations that were "steeped in classic ragtime."[23] The group was exceptionally popular and, subsequently, toured extensively, covering the college concert circuit, and also appearing as an opening act in Las Vegas. The music of Joe Lamb and other revered composers traveled with them — as well as with Max Morath, who was also to spend the next decades touring the country with his one-man ragtime and old-time music shows.

By the time that the 1970s arrived, ragtime was still on the rise and was embraced by an even wider general audience. In many cases, similar to the Original Rag Quartet, its popularity was raised by the efforts of musicians who researched, wrote, and performed in disparate genres.

Joshua Rifkin, a musically eclectic young man, helped to drive the continued ragtime craze during this decade. Rifkin was known for his musicological theories on J.S. Bach and had pursued serious studies at the Juilliard School of Music. He had also performed and conducted the most highly regarded classical works on the planet.

Rifkin went on to exhibit a whole other side to his musical personality, though, one which would certainly establish the breadth of his interests and his scholarship as well as continue to spotlight his ability to discover the best in all branches of music. In his landmark recordings, he ignited a chain reaction on behalf of ragtime, all with the help of the unique record company who stood behind him.

Nonesuch Records was a pioneering label during this time. However it was through the efforts of its ingenious director, Teresa Sterne, that some of its most singular recordings were produced.[24] Among these albums was the set of Scott Joplin rags as performed by Joshua Rifkin, the first volume issued in 1970. It was an astounding success. A second album was to follow several years later.

While Rifkin's albums were selling in record numbers, *The Collected Works of Scott Joplin*, edited by Vera Brodsky Lawrence and published by The New York Public Library, was achieving its own widespread recognition. The first volume contained piano works and the second, works for voice.

An extensive essay by Rudi Blesh appeared as an introduction to Volume One of Lawrence's work. While Blesh covered much ground pertaining to the ragtime style and Scott Joplin himself, he also devoted significant space to recounting the now famous story of Joseph Lamb's meeting with Joplin. The music for "Sensation" appeared in the section entitled "Miscellaneous Works," definitely separate from another grouping which contained collaborative pieces. Both in the essay as well as in the accurate reproduction of "Sensation," including its cover, Lamb's credentials as an independent composer, and one who was certainly recognized as such by Joplin, were clearly established.[25]

During this time, other ragtime was being performed on a wider scale, and the style was increasingly heard live not only in clubs and on college campuses but also at other eclectic venues. In 1972, the Whitney Museum in New York was the scene of a concert during which a group of performers played their own compositions. However, it was Max Morath and William Bolcom who also performed works by Joplin, Turpin, and "the much underrated Joseph Lamb."[26] Such types of events were to continue.

In 1973, the hit film *The Sting* was released with its soundtrack of Joplin rags as scored by Marvin Hamlisch. A recording followed. The public rushed to be entertained by the genial con men, played by Paul Newman and Robert Redford, all to the background music of ragtime (although the film's action took place in a post-ragtime era). The passion for ragtime music was now reaching an all-time high.

During the same year, and shortly before the music from *The Sting* had risen on the charts, an album titled *The Classic Rags of Joe Lamb* was released by Golden Crest Records. Pianist Milton Kaye was the featured performer. Kaye was another accomplished musician with a fine and eclectic background. He had been accompanist to Jascha Heifitz on a European tour in the 1930s and had also been a part of Toscanni's NBC Symphony of the Air. In contrast to this, however, he was well known on the popular music scene for his work on radio and television. He even wrote the theme song for the television show *Concentration.*[27]

Kaye performed a varied selection of Lamb's compositions on the recording, including a number of the Stark classics as well as several pieces from *Ragtime Treasures* and others. The comprehensive album liner notes by its producer Rudi Blesh suggest that, given Kaye's background, he was also especially aware of the classical influence of these works.

A second disc (one side only) was included in the album package. It offered a unique conversation between Kaye and Blesh, with a genial exchange between the two men about Joe Lamb's music and ragtime in general. Kaye admitted that he was drawn to Lamb's compositions because of something "melodic and beautiful about them,"[28] and the two went on to discuss everything from the way the musical establishment originally turned its back on ragtime, to the question of whether improvisations and embellishments should be added to the original works as written. On this subject they both heartily concluded that the creative additions were permissible and that Lamb would have approved.[29] (Subsequently, though, family members expressed disagreement, reacting strongly on the question.[30] "Joe Lamb would have *hated* any alteration, speed-up or addition to any of his rags,"[31] wrote his nephew. As to interpretation, he recalled that his uncle "*never* banged rags and never ended fortissimo,"[32] and he also didn't add any extras, such as arpeggios or tremolos, "because they don't suit rags."[33])

Despite the continuing debates over improvisation, this album became its own form of classic and was reviewed by John S. Wilson in *The New York Times.* He, too, repeated the story of Lamb's rediscovery and commended Kaye for a performance that reflected the "beauty ... and joyful, good-time spirit"[34] of these compositions. A second album, now a rare find, was issued later. It contained works that were unpublished and unrecorded at the time, including "Walper House Rag" and "Ragged Rapids Rag." "Scott Joplin's Dream" was also a part of this recording. (Although interesting from a historical perspective since it is supposed to represent the collaborative efforts of Lamb and Joplin in 1910, most scholars believe that this arranged work is not in the style of either composer and presume that the original manuscript may have been lost over time.[35])

In 1974, Gunther Schuller, acclaimed for his jazz and classical work and for his position as president of the famed The New England Conservatory of Music, made a recording of the Stark Music Company arrangements from *The Red Back Book*. Schuller was another eclectic musician who recognized and appreciated the merits of the ragtime style. The album, issued by Angel records, was highly successful and among the label's best sellers. It contained the music of Joplin. Schuller, however, continued work within the genre and subsequently made another recording, issued by Golden Crest Records, this time with a student ensemble from the New England Conservatory of Music. It contained his own orchestrations and included the work of Joseph Lamb. He graciously sent copies of these orchestrations to members of the Lamb family. "Did you [get] the score of Nightingale Rag that Gunther Schuller arranged," asked Melie in a letter to researcher Joseph Scotti. "He also sent me copies for my five children. That was nice of him."[36] Such recognition by a major figure like Schuller brought additional attention from the classical sector to the work of both Lamb and Joplin, something that Joplin had longed to achieve for the classic ragtime form as a whole during his own lifetime.

Keen interest in Lamb was still tremendously evident at a location that he always held dear — Canada. From his days in school at St. Jerome's, through his association with Harry Sparks, to his famous appearance in 1959 at Toronto's Club 76, Canada had been both a musical and a personal connection that had been important to him. Even after his death, that link was a strong one.

By the 1970s, the Toronto Ragtime Society, five hundred members strong, was holding regular meetings and promoting special events. The group had originally been organized just to keep pure ragtime alive after the closing of the beloved Club 76.[37] In 1974, the Cara Inn was the site of this group's twelfth annual Ragtime Bash. Four hundred of its members attended. This time Amelia Lamb and Joe Lamb, Jr., were guests at the event and, thereafter, Melie always attended. By 1976, daughter Patricia and her husband Bill were able to arrange for care of their children, and joined them. They, too, continued to attend annually. Lamb's music was, of course, always a part of the line-up, and his fans were happy to hear his works performed as well as to meet and speak with his family about the composer himself.

In the meantime, Lamb was becoming a popular subject in the field of scholarly research. In 1975, Brooklyn College graduate student Marjorie Freilich-Den chose to write her master's thesis on Lamb's life and accomplishments. She was able to conduct valuable personal and phone interviews as well as to exchange correspondence with Amelia Lamb, Anastasia Lamb

Van Gieson, Patricia Lamb Conn, Robert Lamb, Richard Lamb, Joseph Lamb, Jr., George and Paul Van Gieson, Rudi Blesh, Lamb's childhood friend Paul Hughes, and co-workers at Dommerich, among others. Freilich-Den's research also led to her discovery of Adaline Bunten McMillan, who provided significant information about Lamb's "Joplin years." The resulting thesis— "Joseph F. Lamb: A Ragtime Composer Recalled"—is an original and important resource on the composer's life, filling in innumerable details and offering much insight into the people and the eras during which Lamb lived.

In 1977, a doctoral candidate at the University of Cincinnati presented a dissertation entitled "Joe Lamb: A Study of Ragtime's Paradox." Joseph R. Scotti conducted extensive research to support his work, and his subsequent findings, in-depth analyses, and thorough commentary remain a critical resource in studying Lamb's life and body of compositions. "Joe Lamb may be the key to making the 'Joplin' revival a true 'Ragtime' revival," he wrote to Melie Lamb. "In many ways Joe symbolizes an American music valid for all races and nationalities in the United States. The fact that he worked alone for the most part and achieved the status of genius makes him truly unique."[38]

During the 1990s, Scotti was doing additional research while preparing to write a book about Lamb. During the course of scrutinizing many papers and artifacts, he found a small sketchbook. Inside was a valuable treasure. As Patricia Lamb Conn describes it, Scotti called her up very excited one day and said that he had discovered a new rag in that sketchbook. He subsequently edited it and prepared it for publication. She recalled that the words "Ragtime Reverie" kept coming to her while playing the piece, tears in her eyes as she fondly recalled her father. This became the title of the work,[39] one that was ultimately premiered by Trebor Tichenor and the St. Louis Ragtimers in Sedalia, Missouri.

Another composition, one that had been incorporated into the "Hot Cinders" recording was also transcribed by Joe Scotti and made available in sheet music form. It was titled "Brown Derby #2," in honor of one of the lost Mills pieces of the same name. (The #2 was added in case the original was ever found.[40]) The work was premiered by pianist and conservatory professor, Tony Caramia.

Lamb's compositions were being increasingly performed in a number of new types of settings, some that appeared quite unusual at first in conjunction with ragtime. In 1974, the Royal Ballet premiered a work in London entitled *Elite Syncopations*. Choreographer Kenneth Macmillan was responsible for this lighthearted ballet that incorporated music by a number of ragtime greats, both old and new. "Ragtime Nightingale" and "Alaskan Rag" were included in the work, an interesting selection of one of the Stark classics as well as

A portion of the sketchbook manuscript for "Ragtime Reverie," a new Lamb rag discovered in the early 1990s by Joseph R. Scotti, who also edited the work for publication (courtesy Patricia Lamb Conn).

Lamb's last rag. This was a ragtime reunion of sorts because the ballet also contained works by Scott Joplin and James Scott — the other two members of the "big three" of ragtime — as well as by Max Morath. Two years later, in 1976, the company premiered this innovative creation in the United States on the stage of the Metropolitan Opera House.[41]

In January of 1976, Lamb's music was an important part of another, and particularly spectacular, production in the world of dance, a groundbreaking work on several counts. Choreographer Twyla Tharp chose one of Lamb's compositions along with music of Franz Joseph Haydn to be used as the accompaniment for her highly successful eclectic modern ballet *Push Comes to Shove*, starring Mikhail Baryshnikov with the American Ballet Theatre. This riveting work opened with Baryshnikov dancing to "Bohemia Rag." It was innovative and clever; and audiences loved it. Clive Barnes of *The New*

Lamb's last classic rag, published in 1919, was featured in the 1976 production of *Push Comes to Shove*, choreographed by Twyla Tharp and danced by Mikhail Baryshnikov (courtesy Charles H. Templeton Collection, Special Collections, Mississippi State University Libraries).

York Times called it "a palpable hit."[42] It was a landmark accomplishment for this inventive choreographer as well as for the internationally known Baryshnikov, and audiences responded with "a kind of delirium."[43] Tharp had combined Joplin and Mozart in the past, and in this work she created another ragtime-classical pairing. Later, in her autobiography — which was also titled *Push Comes to Shove* — Tharp referred to both Joplin and Lamb as the "frontiersmen of jazz,"[44] an illuminating perspective.

Later, in the 1980s, Edward Villella created *Legs of Lamb* for the Eglevsky Ballet Company which was premiered at Hofstra University on Long Island, the accompaniment provided by Milton Kaye. A famed dancer who subsequently became artistic coordinator of this company, Villella was also intrigued by ragtime, especially after hearing the performances of Gunther Schuller's ragtime group from The New England Conservatory.[45] He then discovered Milton Kaye's recordings of Lamb's music.[46] The two met, and the rest was history.

In subsequent years, other dance companies were to repeat many of these works as well as include compositions by Lamb in a number of their other productions as well.

In addition to dance presentations, Lamb's music was incorporated into other mediums, spilling onto the stage, screen, television, and radio. "Ragtime Nightingale" and "American Beauty Rag" were used in the Broadway production of *Tintypes* in the 1980-81 theatre season. The show told the story of life in the late nineteenth and early twentieth centuries — the plight of immigrants, the new inventions, politicians, entertainment styles, and beyond — all of it seen through music. Lamb's "Ragtime Nightingale" begins the show and in a touching bit of coincidence, he is reunited with individuals from his past — his work sharing the musical spotlight with Joplin's "The Ragtime Dance" of 1902 and J. Fred Helf's "Teddy Da Roose" of 1910.[47]

Lamb's music was featured in other ways over the years, as well. In a letter to Joseph Scotti in 1975, Lamb's nephew makes reference to a television special entitled "Toys on the Town," during which "they played a couple of U Joes pieces or parts thereof."[48] Onscreen, the cutting edge artist and illustrator Robert Crumb used "Ragtime Nightingale" as background music for his 1994 autobiographical documentary film.

On the radio, Lamb was the featured subject on *A Prairie Home Companion* in 2000, hosted by Garrison Keillor. The program's famed pianist Butch Thompson played several of Lamb's most famous rags, "American Beauty," "Sensation Rag," "Arctic Sunset," "Ethiopia Rag," and "Cottontail Rag," among them. He was joined by cellist Laura Sewell for some of these renditions.[49]

Beyond this, however, Joe Lamb was acknowledged in a number of other unique ways.

The centennial of Joseph Lamb's birth took place in 1987, an anniversary that was certainly well recognized that year by those in attendance at the annual Scott Joplin Ragtime Festival in Sedalia, Missouri. Glenn Jenks, a versatile pianist, composer, and recording artist from Maine, was a regular performer at the festival and, as an admirer of Lamb's music, he took special note of the date.

Jenks was also a connoisseur of flowers— more specifically, of roses. He had been growing roses since he was a student in the ninth grade. Now, whenever visiting Sedalia, he made it a point to stop by the town rose garden at Liberty Park. During his visit in Lamb's centennial year, Jenks developed an intriguing idea. He decided that something further could be done to commemorate Joseph Lamb and his music and, drawing upon his own combined interests, he formulated a plan.

Jenks was well acquainted with Roses of Yesterday and Today in California, and it was his friend there, Pat Wiley, who had been responsible for introducing the work of Dr. Griffith Buck, a rose breeder from Ames, Iowa. Buck had created ninety different types of roses— including his flagship, "Carefree Beauty"— but was especially known for cultivating roses that could withstand the rigorous winters of Iowa. This drew both interest and empathy from Jenks, who lived in similarly cold temperatures in Maine. Many of Buck's roses also possessed musical names— Earth Song, Mountain Music, Music Maker, and Pearlie Mae (named for singer Pearl Bailey), among them.[50]

Jenks wrote to Buck before traveling to the next festival in Sedalia, explaining that he wanted to create a tribute to Joseph Lamb in the form of a special rose. He asked if Buck might be able to help. When Jenks returned home to Maine, a reply was already in his mailbox. It was accompanied by the photo of a beautiful rose, awaiting its new name.[51]

This rose was both lovely and hardy, able to survive rough winters.

The Joseph F. Lamb Rose, a fitting tribute to the composer of "American Beauty," realized through the efforts of Glenn Jenks, in honor of Lamb's birthday centennial (courtesy Glenn A. Jenks).

Jenks tested its durability himself with the rooted cutting sent to him by Buck. It developed beautifully. After talking with Patricia Lamb Conn, they agreed upon a name, and the Joseph F. Lamb Rose became official in 1988.[52]

Blooming a medium red, this rose deepens in color when its gently pointed petals are exposed to sunlight, a slightly white hue emanating from its center along with a delicately understated fragrance.[53] The rose's quiet beauty echoes many of Lamb's reflective compositions, some of which Jenks himself has recorded, among them the famous 1913 "American Beauty," named after another variety of his own favorite flower.[54]

Joe Lamb's hometown of Montclair, New Jersey, did not forget about him either. In 1987, he was honored with the placing of a commemorative stone in the front yard of his boyhood home. A ceremony was held outside the house during which Rudi Blesh dedicated the stone. A ragtime concert, held in conjunction with this at the nearby Unitarian Church, featured several performers who played some of Lamb's works as well as other ragtime repertoire.[55]

Melie was able to enjoy many of these tributes to her late husband and was an important force in keeping his music alive and in encouraging its performance. She attended as many festivals, concerts, and celebratory events as possible.

Amelia Lamb passed away in 1991. Everyone who met her over the years commented on her charm and energetic spirit — as well as her continued joy in and support of her husband's music. She was always spoken of fondly by anyone who had come in contact with her.

Melie's children — Patricia, in particular — continued on with the work of promoting Lamb's music for future generations. Patricia presented a number of seminars about her father's life and work at ragtime festivals, including events at: Niantic, Connecticut, in 1993; Columbia, Missouri, in 2004; Sacramento, California, in 2004; and Sedalia, Missouri, in 2005. Audiences were eager to hear about Lamb's life and to learn additional details about his work.[56] In 2006, she provided much information about the life of Joe Lamb during an interview conducted by David Sager at the Library of Congress, which is now a part of their online resource collection.[57]

The same year as the interview, ragtime pianist/historian "Perfessor" Bill Edwards completed unfinished sections of "Muskoka: An Indian Idyl," the composition written by Lamb during his student days in Canada. He subsequently published the work and also included it on a recording of varied selections from the early twentieth century. This recording became a companion to a historical novel about the Muskoka area — both the music and the written word capturing the essence of the time and place.[58]

Of course Joe Lamb always wanted to share his music with those who would enjoy it — something that he always did during his lifetime. Soon there would be another project under way that would further this aim.

Patricia Lamb Conn approached acclaimed pianist, singer, and composer Sue Keller about the possibility of issuing some of Lamb's unpublished compositions. Keller was familiar with Joe Lamb's work as well as with a wide variety of ragtime repertoire.

She agreed to the project and was soon spending a great deal of time studying and analyzing a large group of Lamb's unpublished manuscripts as well as some of his previously published but lesser known works. She chose a fine representative selection of eighteen compositions, and then carefully prepared, edited, and structured them into a music folio entitled *A Little Lost Lamb*. The contents include some very early works such as "Mignonne" (1901), "Walper House Rag" (1903), and "My Queen of Zanzibar" (1904), as well as Joe Lamb's final work, "The Alaskan Rag." Previously published songs were also incorporated into the folio—"Gee, Kid! But I Like You" (originally issued by Shapiro Music in 1909) and "I'll Follow the Crowd to Coney" (originally issued by Satterlee Music in 1913), among them. The project took three years to complete.

A recording seemed like a natural companion to the folio and came soon afterwards. Keller performed these selections and made sure that Patricia Lamb Conn joined her on the vocals for "I'll Follow the Crowd to Coney," one of the Lamb children's favorites during their family singalongs after dinner. Both the folio and CD were published by The Ragtime Press in 2005[59] and are a unique resource for the further enjoyment and study of Lamb's music, illustrating the

The cover of *A Little Lost Lamb*, the valuable and comprehensive collection of many of Lamb's previously unpublished rags and songs, compiled by Sue Keller and issued in 2005 as a companion to the folio of the same name (© Ragtime Press, 2005).

eclectic range of his output from his student days through just prior to his death.

On October 11, 2007, both Sue Keller and Patricia Lamb Conn were together again singing "I'll Follow the Crowd to Coney," as part of another tribute to Lamb in his hometown of Montclair, New Jersey, sponsored by the local historical society there. Keller performed a number of compositions from the "Stark classics" as well as from *A Little Lost Lamb*, also providing information about Lamb as a part of the event.

Additional such tributes were to follow. On June 5, 2011, the University of Missouri was the site of a two-and-a-half hour concert in honor of Joe Lamb and his music. It was presented as a part of the Blind Boone Ragtime & Early Jazz Festival, a well-respected annual event, known within both ragtime and related musical communities. A roster of more than a dozen stellar performers played the twelve classic rags as well as many other selections ranging from "Alaskan Rag," to "Hot Cinders," to "I'll Follow the Crowd to Coney." Two audio-visual presentations about Lamb's life and work were also shown.

This particular tribute illustrates the impact of Lamb's music and its permanent place in our musical culture. These performers represented a range of individuals—from internationally acclaimed professional musicians to youthful rising stars in the ragtime world; from a well-respected conservatory professor to those who perform as an avocation. Their ages ranged from young to mature, their homes from New York and Iowa, to California and Norway. Their admiration for Lamb's compositions and their willingness to take the time and effort to be a part of this gala were the common denominators.

But Lamb's story — and that of ragtime — does not end with this tribute or with any other single event. His music will, of course, continue to be performed at concerts and festivals, included on recordings, and incorporated into a wide range of mediums—dance, theatre, radio, and more—as it has been in the past. However there is an ongoing interest in delving further, in gaining an even deeper insight into the essence of ragtime music and its creators as well as of their role in our cultural and historical identity. Joseph F. Lamb will be an important part of this as well.

The unique qualities of Lamb's music have made it timeless and worthy of continued study and performance. Its intrinsic beauty and value have been positively recognized by individuals both in the present and in the past.

The late Joseph R. Scotti praised Lamb not only for his position as one of ragtime's big three but also for "contributing most to the development and viability of the form."[60]

Pianist and composer Larisa Migachyov has recorded and performed

Lamb's compositions for contemporary audiences, clarifying why she loves his music and what makes it unique. "It's so full of passion.... I think it has a wider range of emotion than most other ragtime."[61]

And, of course, there are still the words of music publisher, John Stillwell Stark who referred to one of the classic rags as "another of Lamb's inspirations that will live forever."[62] A century later, his words have proven to be true.

Epilogue

Pianist and entertainer Max Morath referred to ragtime as a combination of chaos and discipline — or syncopation over a steady rhythm — drawing parallels between this and his life as a performer.[1]

The same comparison holds true for writing a biography. There is the discipline, or structure, of the subject's chronological existence with its steady progression of events through time, the natural sequence that is a part of any life.

Then there is the chaos of making sense of it all beyond the basic details, at least from the biographer's point of view. It is a varied and syncopated chaos at that — of delving into old letters and mountains of books, studying unpublished documents, weighing the impact of historical events, and speaking with a great many individuals about the old days and the newer ones. What follows is the fashioning of this chaos into a cohesive whole, always with that steady chronological beat of life keeping a march-like time underneath it all. It is a wonderful process.

In organizing the syncopated components of this equation into a reasonably comprehensive melodic line, though, it is impossible to include everything that one might like. Similar to telling our own life story to a listener, there are some parts forgotten and others omitted for lack of space or time. With the story of another, it is no different — tempting to stray too far down the roads of historical context and anecdotal detail while, at the same time, unintentionally neglecting those that are equally important. In this regard, I have tried to balance the two, exploring some side roads but perhaps not too many, with forgotten ones hopefully at a minimum.

Like any life observed through the lens of time, there are unanswered questions. Joe Lamb's is no different. Who else besides Joplin might he have met during the heyday of Tin Pan Alley? Which specific publishers and songwriters hired him to create those freelance arrangements over the years? Did he compose under any additional pseudonyms? What were the specifics of his unknown conversations with Joplin and Stark? Perhaps some answers will come to light one day; perhaps not. As always, everyday details and facts fade into deeper obscurity over time.

There are mysteries, as well. In Lamb's case, some of them arose posthumously. One pertains to the copyrights on some of his works claimed by Robert Darch and the subsequent confusion arising from this, as well as questions about a number of unpublished manuscripts that Darch registered in his name jointly with Amelia Lamb. Another mystery is why Eubie Blake's name appears as "arranger" on "Scott Joplin's Dream" as well as on a number of Lamb's unpublished works ("She's My Girl," "Joe Lamb's Medley Overture," and "Doin' the Lonesome Slow Drag," among others), something that also appears to have been organized by Darch after Lamb's death. These mysteries lead to more questions. What became of the original manuscripts? How did all of this come about? What details were a part of the bigger picture? The principal players are no longer here to comment on the subject, and one may delve into what details are available and engage in speculation but this is beyond both the parameters and intent of this book.

This is Joe Lamb's story, and it is an important one on a number of levels. Similar to his rags, he had balance and creativity, assuming many roles — husband, father, composer, employee, neighbor, friend — playing them well and with his own innovative flair. And just like his music, there was variety to it all — a syncopated sort of variety — captured within the structure of everyday life, its own beautiful harmonies resonating throughout. These harmonies were built on many personal qualities — resilience and perseverance, generosity and perfectionism, curiosity and joy.

Lamb's story is also an American one: a child of immigrants who was fascinated with other cultures; an artistic innovator in an age of technological advances; an individual who incorporated many disparate interests into a unified whole; and a musical eclectic who both represented and superseded the defining elements of the eras in which he lived — from the gilded age to the space age.

And, so, it is also the story of his music — a distinctive sound — and how it came to be. Lamb observed the great world around him — musical, cultural, and otherwise — and drew the finest inspiration from it, molding this material into melodic, syncopated, harmonious and, of course, classic creations — artfully blending the chaos and discipline of it all.

Seen in this light, what better form of music could there have been in which to achieve recognition than ragtime — a music that Aaron Copland called "absolutely American,"[2] and a form in which Lamb was granted lasting fame as a member of its "big three." And, as such, Lamb was an absolutely American ragtime original.

Appendix I

The Compositions of Joseph F. Lamb

Published Works

CANADIAN PUBLISHERS

Harry H. Sparks Music Publisher (copyright dates in parentheses)

Piano Compositions
Celestine Waltzes (1905)
The Lilliputian's Bazaar (1905)
Florentine Waltzes (1906)

Piano Arrangements
Twilight Dreams (1908; composed by Chas. E. Wellinger, arranged by Jos. F. Lamb)

Songs (Words and Music) Written as Harry Moore
Sweet Nora Doone (1907)
The Engineer's Last Good Bye (1908)
She Does'nt Flirt (1908)
I'm Jealous of You (1908)
Three Leaves of Shamrock on the Watermelon Vine (1908; pseudonym for words only)

Songs (Music Only) Written as Earl West
In the Shade of the Maple by the Gate (1908; words by Ruth Dingman)
Somewhere a Broken Heart (1908; words by Samuel A. White)

Songs (Music Only) Written as Joseph (or "Josef") F. Lamb
The Lost Letter (1908; words by Margret Anger Cawthorpe)
Love's Ebb Tide (1908; words by Samuel A. White)
If Love Is a Dream Let Me Never Awake (1908; words by Llyn Wood)
Dear Blue Eyes (1908; words by Llyn Wood)

Songs (Words and Music) Written as Joseph (or "Jos." or "Josef") F. Lamb
The Homestead Where the Suwanee River Flows (1909)
I Love You Just the Same (1910)

202 Appendix I: The Compositions of Joseph F. Lamb

Playmates (1910; words by Will Wilander; cover attributes words to
Lamb)
My Fairy Iceberg Queen (1910; words by Murray Wood; cover attrib-
utes words to Lamb)

Musgrave Bros. & Davies
Songs (Words & Music) Written as Harry Moore
The Ladies' Aid Song (1913)

AMERICAN PUBLISHERS

Stark Music Company (original publisher of the twelve classic rags)
Sensation — A Rag (1908)
Excelsior Rag (1909)
Ethiopia Rag (1909)
Champagne Rag, March & Two-Step (1910)
American Beauty Rag (1913)
Cleopatra Rag (1915)
Ragtime Nightingale (1915)
Contentment Rag (1915)
Reindeer — Ragtime Two-Step (1915)
Patricia Rag (1916)
Top Liner Rag (1916)
Bohemia Rag (1919)

Shapiro Music Publisher
Gee, Kid! But I Like You (1909; words and music)

Gordon Hurst Music Company
Love in Absence (1909; words by Mary A. O'Reilly)

G. Satterlee Music Co.
I'll Follow the Crowd to Coney (1913; words by G. Satterlee)
I Want to Be a Bird-Man (1913; words by G. Satterlee)

Patricia Lamb Conn
Brown Derby #2 (transcribed and edited by Joseph R. Scotti from an
audio tape of Lamb's performance as recorded by Michael Mont-
gomery; issued 1988, 1993)
Ragtime Reverie (edited from a Joseph F. Lamb Sketchbook by Joseph R.
Scotti; issued 1992/1993)

Signal Sounds
Muskoka Falls: An Indian Idyl (1902/2006; Joseph F. Lamb/Bill Edwards)

PUBLISHED COLLECTIONS
  Belwin Mills Publishing Corp.
    Ragtime Treasures: Piano Solos by Joseph F. Lamb (1964)
      Alabama Rag
      Arctic Sunset
      Bird-Brain Rag
      Blue Grass Rag
      Chimes of Dixie
      Cottontail Rag
      Firefly Rag
      Good and Plenty Rag
      Hot Cinders
      The Old Home Rag
      Ragtime Bobolink
      Thoroughbred Rag
      Toad Stool Rag

  Ragtime Press
    A Little Lost Lamb: Piano Music by Joseph F. Lamb (2005)
      The Alaskan Rag (originally published in *They All Played Ragtime*, third edition)
      *The Beehive Rag
      Chasin' the Chippies: Characteristic Two-Step (1914)
      Gee, Kid! But I Like You (originally published by Shapiro Music Publisher in 1909)
      *Greased Lightening Rag
      I Want to Be a Bird-Man (originally published by G. Satterlee Music Co., in 1913)
      I'll Follow the Crowd to Coney (originally published by G. Satterlee Music Co., in 1913)
      *The Jersey Rag
      *Joe Lamb's Old Rag (originally titled "Dynamite Rag")
      Lorne Scots on Parade (1904)
      Mignonne (1901)
      My Queen of Zanzibar (1904)
      Ragged Rapids Rag: Ragtime March and Two-Step (1905)
      *The Rag-Time Special: A Slow Drag Two-Step
      *Rapid Transit
      Red Feather (1906)
      Spanish Fly (1912)
      Walper House Rag (1903)
        *These compositions (or segments of them) were originally written between 1907 and 1914, subsequently revised by Lamb, and eventually

dated as 1959. "Joe Lamb's Old Rag," originally titled "Dynamite Rag," was one of the pieces that Lamb played for Joplin.

Unpublished Works

DATED

1900: Meet Me at the Chutes; Idle Dreams
1901: Lenonah
1902: Dora Dean's Sister; Muskoka Falls: An Indian Idyl
1903: Golden Leaves: Canadian Concert Waltzes; Le Premier: French Canadian March; Midst the Valleys of the Far Off Golden West; When Winter is Over
1904: The Ivy Covered Homestead on the Hill; Tell Me That You Will Love Me as I Love You
1905: A Rose and You; The Eskimo Glide; Florida: Intermezzo Two-Step; My Little Glow Worm
1906: The Sourdough March
1907: Hyacinth Rag; Symphonic Syncopations (c. 1907–1914)
1908: Joseph Lamb's Medley Overture #1; Samuel: Coon Song; Sunset: A Ragtime Serenade
1909: Dear Old Rose
1910: Scott Joplin's Dream
1912: Let's Do It Again
1913: A Little Girl Like You; Romance Land
1914: Wal-Yo (words by Mrs. Joseph Lamb); That Wonderful Melody
1915: Just for You; I'd Give the World to Have You Back Again
1916: Oh! You With Hair Like Mine; For the Cause of Liberty
1926: Love Me Like I Love You
1959: It Breaks My Heart to Leave You Melie, Dear

UNDATED

Wanda
Only You
She's My Girl
I'd Like You to Love Me
Ilo-Ilo
Since You Took My Heart Away

The Dying Hero
Don't You Be Lonely
The 22nd Regiment March
Doin' the Lonesome Slow Drag
I Should Have Known
I'm Going to Go Somewhere

THE MILLS NOVELETTES

All Wet
Apple Sauce

Chime In
Cinders

Shooting the Works
Soup & Fish

Banana Oil	Crimson Ramblers	Sweet Pickles
The Berries	Knick Knacks	Waffles
Brown Derby	Ripples	

Manuscripts Not Located

Jennie Song	In Gay Old Golden Gate	Nemesis
Farewell My Love	Down in Dear Old Florida	Our Empire
Our Emperor	Cheese It	

Selected Minstrel Show Songs

1929: Barbeque (Lamb/Gus Collins); Coming After You (Lamb)

1930: Purple Moon (Lamb/Gus Collins)*; So Here We Are (Lamb/Gus Collins)*

1933: Here We Are Again (Lamb/Dorrie Collins)*

1935: Hi, Everybody (Lamb)*

*Music/lyrics in "The Black Lamb of the Family," by Galen Wilkes (*The Rag Time Ephemeralist* I, 1998).

Appendix II

Selected Recordings

In Print

Joseph Lamb: A Study in Classic Ragtime
Joseph Lamb, piano
Smithsonian Folkways (FW03562)
Label/Archive: Folkways Records, 1960
www.folkways.si.edu

Joseph F. Lamb: The Complete Stark Rags, 1908–1919
Guido Nielsen, piano
Notes by Galen Wilkes
Basta Disc (30-9087-2)
www.amazon.com

A Little Lost Lamb: Music of Joseph F. Lamb
Sue Keller, piano, vocals
with Patricia Lamb Conn as special guest vocalist
Ragtime Press (HVR 0502)
http://www.rtpress.com
www.amazon.com

Larisa Had a Little Lamb
Larisa Migachyov, piano
www.ragtimechick.com
www.cdbaby.com
www.amazon.com

American Beauties: The Rags of Joseph Lamb
Virginia Eskin, piano
Northeastern, Classical Arts (NR 257-CD)
www.amazon.com

Out of Print

Champagne Rags: The Classic Piano Rags of Joseph Lamb
John Arpin, piano
Pro Arte Digital (CDD 497)

The Classic Rags of Joe Lamb, Volume I
Milton Kaye, pianist
Golden Crest Record #GRS4127)

The Classic Rags of Joe Lamb, Volume II
Milton Kaye, pianist
Golden Crest Record #CRS31035

Hot Cinders: Joe Lamb Plays Joe Lamb (1959)
Contains Lamb's renditions of twenty-four of his compositions as recorded by Michael Montgomery as well as five selections performed by Lamb at Club 76 in Toronto (see Chapter Nine). This recording was privately issued and is currently unavailable. However, a copy of the portion recorded by Montgomery is available for in-library listening at the New York Public Library, Lincoln Center, Performing Arts Research Collection and is listed as Joseph Lamb Plays Ragtime (Miscellaneous Recording).

Appendix III

Selected Folios of Joseph F. Lamb Compositions

Although some of Lamb's works are currently unpublished or out-of-print, the possibility always exists that new publications, reprints, or discoveries of additional material may occur at any time, and it is advisable to periodically check appropriate retail and online sources for updates.

Joseph F. Lamb: 12 Piano Rags
(Originally published by John Stark between 1908 and 1919)
Edited by Christopher Frieman
www.fourbeats.com
www.amazon.com

A Little Lost Lamb: Piano Music by Joseph F. Lamb
Edited by Sue Keller
Ragtime Press, Oak Forest, Illinois
Contains eighteen previously unpublished compositions by Lamb.
www.rtpress.com
www.amazon.com

"Ragtime Reverie" and "Brown Derby #2"
(individual sheet music)
The Scott Joplin International Ragtime Foundation (Store)
http://www.scottjoplin.org/index.htm

Ragtime Treasures: Piano Solos by Joseph F. Lamb
Belwin Mills, 1964 (Out of print)

Some collections that contain classic compositions by Joseph F. Lamb include:

Classic Piano Rags: Complete Music for 81 Rags
Selected and with an introduction by Rudi Blesh
Dover Publications

Fifty Classic Piano Rags
Edited by Rudi Blesh
Dover Publications

Appendix IV

Additional Resources

Many of these websites also include a wealth of links to additional valuable resources, performers, recordings, information, and events pertaining to ragtime music in general.

The Library of Congress
Performing Arts Encyclopedia
http://www.loc.gov/performingarts/

Articles, biographies, and many resources on ragtime. A search for Joseph F. Lamb will provide links to a short biography, a comprehensive interview with Patricia Lamb Conn, and many copies of the classic rags (covers and music) that may be accessed.

Sheet Music Consortium
digital2.library.ucla.edu/sheetmusic/browse.html

A grouping of major university and related large collections of sheet music with digital access and much information.

Classic Ragtime Piano Website, by Ted Tjaden
http://www.ragtimepiano.ca/index.htm

A wealth of information on ragtime, composers, Canadian ragtime, etc. There is a detailed and comprehensive section on Joseph F. Lamb, including biographical information, extensive resource lists, downloadable sheet music, midi recordings, and bibliography. Also, there are digitalized editions of Axel Christensen's *Ragtime Review* between the years of 1914–1918.

Ragtime Press
www.rtpress.com

Listings of Sue Keller's recordings and publications, including *A Little Lost Lamb* folio and CD.

Many valuable links to ragtime music sites.

"Perfessor" Bill Edwards
www.ragpiano.com

An education in ragtime and old-time music — extensive biographies, midi recordings (with sheet music covers and detailed descriptions to match), historical background information, many useful links, and CD/music store. There is a section on Joseph F. Lamb and other classic ragtime composers, with photos, composition lists, detailed backgrounds, etc.

Glenn Jenks
http://www.glennjenks.com
Ragtime composer, performer, recording artist, and catalyst for the introduction of the Joseph F. Lamb Rose. (Information on this rose and on the work of the late Dr. Griffith Buck, may be found on the Iowa State University Extension website at http://www.extension.iastate.edu/hancock/info/Buck+Roses.htm, and details on "Buck Roses" may be found at Roses Unlimited at http://www.rosesunlimiteddownroot.com).

Reginald Robinson
www.reginaldrobinson.com
A composer, performer, recording artist, and MacArthur Foundation genius award recipient, who will be releasing a documentary film on the history and development of ragtime, which will include a major segment on Joseph Lamb as well as numerous other leading figures.

The Scott Joplin International Ragtime Foundation
www.scottjoplin.org
Contains much information about Joplin, ragtime, festivals, events, and performers, and offers an online store for the purchase of recordings and folios, as well as valuable links.

World Championship Old-Time Piano Playing Contest
www.oldtimepiano.tripod.com/index.htm
Established supporters of ragtime and old-time music for all ages. Valuable links to websites of performers, organizations, resources, and events.

Dowling Music
www.dowlingmusic.com
A New York and Houston music store, owned by concert and recording artist Richard Dowling, who has performed works by Joseph Lamb and other ragtime composers, among many other styles of music. The store provides excellent online resources for the purchase of music, recordings, and accessories.

The Music Trade Review
www.mbsi.org/mtr
Digitalized issues of this publication (1880–1933; 1940–1954), offering a historical overview of music, music publishing, and related industries (International Arcade Museum Library, Inc.).

Chapter Notes

Introduction

1. Gene Jefferson (words), Robert S. Roberts (music), "I'm Certainly Living a Ragtime Life" (Chicago: Sol Bloom, 1900).

Chapter One

1. Grover Cleveland, "Third Annual Message (December 6, 1887)," Presidential Speech Archive, *University of Virginia, Miller Center,* http://www.millercenter.org/president/speeches/detail/3757.
2. Marjorie Freilich-Den, "Joseph F. Lamb: A Ragtime Composer Recalled" (master's thesis, Brooklyn College, 1975), 7–8.
3. Ibid.
4. "Rose Cleveland, Frances Cleveland," U.S. Presidents, *University of Virginia, Miller Center,* http://www.millercenter.org/president/cleveland/essays/firstlady.
5. "First Lady Biography: Frances Cleveland," *The National First Ladies' Library,* http://www.firstladies.org/biographies/firstladies.aspx?biography=23.
6. *The Montclair Times,* December 3, 1887.
7. George Inness, "Home at Montclair," *George Inness: The Complete Works,* http://www.georgeinness.org.
8. Joseph F. Lamb, letter to Allan Meyer, June 16, 1960.
9. Freilich-Den, "Ragtime Composer Recalled" (quoting interview with Anastasia C. Van Gieson, October 28, 1974), 5, note 9.
10. *The Montclair Times,* December 3, 1887, back page advertisements.
11. "Picturesque Montclair" (Mercantile Illustrating Company, 1894) as quoted in *Those Were the Days, Volume 6, Montclair in the Decade 1890–1899,* compiled by Gladys Segar (Montclair, NJ: The Montclair Library, 1951), 1.
12. S. C. G. Watkins, D.D.S., *Reminiscences of Montclair* (New York: A. S. Barnes, 1929), 93–95.

13. *The Montclair Times,* December 3, 1887, 3.
14. Ibid., 1.
15. Ibid., 2.
16. "Social Doings in Montclair," *The New York Times,* October 6, 1895, www.nytimes.com.
17. "Montclair Social Matters," *The New York Times,* October 5, 1895, www.nytimes.com.
18. *The Montclair Times,* December 7, 1895.
19. Freilich-Den, "Ragtime Composer Recalled" (quoting A. C. Van Gieson, October 28, 1974), 5, note 9.
20. *Montclair 1694–1982: An Inventory of Historic, Cultural and Architectural Resources,* Volume III (Preservation Montclair — A Project of the Jr. League Montclair/Newark, Inc., April 1982). Descriptive details state: "This home was built in 1885 by James Lamb, the father of Joseph Lamb, a well known rag-time composer." It describes the house as being in the vernacular style with Queen Anne elements, possessing a stone foundation, and residing on a 52' × 118' plot of land.
21. Freilich-Den, "Ragtime Composer Recalled" (quoting letter from Paul Hughes), 6.
22. Joseph F. Lamb, letter to Allan Meyer, March 31, 1960.
23. Freilich-Den, "Ragtime Composer Recalled" (quoting phone conversations with and letters from Paul Hughes), 7, notes 13 and 14.
24. Elizabeth Shepard and Royal Shepard, Jr., *Images of America: Montclair* (Portsmouth, NH: Arcadia, 2003), 41.
25. Philip Edward Jaeger, *Images of America: Montclair: A Postcard Guide to Its Past* (Charleston, SC: Arcadia, 1998), 63.
26. Harry Moore (pseudonym for Joseph F. Lamb), "Sweet Nora Doone" (Toronto, Canada: Harry H. Sparks Music Publisher, 1907).
27. Harry Moore, "Three Leaves of Shamrock on the Watermelon Vine" (1908).
28. George Van Gieson, Jr., letter to Joseph R. Scotti, August 20, 1978.

29. G. Van Gieson, Jr., to Scotti, December 22, 1978.

30. G. Van Gieson, Jr., to Scotti, August 20, 1978.

31. State of New Jersey Department of State, New Jersey State Archives Searchable Database. Index to Marriage Records, May 1848-May 1878, https://wwwnet1state.nj.us/DOS/Admin/ArchivesDBPortal/Marriage1867.aspx.

32. Ibid., William S. Stryker's Record of Officers and Men of New Jersey in the Civil War, 1861–1865, p. 127, 332, https://wwwnet1st ate.nj.us/DOS/Admin/ArchivesDBPortal/Stry kerCivilWar.aspx.

33. James Lamb (1846–1900; memorial #14 764451), http://www.findagrave.com/cgi-bin/fg.cgi. (Author also verified this information in person.)

34. United States Federal Census 1900, Montclair Ward 1, Essex, New Jersey; Roll: T623-970; Page 9B; Enumeration District 205 (James Lamb), http://www.ancestry.com/.

35. The Montclair Times, October 6, 1900.

36. G. Van Gieson, Jr., to Scotti, August 20, 1978.

37. Freilich-Den, "Ragtime Composer Recalled," 7.

38. Shepard, Images/Montclair, 43.

39. Freilich-Den, "Ragtime Composer Recalled," 7.

40. Shepard, Images/Montclair, 45.

41. Freilich-Den, "Ragtime Composer Recalled" (quoting A. C. Van Gieson, October 28, 1974), 7, note 15.

42. The Montclair Times, November 23, 1929.

43. Ibid.

44. Freilich-Den, "Ragtime Composer Recalled" (quoting A. C. Van Gieson, October 28, 1974), 7, note 15.

45. Jaeger, Postcard Guide, 79.

46. Lamb to Meyer, April 13, 1960.

47. Freilich-Den, "Ragtime Composer Recalled" (quoting A. C. Van Gieson, October 28, 1974), 8, note 18.

48. Gerald Carson, "The Piano in the Parlor," American Heritage, December 1965, 55.

49. Richard K. Lieberman, Steinway and Sons (New Haven: Yale University Press, 1995), 104.

50. "First Lady Biography, Frances Cleveland."

51. The Montclair Times, December 7, 1895.

52. Carson, "Piano in Parlor," 55.

53. Ruth Hume, "The Great Chicago Piano War," American Heritage.com, October 1970, http://www.americanheritage.com/content/great-chicago-piano-war.

54. Joseph F. Lamb, letter to Robert Darch, undated.

55. Paul Van Gieson, letter to Joseph R. Scotti, January 27, 1976.

56. Ibid.

57. Ibid.

58. The Montclair Times, December 21, 1907, 1.

59. P. Van Gieson to Scotti, January 27, 1976.

60. Paul Van Gieson, letter to Marjorie Freilich-Den, January 6, 1975.

61. P. Van Gieson to Scotti, January 27, 1976.

62. A Little Lost Lamb: Piano Music by Joseph F. Lamb, edited by Sue Keller (Oak Forest, IL: Ragtime Press, 2005), 34.

63. P. Van Gieson to Scotti, January 27, 1976.

64. Ibid., December 8, 1975.

65. Lamb to Darch, undated.

66. Russ Cassidy, "Joseph Lamb—Last of the Ragtime Composers" (four-part series), Jazz Monthly, August 1961, 4.

67. Ibid.

68. Ibid.

69. Ibid.

70. "The Ages and Historical Records of Pianos Sold in America," Part VI: Sohmer & Co., Bluebook of Pianos, http://www.bluebookofpi anos.com/kron6.htm.

71. Lamb to Darch, undated.

72. Henry T. Finck, My Adventures in the Golden Age of Music (New York: Funk and Wagnalls, 1926), 416.

73. Lamb to Darch, undated.

74. P. Van Gieson to Scotti, January 27, 1976.

75. Lamb to Darch, May 5, 1959.

76. Ibid., May 6, 1959.

77. G. Van Gieson, Jr., to Scotti, December 6, 1975.

78. E. Douglas Bomberger, An Index to Music Published in The Etude Magazine, 1883–1957 (Scarecrow, with Music Library Association, 2004).

79. Charles K. Harris, After the Ball: Forty Years of Melody (New York: Frank-Maurice, 1926), 360.

80. "Picturesque Montclair," 43.

81. Ibid.

82. W. Waugh Lauder, "Music at the World's Fair: Fifth Columbian Letter," The Musical Courier, June 7, 1893, 15.

83. Ibid., 16.

84. Edward A. Berlin, King of Ragtime: Scott Joplin and His Era (New York: Oxford University Press, 1994), 12.

85. Charles Hamm, Yesterdays: Popular Song in America (New York: W. W. Norton, 1983), 318.

86. G. Van Gieson, Jr., to Scotti, October 31, 1975.

87. Cassidy, "Last of Ragtime Composers," August 1961, 4.

Chapter Two

1. *The Montclair Times*, January 6, 1900, 5.
2. Rudi Blesh and Harriet Janis, *They All Played Ragtime* (New York: Oak, 4th ed., 1971), 98.
3. Adam Geibel, "South Car'lina Tickle: Cake Walk," *The Etude*, December 1898, 23–25.
4. *Baldwin's Directory of Montclair, Bloomfield, Verona and Caldwell: May, 1903* (Orange, NJ: J. H. Baldwin, 1902).
5. Charles K. Harris, *After the Ball: Forty Years of Melody* (New York: Frank Maurice, 1926), 209.
6. *The Music Trade Review*, January 6, 1900, 1, www.mbsi.org.
7. *The Music Trade Review*, January 5, 1901, 41.
8. John F. Kasson, *Amusing the Million: Coney Island at the Turn of the Century* (New York: Hill and Wang, 1978), 34.
9. Joseph F. Lamb, "Meet Me at the Chutes" (unpublished manuscript, 1900).
10. Blesh and Janis, *They All Played Ragtime*, 240.
11. Cassidy, "Last of Ragtime Composers," October 1961, 13.
12. "Montclair: The Queen Suburb of the Metropolis" (*Industrial Recorder*, 1903): 17.
13. Ibid.
14. John Graziano, "Music in William Randolph Hearst's *New York Journal*," *Notes*, Second Series 48/2 (December 1991): 387–9.
15. Ibid., 399–403.
16. Ibid., 394.
17. Harris, *After the Ball*, 230.
18. Bonny H. Miller, "A Mirror of Ages Past: The Publication of Music in Domestic Periodicals," *Notes*, Second Series 50/3 (March 1994): 884.
19. The University of Minnesota, Media History Project, http://www.mediahistory.umn.edu/timeline/1900-1909.html.
20. Freilich-Den, "Ragtime Composer Recalled," 6.
21. *The Montclair Times*, October 6, 1900, 1.
22. Joseph R. Scotti, "Joe Lamb: A Study of Ragtime's Paradox" (doctor of philosophy dissertation, University of Cincinnati, 1977), 16.
23. Lamb to Darch, May 6, 1959.
24. *The Canadian Year Book for 1904*, Volume 7 (Toronto, Canada: Alfred Hewett, 1904), 322.
25. Ibid.
26. Eugene McCarthy, "U.S. Ragtime Great Started Composing in Kitchener," *Kitchener-Waterloo Record*, October 21, 1974, Section 2, 17.
27. Lamb to Meyer, April 13, 1960.
28. *The Canadian Encyclopedia*, Year 2000 Edition (Toronto, Ontario, Canada: McClelland and Steward, 1999), 1251.
29. Ibid.
30. "Busy Berlin," *Kitchener Trivia*, Kitchener, Ontario Public Library Local History Information, http://www.kpl.org/ref/gsr/trivia.html.
31. *The Canadian Encyclopedia*, p. 1251.
32. Joseph F. Lamb, letter to Michael Montgomery, November 3, 1958.
33. McCarthy, "U.S. Ragtime Great," Section 2, 17.
34. Freilich-Den, "Ragtime Composer Recalled," 9.
35. McCarthy, "U.S. Ragtime Great," Section 2, 17.
36. George A. Borgman, "Joseph F. Lamb, Classic Ragtimer, Part I," *The Mississippi Rag*, August 2001.
37. Lamb to Darch, May 6, 1959.
38. G. Van Gieson, Jr., to Scotti, October 31, 1975.
39. *A Little Lost Lamb*, ed. Keller, 34.
40. Graziano, "Music in *New York Journal*," 407.
41. Lamb to Meyer, April 13, 1960.
42. *The Toronto City Directory* (Toronto, Canada: Might Directories, 1904).
43. Helmut Kallmann, "H. H. Sparks Music Co.," *The Canadian Encyclopedia/The Encyclopedia of Music in Canada*, http://www.thecanadianencyclopedia.com.
44. Scotti, "Ragtime's Paradox," 19.
45. Freilich-Den, "Ragtime Composer Recalled" (quoting A. C. Van Gieson, October 28, 1974), 10, note 26.
46. Scotti, "Ragtime's Paradox," 34.
47. Ted Tjaden, "Joseph F. Lamb: The Humble Ragtime 'Sensation,'" *Classic Ragtime Piano*, http://www.ragtimepiano.ca/.
48. *On Dress Parade: The United States Air Force Band*, Washington D.C., Colonel Lowell E. Graham, Commander/Conductor (January 2000), liner notes.
49. David A. Jasen, *Tin Pan Alley: The Composers, the Songs, the Performers and their Times* (New York: Donald I. Fine, 1988), 51–52.
50. "Musquakie," *Dictionary of Canadian Biography Online*, Vol. IX, www.biographi.ca/009004-130-e.html.
51. "History," *Visit Muskoka*, www.visitmuskoka.com/history.htm.
52. Ibid.
53. *Muskoka Falls Tourism 75th Anniversary*, www.discovermuskoka.ca/about.php?s=about_243&r_ro-0.

54. Blesh and Janis, *They All Played Ragtime*, 92.
55. "Hotel History," Walper Hotel, http://www.walper.com.
56. Isidore Witmark and Isaac Goldberg, *From Ragtime to Swingtime: The Story of the House of Witmark* (New York: Lee Furman, 1939), 176.
57. Joseph F. Lamb, "Walper House Rag" (1903). This work was published and recorded in the 2005 folio collection/companion CD, *A Little Lost Lamb*. Further discussion of these collections appears in Chapter Ten.
58. Joseph F. Lamb, letter to Trebor Tichenor, April 11, 1958.
59. Blesh and Janis, *They All Played Ragtime*, 238.
60. Tjaden, "Ragtime Music in Canada: Charles Wellinger," *Classic Ragtime Piano*.
61. Alfred, Lord Tennyson, *The Princess* (New York: Maynard, Merrill & Co., 1897) from Maynard's English-Classic Series.
62. Lamb to Meyer, April 13, 1960.
63. Joseph F. Lamb, letter to George (Sr.) and Anastasia Van Gieson, October 19, 1959.
64. Lamb to Meyer, April 13, 1960.
65. Ibid.
66. Park Lawn Cemetery, Toronto, Canada, correspondence with administrator, July 7, 2011.
67. Lamb to Montgomery, October 21, 1959.

Chapter Three

1. "The 1904 St. Louis World's Fair, Day-by-Day Calendar of Events, April 30, 1904," World's Fair Links, *The 1904 World's Fair Society*, www.1904worldsfairsociety.org/.
2. "The World's Fair at St. Louis, 1904," *The Evening Bulletin* (Maysville, KY), April 30, 1904, 1, http://www.chroniclingamerica.loc.gov/.
3. "August 5, 1904, Friday," *1904 World's Fair Society*.
4. "Daily Official Program-World's Fair St. Louis," Thursday, June 16, 1904," *1904 World's Fair Society*.
5. *Baldwin's Directory*, 1903.
6. George A. Van Gieson, Sr., "Recollections of Early Montclair," *The Montclair Times*, December 1, 1955, 21.
7. Ibid.
8. Berlin, *King of Ragtime*, 136, note 14.
9. Cassidy, "Last of Ragtime Composers," August 1961, 5.
10. Ibid.
11. Whitney Balliett, "The Ragtime Game," *The New Yorker*, July 2, 1960, 21.
12. *The Evening World*, February 2, 1904, 7.
13. Ibid.
14. Karen Plunkett-Powell, *Remembering Woolworth's: A Nostalgic History of the World's Most Famous Five-and-Dime* (New York: St. Martin's, 1999), 194.
15. Cassidy, "Last of Ragtime Composers," August 1961, 7.
16. Ibid., 5.
17. Ibid.
18. Joseph F. Lamb, "The Ivy-Covered Homestead on the Hill" (unpublished manuscript, 1904).
19. Lamb to Meyer, April 29, 1960.
20. Katherine Schouten, letter to George Van Gieson, Jr., October 12, 1972.
21. Lamb to Meyer, April 29, 1960.
22. Schouten to G. Van Gieson, Jr., October 12, 1972.
23. P. Van Gieson to Scotti, December 8, 1975.
24. Schouten to G. Van Gieson, Jr., October 12, 1972.
25. Calendar, *1904 World's Fair Society*.
26. Lamb to Meyer, July 4, 1960.
27. Lamb to Meyer, March 31, 1960 and April 29, 1960.
28. Lamb to Meyer, July 4, 1960.
29. Harry Moore, "The Engineer's Last Goodbye," (Toronto, Canada: Harry H. Sparks, 1908).
30. Lamb to Meyer, April 29, 1960.
31. Lamb to Darch, January 8, 1959.
32. Peter Booth Wiley, *National Trust Guide San Francisco: America's Guide for Architecture and History Travelers* (New York: John Wiley and Sons, 2000), 50–54.
33. Ibid., 54.
34. Schouten to Van Gieson, Jr., October 12, 1972.
35. Lamb to Meyer, March 31, 1960.
36. Ibid.
37. Ibid.
38. "Our History," *Sherman Clay*, http://www.shermanclay.com/sherman-clay-history.shtml.
39. *The Music Trade Review*, September 30, 1905, 24.
40. David A. Jasen and Gene Jones, *That American Rag: The Story of Ragtime from Coast to Coast* (New York: Schirmer, 2000), 201.
41. "A Pioneer Music Store," *The Virtual Museum of the City of San Francisco*, http://www.sfmuseum.org/hist/kandc.html.
42. Nan Bostick, e-mail message to author, June 15, 2011.
43. Ibid.
44. *The Music Trade Review*, September 30, 1905, 45.
45. Ibid., 31.
46. Lamb to Meyer, March 31, 1960.
47. Freilich-Den, "Ragtime Composer Recalled" (quoting A. C. Van Gieson, October 28, 1974), 11, note 31.

48. Scotti, "Ragtime's Paradox," 34–36.
49. Lamb to Meyer, March 31, 1960.
50. Ibid.
51. "Cliff House & Sutro Baths," Golden Gate National Recreation Area, National Park Service, U.S. Department of the Interior, www.nps.gov/goga/clho.htm.
52. Lamb to Meyer, March 31, 1960.
53. Lamb to Meyer, May 12, 1960.
54. Lamb to Meyer, March 31, 1960.
55. Cassidy, "Last of Ragtime Composers," August 1961, 5.
56. Schouten to G. Van Gieson, Jr., October 12, 1972.
57. Lamb to Meyer, March 11, 1960.
58. Ibid.
59. Lamb to Meyer, March 31, 1960.
60. Ibid.
61. Lamb to Meyer, June 16, 1960.
62. Lamb to Darch, March 16, 1959.
63. "Enrico Caruso and the 1906 Earthquake," *The Virtual Museum of the City of San Francisco,* http://www.sfmuseum.org/1906/ew19.html.
64. Schouten to Van Gieson, October 12, 1972.
65. Lamb to Meyer, March 31, 1960.

Chapter Four

1. Blesh and Janis, *They All Played Ragtime,* 45–49.
2. William W. Scott, *History of Passaic and its Environs* (New York: Lewis Historical, 1922), 85–87.
3. "Syndicate Trading Company," *The Lucile Project,* http://sdrc.lib.uiowa.edu/lucile/publishers/syndicate/syndicate.htm.
4. *The Publishers' Weekly,* August 2, 1919, 37.
5. Witmark and Goldberg, *From Ragtime to Swingtime,* 287–293.
6. Ibid.
7. Borgman, "Classic Ragtimer, Part I," August 2001.
8. "Menu [held by] Flatiron Restaurant & Café [at] 'New York, NY' (REST;) (1906)," New York Public Library Digital Gallery Image ID 473853 and 40000194365/6, http://digitalgallery.nypl.org/nypldigital/.
9. *The New York Clipper,* April 21, 1906, 258.
10. Harry Moore, "Nora Doone" (Toronto, Canada: Harry H. Sparks, 1907).
11. Balliett, "The Ragtime Game," 21.
12. Lamb to Meyer, April 13, 1960.
13. J. Jousse, *A Catechism of Music,* "Conservatory Edition," revised and edited by Louis C. Elson and H. L. Heartz (Boston and New York: White-Smith Music, 1907). Previous editions of this work contained varying material.
14. *The Intermezzo: A Musical Monthly*, January 1906, inside back cover.
15. Lamb to Meyer, May 28, 1960.
16. David A. Jasen and Trebor Jay Tichenor, *Rags and Ragtime: A Musical History* (New York: Dover, 1978), 111.
17. *The Montclair Times,* October 26, 1907.
18. *The Montclair Times,* November 2, 1907.
19. *The Montclair Times,* August 24, 1907.
20. *The Montclair Times,* September 7, 1907.
21. *The Montclair Times,* December 7, 1907.
22. P. Van Gieson to Scotti, undated.
23. G. Van Gieson, Sr., "Recollections," September 8, 1955, 16.
24. Lamb to G. Van Gieson, Sr., February 6, 1960.
25. Freilich-Den, "Ragtime Composer Recalled," 14.
26. G. Van Gieson, Sr., "Recollections," December 1, 1955, 21.
27. G. Van Gieson, Jr., to Scotti, January 6, 1975.
28. *Directory of Montclair, Bloomfield, Caldwell, Essex Fells, Glen Ridge and Verona 1908* (Newark, NJ: Price and Lee, 1908).
29. *The Music Trade Review,* August 13, 1910, 5.
30. G. Van Gieson, Jr., to Scotti, January 6, 1975.
31. George Van Gieson, Sr., unpublished autobiography, May 1947, 7.
32. Freilich-Den, "Ragtime Composer Recalled," G. Van Gieson, Sr., letter to Joseph F. Lamb (undated), Appendix.
33. Ibid.
34. Lamb to G. Van Gieson, Sr., February 6, 1960.
35. United States Federal Census 1900, Brooklyn Ward 26, Kings, New York; Roll T623-1064; Page 21B; Enumeration District: 470 (Theodore H. Gatlin).
36. G. Van Gieson, Jr., to Scotti, October 31, 1975.
37. Census 1900 (Theodore H. Gatlin).
38. Lamb to G. Van Gieson, Sr., February 6, 1960.
39. Berlin, *King of Ragtime,* 52–56.
40. Tjaden, "*Christensen's Ragtime Review,* August 1915," *Classic Ragtime Piano,* 2.
41. Edward B. Marks as told to Abbott J. Liebling, *They All Sang: From Tony Pastor to Rudy Vallee* (New York: Viking, 1934), 159.
42. Many sources cite 1907 as the date of the meeting, although Joseph Lamb himself mentioned both 1907 as well as 1908 in letters and interviews during later years. A viable case may be made for either date.
43. Balliett, "Ragtime Game," 21.
44. Blesh and Janis, *They All Played Ragtime,* 236.

45. Joyce Mendelsohn, "Madison Square," *The Encyclopedia of New York City*, edited by Kenneth T. Jackson (New Haven: Yale University Press, and New York: New-York Historical Society, 1995), 711–12.
46. Christopher Gray, "Tracing Scott Joplin's Life Through His Addresses," Streetscapes Column, *The New York Times* (February 4, 2007).
47. G. Van Gieson, Jr., to Scotti, October 31, 1975.
48. Lamb to Montgomery, January 25, 1958.
49. Lamb to Darch, March 16, 1959.
50. Ibid., January 8, 1959.
51. Blesh and Janis, *They All Played Ragtime*, 236–237.
52. Scotti, "Ragtime's Paradox," 43.
53. Tjaden, "*Christensen's Ragtime Review*," *Classic Ragtime Piano*.

Chapter Five

1. *The New York Times*, January 1, 1908, 1.
2. "Panic of 1907," Federal Reserve Bank of Boston, http://www.bos.frb.org/about/pubs/panicof1.pdf.
3. *The Music Trade Review*, January 4, 1908, 4.
4. Ibid., 45.
5. Ibid., 36.
6. Ibid., 12.
7. Ibid., 43.
8. Trebor Jay Tichenor, "The World of Joseph Lamb—An Exploration," (four-part series), *Jazz Monthly*, August 1961, 8.
9. Balliett, "Ragtime Game," 21.
10. Cassidy, "Last of Ragtime Composers," August, 1961, 6.
11. Joseph F. Lamb, letter to Arthur Marshall, April 13, 1960.
12. Bruce Anderson, "The National Pastime's Anthem," *Sports Illustrated*, April 15, 1991, 20.
13. Jasen, *Tin Pan Alley*, 289–292.
14. Ibid.
15. *The Evening World*, May 28, 1908, p. 13.
16. *The New York Clipper*, February 22, 1908, p. 36D.
17. Information on all of the "Sparks songs" appears in Appendix I.
18. Blesh and Janis, *They All Played Ragtime*, 238.
19. See Epilogue.
20. Scotti, "Ragtime's Paradox," 56.
21. Blesh and Janis, *They All Played Ragtime*, 92.
22. Ibid., 93.
23. Harry Moore, "She Does'nt Flirt" (Toronto, Canada: Harry H. Sparks, 1908).
24. G. Van Gieson, Sr., autobiography, 8.
25. Ibid.

26. Freilich-Den, "Ragtime Composer Recalled," 13. ("Bunton" is used in Ms. Freilich-Den's thesis as well as in Dr. Scotti's dissertation in referring to Adaline B. McMillan. However the dedication to the published work, "Gee, Kid! But I Like You," as well as family listings in Montclair directories and other sources are recorded as "Bunten," which I have used in this text.) Ms. Freilich-Den was responsible for discovering Mrs. McMillan and for eliciting a wealth of valuable, first-hand research material, as presented in her thesis. References to and quotations from this information are included in this chapter with her permission and with my sincere thanks.
27. Ibid.
28. Ibid. (quoting correspondence from "Adaline B. McMillan," in 1975).
29. Lamb to Meyer, March 30, 1960.
30. Lamb to Darch, undated.
31. David A. Jasen, *Ragtime: An Encyclopedia, Discography, and Sheetography* (New York: Routledge, 2007), xix.
32. Scotti, "Ragtime's Paradox," 67–71.
33. Tichenor, "World of Joseph Lamb," August 1961, 8.
34. Borgman, "Classic Ragtimer, Part I," August 2001.
35. Cassidy, "Last of Ragtime Composers," August 1961, 6.
36. *Encyclopedia of Recorded Sound*, Volume I, edited by Frank Hoffmann (New York: Routledge, 2005), 37.
37. Gilbert Chase, *America's Music: From the Pilgrims to the Present* (New York: McGraw-Hill, 1955), 292–293.
38. Cassidy, "Last of Ragtime Composers," August 1961, 6.
39. Ibid.
40. Scotti, "Ragtime's Paradox," 59.
41. Ibid.
42. Ibid., 60.
43. Freilich-Den, "Ragtime Composer Recalled" (quoting letter from McMillan, February 22, 1975), 13, note 36.
44. "The Fortune Teller," *The New York Times*, September 15, 1898.
45. Ibid., "Some Good Fun," September 21, 1906.
46. Jasen, *Tin Pan Alley*, 31–32.
47. Joseph F. Lamb, "Dear Old Rose" (unpublished manuscript, 1909).
48. Bordman, Gerald, *American Musical Theatre: A Chronicle*, 3d ed. (New York: Oxford University Press, 2001).
49. Freilich-Den, "Ragtime Composer Recalled," (quoting conversation with McMillan, March 16, 1975), 13, note 39.
50. Tichenor, "World of Joseph Lamb," August 1961, 9.

ning the.

51. Freilich-Den, "Ragtime Composer Recalled," 14.
52. "Syndicate Trading," *The Lucile Project*.
53. Lamb to Darch, March 16, 1959.
54. Lamb to Darch, May 6, 1959 (completed questionnaire).
55. Blesh and Janis, *They All Played Ragtime*, 242.
56. Lamb to Meyer, April 13, 1960.
57. Ibid.
58. Freilich-Den, "Ragtime Composer Recalled," 15.
59. Cassidy, "Last of Ragtime Composers," August 1961, 6.
60. Blesh & Janis, *They All Played Ragtime*, 242.
61. See Epilogue.
62. Freilich-Den, "Ragtime Composer Recalled" (quoting letter from McMillan, February 22, 1975), 14–15, note 42.
63. Lamb to Meyer, March 31, 1960.
64. Blesh and Janis, *They All Played Ragtime*, 46–47.
65. Cassidy, "Last of Ragtime Composers," August 1961, 7.
66. Kallmann, "H. H. Sparks Music Co.," *Canadian Music Encyclopedia*.
67. Josef F. Lamb, "I Love You Just the Same," (Toronto, Canada: Harry H. Sparks, 1910).
68. Scotti, "Ragtime's Paradox," 72.
69. Elliott L. Adams, "The Joseph F. Lamb Story, Part I," *Sacramento Ragtime Society Newsletter*, October 1989, 6.
70. Josef. Lamb, "My Fairy Iceberg Queen" (Toronto, Canada: Harry H. Sparks, 1910).
71. *The Brooklyn Daily Eagle*, November 9, 1910, 13.
72. *The Music Trade Review*, August 31, 1907, 40.
73. Witmark and Goldberg, *From Ragtime to Swingtime*, 231.
74. Ibid.
75. *The Music Trade Review*, October 3, 1908, 43.
76. *The Music Trade Reviews*, December 12, 1908, 47.
77. Lamb to Meyer, April 13, 1960.
78. *The Music Trade Review*, July 2, 1910, 1.
79. Lamb to Meyer, April 13, 1960.
80. Ibid.
81. Lamb to Darch, March 16, 1959.
82. Ibid.
83. Amelia Lamb, letter to Joseph R. Scotti, March 10, 1975.
84. Plunkett-Powell, *Remembering Woolworth's*, 194.
85. Lamb to Meyer, April 13, 1960.
86. Ibid.
87. A. Lamb to Scotti, March 10, 1975.
88. Adams, "Lamb Story, Part V," February

1990, 3. Adams provides stylistic examples of arrangements possibly completed by Lamb for Helf.
90. Jasen, *Tin Pan Alley*, 82.
90. G. Van Gieson, Jr., to Scotti, October 31, 1975.
91. Lamb to Meyer, April 13, 1960.
92. Borgman, "Classic Ragtimer, Part I," August 2001.
93. Freilich-Den, "Ragtime Composer Recalled," 15.

Chapter Six

1. Cassidy, "Last of Ragtime Composers," October 1961, 13–14.
2. There are some discrepancies as to whether Lamb returned to Syndicate Trading at this time or was employed by another, unidentified firm after his employment with Helf.
3. G. Van Gieson, Jr., to Scotti, October 31, 1975.
4. P. Van Gieson to Scotti, December 8, 1975.
5. Freilich-Den and some family members state that Henrietta was called "Ettie." Her name is also handwritten on a number of the "Sparks" sheet music covers as "Etta" Schultz, photocopies of which are in the Library of Congress Music Division archives as well as in family collections. George Van Gieson, Jr., also refers to her as "Etta" in his letter to Joseph R. Scotti of December 17, 1978.
6. United States Federal Census 1910, Brooklyn Ward 29, Kings, New York; Roll T624-982; Page 26A; Enumeration District: 0920; Image 645; FHL Number: 1374995 (Henrietta Schultz).
7. Margaret Latimer, "Brooklyn," *Encyclopedia of New York City*, 152.
8. Prospect Park Alliance, www.prospect park.org/about/history.
9. "Spanish Fly: Intermezzo" (1912) was published in *A Little Lost Lamb* in 2005.
10. Adams, "Lamb Story, Part VII," April 1990, 4.
11. Plunkett-Powell, *Remembering Woolworth's*, 194.
12. "Waltzed Facing Death: Titanic Survivor in Hospital Says Music Prevented Panic," *The New-York Tribune*, April 22, 1912, 2.
13. Eve Golden, *Vernon and Irene Castle's Ragtime Revolution* (Lexington: University Press of Kentucky, 2007), 70.
14. Ibid., 87.
15. Jasen and Tichenor, *Rags and Ragtime*, 144.
16. *Utica* (NY) *Herald-Dispatch*, December 7, 1912, 1C.
17. Golden, 84.

18. Ibid., 85.
19. Ibid., 81.
20. Eileen Bowser, *History of the American Cinema, Volume 2, The Transformation of Cinema* (New York: Charles Scribner's Sons, 1990), 13.
21. *The Music Trade Review*, June 6, 1914, 97.
22. G. Van Gieson, Jr., to Scotti, October 31, 1975.
23. "Ellen Wilson," *National First Ladies' Library*.
24. "Millions of Roses and Pinks; Increasing Demand for Cut Flowers in This City," *The New York Times*, January 27, 1896.
25. "Three American Beauties," in *Edison: The Invention of the Movies* (Museum of Modern Art in cooperation with the Library of Congress; New York: Kino Video, 2005).
26. "Ragtime Kalamazoo," Kalamazoo, Michigan Public Library, www.kpl.gov/local/arts-entertainment/ragtime-kalamazoo.aspx.
27. "Henry Reichard," Sheet Music Cover Art History, *Perfessor Bill Edwards*, www.ragpiano.com.
28. Lamb to Darch, undated.
29. Lamb to Meyer, May 28, 1960.
30. Tichenor, "World of Joseph Lamb," August 1961, 9.
31. Cassidy, "Last of Ragtime Composers," August 1961, 7.
32. Photocopy of material from Stark Music Company publication, Library of Congress, Music Division, Joseph F. Lamb Collection.
33. Ibid.
34. "Entertainments: His Majesty's Theatre," *Evening Post* (New Zealand), January 4, 1915, www.paperspast.natlib.govt.nz/.
35. "Rocco Venuto," *In Harmony*, Sheet Music from Indiana, www.dlib.indiana.edu/projects/inharmony.
36. Joseph F. Lamb, letter to Thornton (Tony) Hagert, October 21, 1959.
37. *The Brooklyn City Directory 1912*, Volume 3 (Brooklyn, New York: Brooklyn Directory, 1912).
38. United States Federal Census 1920, Brooklyn Assembly, District 12, Kings New York; Roll T625-1162; Page 12B; Enumeration District: 679; Image 471 (George J. Satterlee).
39. Platzmann was an arranger for a series of dance folios, including Shapiro, Bernstein & Company's annual *Gem Dance Folios,* as well as for other individual works, from approximately 1911 through at least 1918.
40. *The New York Clipper*, September 28, 1912, 19.
41. Joseph Lamb (music), G. Satterlee (words), "I'll Follow the Crowd to Coney" (Brooklyn, New York: G. Satterlee, 1913).
42. *The Toronto City Directory 1904*, 1036.
43. Kallmann, "Musgrave," *The Canadian Encyclopedia/The Encyclopedia of Music.*
44. Tjaden, "Humble Ragtime 'Sensation,'" *Classic Ragtime Piano.*
45. Lamb to Darch, March 16, 1959.
46. Gray, "Tracing Joplin's Life."
47. Lamb to Montgomery, January 25, 1958.
48. Ibid.
49. G. Van Gieson, Jr., to Scotti.
50. Cassidy, "Last of Ragtime Composers," October 1961, 14.
51. Ibid.
52. Tichenor, "World of Joseph Lamb," October 1961, 16.
53. Adams, "Lamb Story, Part VI," March 1990, 7.
54. "Joseph Francis Lamb — Cleopatra Rag," *Perfessor Bill Edwards.*
55. *The Classic Rags of Joe Lamb*, Volume I, Golden Crest Records #GRS4127, liner notes, Rudi Blesh.
56. Lamb to Darch, undated.
57. Ibid.
58. *The Music Trade Review*, June 26, 1915, 16.
59. Ibid., September 25, 1915.
60. Lamb to Darch, undated.
61. Adams, "Lamb Story, Part VIII," June 1990, 4.
62. Lamb to Darch, undated.
63. Lamb to Montgomery, January 25, 1958.
64. Tjaden, "*Christensen's Ragtime Review,*" *Classic Ragtime Piano.*
65. Photocopy of letter from a Stark Music Company publication, dated May 16, 1916, Library of Congress, Music Division, Lamb Collection.
66. Joseph F. Lamb, "The Cause of Liberty" (unpublished manuscript, 1916).
67. Freilich-Den, "Ragtime Composer Recalled," 17.
68. "WWI Draft Card Essays, Joseph Francis Lamb," *Ragtime, Blues, Hot Piano*, www.doctorjazz.co.uk/draftcard3.htmml.
69. United States Federal Census 1920; Brooklyn Assembly District 12, Kings, New York; Roll: T625-1163; Page: 8A; Enumeration District: 704; Image: 75 (Joseph F. Lamb).
70. Freilich-Den, "Ragtime Composer Recalled" (quoting interview with Amelia Lamb, October 13, 1974), 17, note 50.
71. Ibid.
72. Ibid.
73. Ibid.
74. *Classic Rags of Joe Lamb*, Volume I, liner notes.
75. Tichenor, "World of Joseph Lamb," October 1961, 16.
76. P. Van Gieson to Freilich-Den, June 6, 1975.

77. Scotti, "Ragtime's Paradox," 108.

78. "The Deadly Virus: The Influenza Epidemic of 1918," National Archives & Records Administration, www.archives.gov/exhibits/influenza-epidemic/.

79. Freilich-Den, "Ragtime Composer Recalled," 18, note 51.

Chapter Seven

1. Freilich-Den, "Ragtime Composer Recalled," 18.

2. United States Federal Census 1920, Brooklyn Assembly District 12, Kings, New York; Roll T625-1163; Page 8A; Enumeration District: 704; Image 75 (Joseph F. Lamb).

3. G. Van Gieson, Jr., to Scotti, December 17, 1978.

4. Scotti, "Ragtime's Paradox" (quoting interview with Amelia Lamb and Joseph Lamb, Jr., on December 28, 1975), 108–109.

5. Copies of these and other sheet music covers in the Library of Congress, Music Division, Joseph F. Lamb Collection, as well as in personal collection of Patricia Lamb Conn.

6. Joseph F. Lamb, "Wal-Yo" (unpublished manuscript, 1914).

7. Freilich-Den, "Ragtime Composer Recalled," 17.

8. United States Federal Census 1920, Brooklyn Assembly District 12, Kings, New York: Roll T625-1163; Page 8A; Enumeration District: 704; Image 75 (Herman D. Schultz).

9. Ibid. (William M. K. Schultz).

10. Ibid. (Herman Schultz).

11. United States Federal Census 1900, Brooklyn Ward 8, Kings, New York; Roll T623-1047; Page 17B; Enumeration District: 95 (Herman D. Schultz).

12. United States Federal Census 1910, Brooklyn Ward 29, Kings, New York; Roll T624-982; Page 26A; Enumeration District: 0920; Image: 645; FHL Number: 1374995 (Herman Schultz).

13. Ibid. (Elizabeth Schultz).

14. Lamb to Meyer, April 13, 1960.

15. Ibid.

16. G. Van Gieson, Jr., to Scotti, October 31, 1975.

17. Conversations with Patricia Lamb Conn.

18. G. Van Gieson, Jr., to Scotti, January 6, 1975.

19. United States Federal Census, 1920 (Joseph F. Lamb).

20. G. Van Gieson, Jr., to Scotti, October 31, 1975.

21. Mark Tucker, "Confrey, Zez," *The New Grove's Dictionary of Music and Musicians,* 2d ed., edited by Stanley Sadie, Volume 6, 283.

22. Ibid.

23. G. Van Gieson, Jr., to Scotti, October 31, 1975.

24. Scotti, "Ragtime's Paradox" (quoting phone interview with George Van Gieson, Jr., April 3, 1977), 109.

25. G. Van Gieson, Jr., to Scotti, October 31, 1975.

26. Scotti, "Ragtime's Paradox" (quoting phone interview with Paul Van Gieson, April 2, 1977), 109–110.

27. G. Van Gieson, Jr., to Scotti, October 31, 1975.

28. P. Van Gieson to Scotti, December 8, 1975.

29. Freilich-Den, "Ragtime Composer Recalled" (quoting interview with Joseph Lamb, Jr., December 28, 1974), 19, note 55.

30. Ibid.

31. Ibid., (quoting letter of Paul Van Gieson, February 12, 1975), 18, note 54.

32. G. Van Gieson to Scotti, January 6, 1976.

33. Anne Shaw Faulkner, "Does Jazz Put the Sin in Syncopation?" *Ladies' Home Journal,* August, 1921.

34. Freilich-Den, "Ragtime Composer Recalled," (quoting interview with George Van Gieson, Jr., October 28,1974), 18, note 53. (In a letter to Joseph R. Scotti on October 31, 1975, however, Van Gieson says that it was a clarinet and a flute and that Lamb did play them.)

35. Ibid.

36. P. Van Gieson to Scotti, December 8, 1975.

37. 1923 Kissel Speedster, http://www.forneymuseum.org/FE_AmeliaEarhartGoldBug.html and Anita King: The Paramount Girl Who Conquered a Continent, www.welcometosilentmovies.com/anitaking.

38. G. Van Gieson to Scotti, December 6, 1975.

39. Freilich-Den, "Ragtime Composer Recalled," 19.

Chapter Eight

1. United States Federal Census 1910, Brooklyn Ward 29, Kings, New York; Roll T624-983; Page 2A; Enumeration District: 1016; Image: 582; FHL Number 1374996 (Augustus F. W. Collins).

2. United States Federal Census 1930, Brooklyn, Kings, New York; Roll 1496; Page 12A; Enumeration District 1281; Image 582.0.

3. Louis Werba had a number of theaters in Brooklyn and surrounding areas. See "The Final Curtain: Louis F. Werba," *The Billboard* (November 28, 1942): 27. Family members recall Werba's and the fact that Augustus Collins had been employed locally, although there are

no further details. However, both Patricia Lamb Conn and Robert Lamb definitely remember their father saying that he played piano for silent films at one time, both of them assuming that this took place sometime prior to the 1920s. Augustus Collins would have been a viable connection for this during the latter part of this time period. J. Fred Helf, who had wanted Lamb to play in theaters, would have been a much earlier connection, as well.

4. Freilich-Den, "Ragtime Composer Recalled" (quoting interview with Joseph Lamb, Jr., December 28, 1974), 21–22, note 63.

5. Ibid. (quoting interview with Amelia Lamb, October 13, 1974), 19, note 56.

6. G. Van Gieson, Jr., letter to Scotti, December 6, 1975.

7. Edo McCullough, *Good Old Coney Island: A Sentimental Journey into the Past* (New York: Fordham University Press, 1957, 2000), 127–129.

8. Ellen Fletcher, "Sheepshead Bay," *Encyclopedia of New York City*, 1065–106, 6.

9. Ellen M. Snyder-Grenier, *Brooklyn! An Illustrated History* (Philadelphia: Temple University Press, 1996), 110.

10. Freilich-Den, "Ragtime Composer Recalled" (quoting interview with Amelia Lamb, October 13, 1974), 19, note 56.

11. Ibid.

12. Lamb to Meyer, May 12, 1960.

13. McCarthy, "U.S. Ragtime Great," October 21, 1974, Section 2, 17.

14. Conversations with Robert Lamb.

15. A. Lamb to Scotti, March 19, 1975.

16. Jasen and Jones, *That American Rag*, 299.

17. Ibid., 300.

18. Lamb to Darch, March 16, 1959.

19. Blesh and Janis, *They All Played Ragtime*, 265–266.

20. Lamb to Tichenor, April 11, 1958.

21. Borgman, "Classic Ragtimer," August 2001.

22. Arndt may have briefly played the organ at New York's Trinity Church.

23. "Felix Arndt," *Perfessor Bill Edwards*.

24. Scotti, "Ragtime's Paradox," 112.

25. Lamb to Darch, March 16, 1959.

26. Lamb to Meyer, March 31, 1960.

27. A. Lamb to Scotti, March 10, 1975.

28. The information about L. F. Dommerich and its staff that is referenced and quoted here with permission is from original research completed by Marjorie Freilich-Den for her thesis, "Joseph F. Lamb: Ragtime Composer Recalled."

29. Freilich-Den, "Ragtime Composer Recalled" (quoting letter from Frank Stayskal, October 29, 1974), 23, note 69.

30. Ibid.

31. Ibid. (quoting letter from Frances Steinhagen, February 13, 1975), 24, note 71.

32. Ibid. (quoting interview with Michael N. Barbatelli, September 25, 1974), 24, note 72.

33. Ibid. (quoting interview with Marietta Hanley, October 13, 1974), 24, note 73.

34. Lamb to Tichenor, April 11, 1958.

35. Lamb to Meyer, June 16, 1960.

36. Witmark, *From Ragtime to Swingtime*, 279–282.

37. Further information, photographs, and selected songs from the "Blackberries" minstrel shows produced at St. Edmund's Church are contained in the excellent, although difficult to locate, article by Galen Wilkes in *The Rag Time Ephemeralist I*.

38. Galen Wilkes, "The Black Lamb of the Family: Joseph F. Lamb's Minstrel Shows," *The Rag Time Ephemeralist I* (1998): 93 (quoting *Blackberries of 1931*).

39. Ibid.

40. Conversations with Patricia Lamb Conn.

41. *Blackberries of 1929*, program notes.

42. "Merle T. Kendrick," Kirk Collection: Dance Band Index, Cunningham Memorial Library, Indiana State University, library.indstate.edu.

43. "Merle T. Kendrick," The Internet Movie Database, www.imdb.com/name/nm0447719/.

44. Wilkes, "Minstrel Shows," 93.

45. Ibid., 97.

46. Gus Collins (lyrics), "So Here We Are," 1930.

47. Wilkes, "Minstrel Shows," 97.

48. Ibid., 97.

49. Ibid., 98.

50. Dorrie Collins (lyrics), "Here We Are Again," 1933.

51. Joseph F. Lamb, "Hi, Everybody," 1935.

52. Wilkes, "Minstrel Shows," 93. Conversations with Patricia Lamb Conn.

53. Adrian Bailey, *Walt Disney's World of Fantasy* (New York: Gallery, 1982).

54. Wilkes, "Minstrel Shows," 98.

55. Ibid.

56. Freilich-Den, "Ragtime Composer Recalled" (quoting interview with Robert Lamb), 21, note 62.

57. David Wright, "Barbershop Harmony," Articles and Essays, *The A Cappella Foundation*, www.acappellafoundation.org/.

58. Joel Zoss and John Bowman, *Diamonds in the Rough: The Untold History of Baseball* (Lincoln: University of Nebraska Press, 1989), 7.

59. Arthur Longbrake, "Brother Noah Gave Out Checks for Rain," *In Harmony*, Sheet Music from Indiana.

60. Refer to Chapter 3.

61. Conversations with Patricia Lamb Conn.

62. Ibid.
63. Fred Hoeptner, "Patricia Lamb Conn: Connecting with Ragtime's Glory Days," *The Mississippi Rag,* February 2008.
64. Conversations with Robert Lamb.
65. Lamb to Meyer, April 13, 1960.
66. Freilich-Den, "Ragtime Composer Recalled" (quoting interview with A. Lamb, October 13, 1974), 14.
67. Lamb to Darch, March 16, 1959.
68. Galen Wilkes, "The Whirlwind Pianist," *The Rag Times,* May 1988, 102.
69. Conversations with Patricia Lamb Conn.
70. "Harry Carroll," Songwriters Hall of Fame, www.songwritershalloffame.org/exhibits/C321.
71. "The Trail of the Lonesome Pine," George Willoughby Music, Music Australia, National Library of Australia, http://nla.gov.au/nla.cs-ma-an23234611.
72. Conversations with Robert Lamb.
73. Lamb to Meyer, May 12, 1960.
74. Ibid.
75. Lamb to Meyer, July 4, 1960.
76. Conversations with Patricia Lamb Conn.
77. Conversations with Robert Lamb.
78. Terry Waldo, *This is Ragtime* (New York: Da Capo, 1976), 134.
79. Ibid., 135.
80. Jasen and Tichenor, *Rags and Ragtime,* 260.
81. Waldo, *This is Ragtime,* 133–155.
82. Ibid., 154.

Chapter Nine

1. John Edward Hasse, "Rudi Blesh and the Ragtime Revivalists," *Ragtime: Its History, Composers, and Music,* edited by John Edward Hasse (New York: Schirmer, 1985), 181.
2. Ibid., 181–2.
3. Conversations with Patricia Lamb Conn. (Also see Borgman, "Classic Ragtimer, Part II," *The Mississippi Rag,* September 2000.)
4. Stephen Holden, "Rudi Blesh, 86, Dies; A Historian of Jazz, Author and Teacher," *The New York Times,* August 28, 1985.
5. "Mrs. Sidney Janis, 65, Artist, Ran Gallery," *The New York Times,* November 12, 1963.
6. Hasse, "Blesh and the Revivalists," 181.
7. Blesh and Janis, *They All Played Ragtime,* 237–8.
8. Conversations with Patricia Lamb Conn.
9. Scotti, "Ragtime's Paradox," 123.
10. Freilich-Den, "Ragtime Composer Recalled" (quoting an interview with Rudi Blesh, January 29, 1975), 27, note 76.
11. Lamb to Meyer, March 31, 1960.
12. Ibid.

13. Ibid.
14. G. Van Gieson, Jr., to Scotti, October 16, 1975.
15. Freilich-Den, "Ragtime Composer Recalled" (quoting Hanley, October 13, 1974), 24, note 73.
16. Lamb to Meyer, June 16, 1960.
17. *The Classic Rags of Joe Lamb,* Volume I, Golden Crest Records #GRS4127, played by Milton Kaye. A conversation between Kaye and Rudi Blesh is a part of this recording, during which Kaye mentions the correlation between "Ragtime Bobolink" and Chaminade's "Scarf Dance."
18. Conversations with Robert Lamb.
19. *Joe Lamb: A Study in Classic Ragtime,* Folkways Record #FG3562, original liner notes by Sam Charters.
20. Lamb to Meyer, March 11, 1960.
21. Ibid., June 10, 1960.
22. Michael Montgomery, "A Visit with Joseph Lamb," *The Second Line,* November–December 1957, 3–5, 30.
23. Ibid.
24. Lamb to Montgomery, January 25, 1958.
25. Ibid.
26. Lamb to Montgomery, April 2, 1958.
27. Freilich-Den, "Ragtime Composer Recalled" (quoting Steinhagen, February 13, 1975), 24, note 71.
28. Lamb to Montgomery, November 3, 1958.
29. A. Lamb to Scotti, March 10, 1975.
30. Cassidy, "Last of Ragtime Composers," August 1961, 1.
31. Ibid.
32. Joseph F. Lamb, letter to Thorton (Tony) Hagert, October 21, 1959.
33. Ibid.
34. Ibid.
35. Lamb to Meyer, April 13, 1960.
36. Lamb to Meyer, July 13, 1960.
37. Ibid.
38. *Study in Classic Ragtime,* liner notes.
39. Joseph F. Lamb, letter to Mr. Asch, February 15, 1960.
40. Ibid.
41. *Study in Classic Ragtime,* liner notes.
42. *Classic Rags of Joe Lamb,* Blesh/Kaye interview.
43. *Study in Classic Ragtime,* liner notes.
44. *Classic Rags of Joe Lamb,* Blesh/Kaye interview.
45. Lamb to Asch, February 15, 1960.
46. Joseph F. Lamb, letter to Arthur Marshall, April 13, 1960.
47. Lamb to Meyer, March 11, 1960.
48. Lamb to Meyer, May 12, 1960.
49. Lamb to Hagert, October 21, 1959.
50. Lamb to Montgomery, October 3, 1959.
51. Lamb to Hagert, October 21, 1959.

52. Lamb to G. and A. Van Gieson, October 19, 1959.
53. Lamb to Montgomery, October 21, 1959.
54. Lamb to Hagert, October 21, 1959.
55. *Classic Rags of Joe Lamb*, liner notes.
56. Lamb to Montgomery, October 21, 1959.
57. Ibid.
58. Helen McNamara, "Forgotten Jazz Genius Plays Again," *Toronto Telegram*, October 8, 1959.
59. The engraved sterling silver award plate is in the Library of Congress, Music Division, Lamb Collection. The inscription reads: "To Joseph F. Lamb 1887 from The Ragtime Music Lovers of Toronto, Ont., Canada 7 Oct. 59 — 76 Club."
60. William Eccles, "Mr. Ragtime Comes Home," *The (Toronto) Star Weekly*, November 21, 1959.
61. Freilich-Den, "Ragtime Composer Recalled" (quoting A. Lamb, October 13, 1974), 33, note 85.
62. Ron Johnson, "Ragtime's Joe Lamb Still Has His Touch," *Toronto Star*, October 8, 1959.
63. Frank Morriss, "Visit in a Rainswept Cemetery: Ragtime Composer Recalls a Debt," *Toronto Globe and Mail*, October 8, 1959.
64. Lamb to Montgomery, October 21, 1959.
65. Ibid.
66. Cassidy, "Last of Ragtime Composers," November 1961, 9. Also see Epilogue.
67. Lamb to Meyer, March 11, 1960.
68. Lamb to Darch, undated.
69. Cassidy, "Last of Ragtime Composers," December 1961, 15.
70. Balliett, "Ragtime Game," 20–21.
71. Cassidy, "Last of Ragtime Composers," November 1961, 10.
72. Lamb to Meyer, July 4, 1960.
73. Borgman, "Classic Ragtimer, Part II," September 2001.
74. Lamb to Marshall, April 13, 1960.
75. Lamb to Meyer, June 19, 1960.
76. *A Little Lost Lamb*, 45.
77. Lamb to Darch, March 16, 1959.
78. Blesh and Janis, *They All Played Ragtime*, 26.
79. Ibid., 20.
80. Lamb to Marshall, April 13, 1960.
81. Ibid.
82. Lamb to Meyer, June 10, 1960.
83. Conversations with Patricia Lamb Conn.
84. Lamb to Hagert, October 21, 1959.
85. Lamb to "children," dated as "tomorrow will be August 28, 1960."
86. Ibid.
87. Borgman, "Classic Ragtimer, Part II," September 2001.
88. Ibid.

Chapter Ten

1. Phone interview with Stella Laufer-Turk, June 20, 2011.
2. Ibid.
3. Ibid.
4. Ibid.
5. Stella Laufer, "The Joseph F. Lamb School: P.S. 206," unpublished essay, February 11, 1974.
6. Ibid.
7. Ibid.
8. Phone interview, Laufer-Turk.
9. "The Joseph F. Lamb School — P.S. 206: 50th Birthday and School Naming Celebration," event program, May 27, 1976.
10. *The Bay News*, June 7, 1976, p. 24.
11. State of New York Department of State Distinguished Service Award in Honor of Joseph Francis Lamb, signed (with official seal) by Mario M. Cuomo, Secretary of State, on May 27, 1976. A copy of this document is in the Library of Congress, Music Division, Joseph Lamb Collection.
12. A. Lamb to Scotti, July 29, 1976.
13. Ibid.
14. See appendix for complete list of compositions included in *Ragtime Treasures*.
15. Rudi Blesh, "Notes on An American Genius." *Introduction to Ragtime Treasures: Piano Solos by Joseph F. Lamb* (New York: Mills Music, Belwin Mills, 1964).
16. David Stewart, "A Ragtime Pianist Shows Public TV How to Have Fun," *Current*, September 30, 1996, www.current.org/music/music9618ragtime-morath.shtml, (posted on July 29, 2008).
17. "Any Rags Today," Program Two Script, page 5, from *The Ragtime Era*, NET TV series, 1959–1960, files of Max Morath.
18. John S. Wilson, "Turn-of-the-Century Music Sparkles," *The New York Times*, September 7, 1963.
19. "Classic Ragtime," Program Four Script, *Turn of the Century*, KRMA Denver, 1961, files of Max Morath.
20. Ashley Kahn, "After 70 Years, The Village Vanguard Is Still in the Jazz Swing," *The Wall Street Journal Online*, February 8, 2005, as reprinted on the Village Vanguard website, www.villagevanguard.com/html/history.html.
21. John S. Wilson, "Max Morath's Original Rag Ensemble is at Redecorated Village Vanguard," *The New York Times*, June 24, 1964.
22. Ibid.
23. Harold Stern, "Max Morath: He's Giving 'Ragtime' a New Image," syndicated review, Bell-McClure Syndicate, June 10, 1964, files of Max Morath.
24. "Teresa Sterne, 73, Pioneer in Making

Classical Records," *The New York Times*, December 12, 2000.

25. *Scott Joplin: Collected Piano Works*, edited by Vera Brodsky Lawrence (New York: New York Public Library, 1971).

26. "Ragtime and All That Jazz," *Billboard*, March 18, 1972, 47.

27. Douglas Martin, "Milton Kaye, 97, Pianist and Arranger, Dies," *The New York Times*, August 17, 2006.

28. *The Classic Rags of Joe Lamb*, conversation with Rudi Blesh and Milton Kaye.

29. Ibid.

30. P. Van Gieson to Freilich-Den, January 6, 1975. Also, author's conversations with Patricia Lamb Conn and Robert Lamb.

31. Ibid.

32. P. Van Gieson to Scotti, December 8, 1975.

33. Ibid.

34. Wilson, "Lamb's Ragtime," October 17, 1973, L53.

35. See Epilogue.

36. A. Lamb to Scotti, March 8, 1976.

37. McCarthy, "U.S. Ragtime Great," Section 2, p. 17.

38. Scotti to A. Lamb, early 1975.

39. Joseph F. Lamb, "Ragtime Reverie," edited from *Joseph F. Lamb Sketchbook* by Joseph R. Scotti, published by Patricia Lamb Conn (a.k.a., "The Lamb Family"), 1992, 1993. Information about this composition from conversations with Patricia Lamb Conn.

40. Joseph F. Lamb, "Brown Derby #2," Transcribed and edited by Joseph R. Scotti from an audio tape of Lamb's performance recorded by Michael Montgomery, published by Patricia Lamb Conn (a.k.a. Joseph Lamb Family), 1988, 1993. Information about this composition from conversations with Patricia Lamb Conn.

41. Anna Kisselgoff, "Royal Ballet Presents 12-Rag Production," *The New York Times*, May 6, 1976.

42. Clive Barnes, "Ballet: A Palpable Hit; Twyla Tharp's 'Push' is Danced at Uris," *The New York Times*, 43.

43. Clive Barnes, "Neumeier Fizzles While Tharp Triumphs," *The New York Times*, January 18, 1976, Arts and Leisure, 80.

44. Twyla Tharp, *Push Comes to Shove: An Autobiography* (New York: Linda Grey/Bantam, 1992), 218.

45. Peter Goodman, "Eglevsky Doing a Ragtime Work," clippings files, Library of Congress, Music Division, Lamb Collection.

46. Jill Silverman, "Villella to Narrate Children's Program," *The New York Times*, Long Island Weekly Section, May 25, 1980, L1.

47. *Tintypes*, Playbill from John Golden Theatre, 1980.

48. G. Van Gieson, Jr., to Scotti, December 6, 1975.

49. *A Prairie Home Companion* with Garrison Keillor, January 29, 2000, http://prairieho me.publicradio.org/programs/20000129/.

50. Phone interview with Glenn Jenks, June 23, 2011.

51. Ibid.

52. Ibid.

53. Ibid.

54. See Appendix IV for further information.

55. *The Montclair Times*, December 10, 1987.

56. Conversation with Patricia Lamb Conn.

57. "Patricia Lamb Conn in an interview with David Sager" (video recording), Library of Congress, 2006, http://lcweb2.loc.gov/diglib/ ihas/loc.natlib.ihas.2000335773/default.html.

58. "Muskoka," *Perfessor Bill Edwards*, www. ragpiano.com.

59. Phone interview with Sue Keller, June 20, 2011. *A Little Lost Lamb*, folio and CD, are published by Ragtime Press.

60. Scotti, "Ragtime's Paradox," 6.

61. Correspondence from Larisa Migachyov, June 13, 2011.

62. Library of Congress, Music Division, Joseph F. Lamb Collection, folders of sheet music, advertisements, and miscellaneous papers.

Epilogue

1. Max Morath, Diane Fay Skomars, with Ralph Schoenstein, *Max Morath: The Road to Ragtime* (Virginia Beach, VA: Donning, 1999), 7.

2. "Voices of American Music: Aaron Copland," interview by Vivian Perlis in 1975 and 1976, Peekskill, NY (Yale University Library, Oral History of American Music), http://www. library.yale.edu/about/departments/oham/aud io_copland.html.

Bibliography

Theses/Dissertations

Freilich-Den, Marjorie. "Joseph F. Lamb: A Ragtime Composer Recalled." M.A. Thesis, Brooklyn College, 1975.

Scotti, Joseph R. "Joe Lamb: A Study of Ragtime's Paradox." Dissertation, University of Cincinnati, 1977.

Books

Ashby, LeRoy. *With Amusement for All: A History of American Popular Culture Since 1830.* Lexington: University Press of Kentucky, 2006.

Bailey, Adrian. *Walt Disney's World of Fantasy.* New York: Gallery, 1982.

Baldwin's Directory of Montclair, Bloomfield, Verona and Caldwell: Year Ending May 1, 1903. Orange, NJ: J. H. Baldwin, 1902.

Berlin, Edward A. *King of Ragtime: Scott Joplin and His Era.* New York: Oxford University Press, 1994.

_____. *Ragtime: A Musical and Cultural History.* Lincoln, NE: iUniverse, 2002 (originally published by the University of California Press, 1980).

_____. *Reflections and Research on Ragtime.* Brooklyn, NY: Brooklyn College of the City University of New York, Institute for Studies in American Music, 1987.

Blesh, Rudi, and Harriet Janis. *They All Played Ragtime,* 4th ed. New York: Oak, 1971.

Bomberger, E. Douglas. *An Index to Music Published in* The Etude *Magazine, 1883–1957.* Lanham, MD: Scarecrow, with Music Library Association, 2004.

Bordman, Gerald. *American Musical Theatre: A Chronicle,* 3d ed. New York: Oxford University Press, 2001.

Bowser, Eileen. *History of the American Cinema, Volume 2: The Transformation of Cinema.* New York: Charles Scribner's Sons, 1990.

Brooklyn City Directory 1912, Volume 3. Brooklyn, New York: Brooklyn Directory, 1912.

Burton, Jack. *The Blue Book of Tin Pan Alley: A Human Interest Anthology of American Popular Music.* Watkins Glen, NY: Century House, 1951.

Cacioppo, Richard K. *The Glory of Montclair: Past and Present.* Montclair, NJ: Dream City, 1995.

The Canadian Encyclopedia. Year 2000 Edition. Toronto, Ontario, Canada: McClelland and Steward, 1999.

The Canadian Year Book for 1904. Toronto, Canada: Alfred Hewett, 1904.

Charters, Samuel B. *Jazz: A History of the New York Scene.* Garden City, NY: Doubleday, 1962.

Chase, Gilbert. *America's Music.* New York: McGraw-Hill, 1955.

Directory of Montclair, Bloomfield, Caldwell, Essex Fells, Glen Ridge and Verona, 1908. Newark, NJ: Price and Lee, 1908.

Dolan, Brian. *Inventing Entertainment: The Player Piano and the Origins of an American Musical Industry.* Lanham, MD: Rowman and Littlefield, 2009.

Durso, Joseph. *Madison Square Garden: 100 Years of History.* New York: Simon and Schuster, 1979.

Encyclopedia of Recorded Sound, Vol. I, edited by Frank Hoffmann. New York: Routledge, 2005.

Ewen, David. *All the Years of American Popular Music.* Englewood Cliffs, NJ: Prentice-Hall, 1977.

Finck, Henry T. *My Adventures in the Golden Age of Music.* New York: Funk and Wagnalls, 1926.

Forma, Warren. *They Were Ragtime.* New York: Grosset and Dunlap, 1976.

Furia, Philip. *The Poets of Tin Pan Alley: A History of America's Great Lyricists.* New York: Oxford University Press, 1992.

Goldberg, Isaac. *Tin Pan Alley: A Chronicle of the American Popular Music Racket.* New York: John Day, 1930.

Golden, Eve. *Vernon and Irene Castle's Ragtime*

Revolution. Lexington: The University Press of Kentucky, 2007.

Groce, Nancy. *New York: Songs of the City.* New York: Watson-Guptill, 1999.

Hamm, Charles. *Yesterdays: Popular Song in America.* New York: W. W. Norton, 1983.

Harris, Charles K. *After the Ball: Forty Years of Melody.* New York: Frank Maurice, 1926.

Jaeger, Philip Edward. *Images of America—Montclair: A Postcard Guide to Its Past.* Charleston, SC: Arcadia, 1998.

Jasen, David A. *Ragtime: An Encyclopedia, Discography, and Sheetography.* New York: Routledge, 2007.

_____. *Tin Pan Alley: The Composers, the Songs, the Performers and their Times.* New York: Donald I. Fine, 1988.

Jasen, David A., and Gene Jones. *That American Rag: The Story of Ragtime from Coast to Coast.* New York: Schirmer, 2000.

Jasen, David A., and Trebor Jay Tichenor. *Rags and Ragtime: A Musical History.* New York: Dover, 1978.

Jousse, J. *A Catechism of Music,* "Conservatory Edition," rev. and edited by Louis C. Elson and H. L. Heartz. Boston and New York: White-Smith Music Publishing Co., 1907.

Kasson, John F. *Amusing the Million: Coney Island at the Turn of the Century.* New York: Hill and Wang, 1978.

Lieberman, Richard E. *Steinway & Sons.* New Haven, CT: Yale University Press, 1995.

A Little Lost Lamb: Piano Music by Joseph F. Lamb, edited by Sue Keller. Oak Forest, IL: Ragtime Press, 2005.

Loesser, Arthur. *Men, Women and Pianos: A Social History.* New York: Dover Publications, 1990, 1982, 1954.

Madison's Directory of Montclair and Glen Ridge, New Jersey for the Year Beginning May 1, 1898. Montclair, NJ: Press of the Montclair Herald; Edward Madison, Publisher, 1898.

Marks, Edward B., as told to Abbott J. Liebling. *They All Sang: From Tony Pastor to Rudy Vallee.* New York: Viking, 1934.

McCullough, Edo. *Good Old Coney Island: A Sentimental Journey into the Past.* New York: Fordham University Press, 1957, 2000.

The Montclair Annual: Who's Who in Montclair 1916. Montclair, NJ: Annual Publications, 1916.

Montclair 1694–1982, An Inventory of Historic, Cultural and Architectural Resources— Volume III, April 1982. Preservation Montclair—A Project of the Junior League Montclair/Newark.

Morath, Max, and Diane Fay Skomars, with Ralph Schoenstein. *Max Morath: The Road to Ragtime.* Virginia Beach, VA: Donning, 1999.

The New Grove Dictionary of Music and Musicians, 2d ed. Edited by Stanley Sadie. New York: Grove's Dictionaries, 2001.

New Jersey: A Guide to Its Present and Past. Compiled and written by the Federal Writers' Project of the Works Progress Administration for the State of New Jersey. New York: Hastings House, 1939.

New Jersey Civil War Record: Introduction, Record of Officers and Men of New Jersey in the Civil War, 1861–1865. William S. Stryker, Adjutant General, Volume I, pp. 585–588. Trenton: John L. Murphy, Steam & Job Printer, 1876. https://wwwnet1.state.nj.us/DOS/Admin/ArchivesDBPortal/StrykerCivilWar.aspx.

Plunkett-Powell, Karen. *Remembering Woolworth's: A Nostalgic History of the World's Most Famous Five-and-Dime.* New York: St. Martin's, 1999.

Ragtime: Its History, Composers and Music. Edited by John Edward Hasse. New York: Schirmer, 1985.

Ragtime Rarities: Complete Original Music for 63 Piano Rags. Selected and with an introduction by Trebor Jay Tichenor. New York: Dover, 1975.

Ragtime Treasures: Piano Solos by Joseph F. Lamb. With an introduction, "Notes on An American Genius," by Rudi Blesh. Rockville Centre, NY: Belwin Mills (Mills Music), 1964.

Roell, Craig H. *The Piano in America 1890–1940.* Chapel Hill: University of North Carolina Press, 1989.

Schafer, William J., and Johannes Riedel. *The Art of Ragtime: Form and Meaning of an Original Black American Art.* Baton Rouge: Louisiana State University Press, 1973.

Scott, William W., *History of Passaic and its Environs.* New York: Lewis Historical, 1922.

Shepard, Elizabeth, and Royal F Shepard. *Images of America: Montclair.* Portsmouth, NH: Arcadia, 2003.

Snyder-Grenier, Ellen M. *Brooklyn! An Illustrated History.* Philadelphia: Temple University Press, 1996.

Suisman, David. *Selling Sounds: The Commercial Revolution in American Music.* Cambridge, MA: Harvard University Press, 2009.

Sullivan, Mark. *Our Times: The United States 1900–1925, Volume I—The Turn of the Century.* New York: Charles Scribner's Sons, 1926.

Tawa, Nicholas E. *The Way to Tin Pan Alley: American Popular Song, 1866–1910.* New York: Schirmer, 1990.

Tharp, Twyla, *Push Comes to Shove: An Autobiography.* New York: Linda Grey/Bantam, 1992.

Those Were the Days; Volume 5, Montclair in the Decade 1880 through 1889; Volume 6, 1890–

1899; *Volume 7, 1900–1909; Volume 7B, 1900–1909.* Compiled by Gladys Segar. Montclair Library, 1951.

Three American Beauties, in *Edison: The Invention of the Movies.* The Museum of Modern Art in cooperation with the Library of Congress. New York: Kino Video, 2005.

Toronto City Directory, The. Toronto, Canada: Might Directories, 1904.

Waldo, Terry. *This is Ragtime.* New York: Da Capo, 1991, 1976.

Watkins, S.C.G. *Reminiscences of Montclair.* New York: Barnes, 1929.

White, H. Loring. *Ragging It: Getting Ragtime into History (and Some History into Ragtime).* New York: iUniverse, 2005.

Wiley, Peter Booth. *National Trust Guide San Francisco: America's Guide for Architecture and History Travelers.* New York: John Wiley and Sons, 2000.

Witmark, Isidore, and Isaac Goldberg. *From Ragtime to Swingtime: The Story of the House of Witmark.* New York: Lee Furman, 1939.

Zoss, Joel, and John Bowman. *Diamonds in the Rough: The Untold History of Baseball.* Lincoln: University of Nebraska Press, 1989.

Articles

Adams, Elliott L. "The Joseph F. Lamb Story." *The Sacramento Ragtime Society Newsletter,* October 1989-April 1990.

"Ages and Historical Records of Pianos Sold in America," Sohmer & Co., *Bluebook of Pianos,* http://www.bluebookofpianos.com/kron6.htm.

Anderson, Bruce. "The National Pastime's Anthem." *Sports Illustrated,* April 15, 1991, 20.

Balliett, Whitney. "The Ragtime Game." *The New Yorker,* July 2, 1960, 20–21.

Barnes, Clive. "Ballet: A Palpable Hit." *The New York Times,* January 11, 1976, www.nytimes.com.

_____. "Neumeier Fizzles While Tharp Triumphs." *The New York Times,* January 18, 1976, Arts & Leisure, 80.

Berlin, Edward A. "Ragtime." *The New Grove Dictionary of Music and Musicians,* 2d ed., edited by Stanley Sadie, Vol. 20. New York: Macmillan, 2001, 755–759.

_____. "Scott Joplin's Treemonisha Years." *American Music,* Volume 9, Number 3, Special Issue (Fall 1991): 260–276.

Bessom, M. E. "From Piano Thumping to the Concert Stage: The Rise of Ragtime." *Music Educators Journal,* Volume 59, Number 8 (April 1973): 53–56.

Boiler, Jr., Paul F. "The Sound of Silents." *American Heritage.com,* Volume 36, Issue 5, August/September 1985.

Borgman, George A. "Joseph F. Lamb, Classic Ragtimer." *The Mississippi Rag,* August/September 2001.

"Carroll, Harry." Songwriters Hall of Fame, www.songwritershalloffame.org/exhibits/C321.

Carson, Gerald. "The Piano in the Parlor." *American Heritage,* December 1965, p. 54–59, 91.

Cassidy, Russell. "Joseph F. Lamb — Last of the Ragtime Composers." *Jazz Monthly* (four-part series), August–December 1961.

"Cliff House and Sutro Baths." National Park Service, U.S. Department of the Interior. Golden Gate National Recreation Area, www.nps.gov/goga/clho.htm.

Cohen, Nathan. Untitled. *Toronto Daily Star,* September 28, 1960.

"Composer Honored." *The Star-Ledger,* October 29, 1978.

"The Deadly Virus: The Influenza Epidemic of 1918." National Archives and Records Administration, www.archives.gov/exhibits/influenza-epidemic/.

Dvorak, Antonin. "Music in America." *Harper's New Monthly Magazine,* February 1895, 428–494.

Edwards, Perfessor Bill. "Joseph Lamb," http://www.ragpiano.com/.

Eccles, William. "Mr. Ragtime Comes Home." *The Toronto Star Weekly,* November 21, 1959, 23–25.

"Ellen Wilson." *National First Ladies' Library,* www.firstladies.org/biographies.

Elliker, Calvin. "Sheet Music Special Issues: Formats and Functions." *Notes,* Second Series 53/1 (September 1996): 9–17.

"Entertainments: His Majesty's Theatre." *Evening Post* (New Zealand), January 4, 1915, www.paperspast.natlib.govt.nz/.

"Enrico Caruso and the 1906 Earthquake." The Virtual Museum of the City of San Francisco, http://www.sfmuseum.org/1906/ew19.html.

Faulkner, Anne Shaw. "Does Jazz Put the Sin in Syncopation?" *Ladies' Home Journal,* August 1921.

"The Final Curtain: Louis F. Werba." *The Billboard,* November 28, 1942, 27.

Fletcher, Ellen. "Sheepshead Bay," *The Encyclopedia of New York City,* edited by Kenneth T. Jackson. New Haven and London: Yale University Press, and New York: The New-York Historical Society, 1995, 1065–1066.

Floyd, Jr., Samuel A. and Marsha J. Reisser. "Social Dance Music of Black Composers in the Nineteenth Century and the Emergence of Classic Ragtime." *The Black Perspective in Music,* Volume 8, Number 2 (Autumn 1980): 161–193.

_____, and _____. "The Sources and Resources of Classic Ragtime Music in Black Music." *Black Music Research Journal*, Volume 4 (1984): 22–59.

Fox, Joseph, "Day of the Player Piano." *American Heritage.com*, Volume 39, Issue 4, May/June 1988.

"Frances Cleveland." *National First Ladies' Library*, www.firstladies.org/biographies.

Geibel, Adam. "South Car'lina Tickle: Cake Walk." *The Etude*, December 12, 1898, 23–25.

Goldmark, Daniel. "Creating Desire on Tin Pan Alley." *The Musical Quarterly* 90/2 (Summer 2007): 197–229.

Gray, Christopher. "Tracing Scott Joplin's Life Through His Addresses." *The New York Times,* February 4, 2007.

Graziano, John. "Music in William Randolph Hearst's *New York Journal.*" *Notes*, Second Series, 48/2 (December 1991): 383–424.

Hamm, Charles. "Alexander and His Band." *American Music*, Volume 14, Number 1 (Spring 1996): 65–102.

Hasse, John Edward. "Rudi Blesh and the Ragtime Revivalists," *Ragtime: Its History, Composers, and Music,* edited by John Edward Hasse. New York: Schirmer, 1985, 181.

"History." Prospect Park Alliance, www.prospectpark.org/about/history.

"History." Visit Muskoka, www.visitmuskoka.com/history.htm.

"History of Ragtime." Library of Congress, Music, Theatre and Dance, www.loc.gov/performingarts/

Hoeptner, Fred. "Patricia Lamb Conn: Connecting with Ragtime's Glory Days." *The Mississippi Rag*, February 2008, http://www.Mississippirag.com/ragonline_feb08/features_feb_lamb.html.

_____. "Rocked in the Cradle of Ragtime." *The Rose Leaf Ragtime Club Review*, 2005.

Holden, Stephen. "Rudi Blesh, 86, Dies; A Historian of Jazz, Author and Teacher." *The New York Times*, August 28, 1985.

"Hotel History." Walper Hotel, http://www.walper.com.

Hume, Ruth. "The Great Chicago Piano War." *American Heritage Magazine* 21/6, October 1970, http://www.americanheritage.com/content/great-chicago-piano-war.

Hylton, John. "The Music of the Louisiana Purchase Exposition." *College Music Symposium* 31 (1991): 59–66.

Jefferson, Margo. "Recapturing Past Delights While Making Them New." *The New York Times*, November 16, 1998, E2.

Johnson, Ron. "Ragtime King Returning." *Toronto Star*, October 2, 1959.

_____. "Ragtime's Joe Lamb Still Has His Touch." *Toronto Star*, October 8, 1959.

Kahn, Ashley. "After 70 Years, The Village Vanguard is Still in the Jazz Swing." *The Wall Street Journal Online*, February 8, 2005, as reprinted on the Village Vanguard website, www.villagevanguard.com/html/history.html.

Kallmann, Helmut. "H.H. Sparks Music Co." *The Canadian Encyclopedia/The Encyclopedia of Musical Canada,* http://www.thecanadianencyclopedia.com.

_____. "Musgrave." *The Canadian Encyclopedia/The Encyclopedia of Musical Canada,* http://www.thecanadianencyclopedia.com.

Kendrick, Merle T. Indiana State University, Cunningham Memorial Library, Kirk Collection: Dance Band Index, library.indstate.edu.

Kendrick, Merle T. *The Internet Movie Database,* www.imdb.com/name/nm0447719.

Kisselgoff, Anna. "Royal Ballet Presents 12-Rag Production." *The New York Times*, May 6, 1976, www.nytimes.com.

Latimer, Margaret. "Brooklyn," *The Encyclopedia of New York City*, edited by Kenneth T. Jackson. New Haven: Yale University Press, and New York: The New-York Historical Society, 1995, 152.

Lauder, W. Waugh. "Music at the World's Fair: Fifth Columbian Letter." *The Musical Courier,* June 7, 1893, 15.

Martin, Douglas. "Milton Kaye, 97, Pianist and Arranger, Dies." *The New York Times*, August 17, 2006, www.nytimes.com.

Massey, Drew. "Unifying Characteristics in Classic Ragtime." *Indiana Theory Review*, Volume 22, Number 2 (Fall 2001): 27–50.

McCarthy, Eugene. "U.S. Ragtime Great Started Composing in Kitchener." *Kitchener-Waterloo Record*, Section 2, October 21, 1974, 17.

McDonald, Gerald D. "A Bibliography of Song Sheets: Sports and Recreations in American Popular Songs, Part IV, Songs of the Silent Film." *Notes*, Second Series, Volume 14, Number 3 (June 1957): 325–352 and Number 4 (September 1957): 507–533.

McNamara, Helen. "Forgotten Jazz Genius Plays Again." *Toronto Telegram*, October 8, 1959.

Mendelsohn, Joyce. "Madison Square," *The Encyclopedia of New York City*, edited by Kenneth T. Jackson. New Haven: Yale University Press, and New York: The New-York Historical Society, 1995, 711–712.

"Menu [held by] Flatiron Restaurant & Café [at] 'New York, NY' REST; (1906)," New York Public Library Digital Image ID 473853 and 40000194365/6, http://digitalgallery.nypl.org/nypldigital/.

Miller, Bonny H. "A Mirror of Ages Past: The Publication of Music in Domestic Periodicals." *Notes*, Second Series 50/3 (March 1994): 883–901.

"Montclair: The Queen Suburb of the Metropolis." *Industrial Recorder*, Vol. II, No. 7, 1903.

"Montclair Social Matters." *The New York Times*, October 5, 1895, http://www.nytimes.com.

Montgomery, Michael. "A Visit with Joseph Lamb." *The Second Line*, November-December 1957, 3–5, 30.

Morriss, Frank. "Visit in a Rainswept Cemetery: Ragtime Composer Recalls a Debt." *Toronto Globe & Mail*, October 8, 1959.

"Mrs. Sidney Janis, 65, Artist, Ran Gallery." *The New York Times*, November 12, 1963.

"Muskoka Falls Tourism 75th Anniversary, *Discover Muskoka*, www.discovermuskoka.ca/about.php?s=about_243&r_ro-0.

"Musquakie," *Dictionary of Canadian Biography Online*, Vol. IX, www.biographi.ca/009004-130-e.html.

"1901 SJF Student Wrote 'Rag' Tunes." *Kitchener-Waterloo Record*, October 10, 1959.

On Dress Parade, The United States Air Force Band. Washington D.C., Colonel Lowell E. Graham, Commander/Conductor, January 2000, liner notes.

Ostendorf, Berndt. "The Musical World of Doctorow's Ragtime." *American Quarterly*, Volume 43, Number 4 (December 1991): 579–601.

"Panic of 1907." Federal Reserve Bank of Boston, http://www.bos.frb.org/about/pubs/panicof1.pdf.

Pfizer Pulse, Obituary, September 7, 1960.

"The Pioneer Music Store." *The Virtual Museum of the City of San Francisco*, http://www.sfmuseum.org/hist/kandc.html.

"Publisher: Syndicate Trading Company, New York." The Lucile Project, http://sdrc.lib.uiowa.edu/lucile/publishers/syndicate/syndicate.htm.

"Rag Composer Remembered." *The Montclair Times*, October 26, 1978.

"Ragtime and All That Jazz." *Billboard*, March 18, 1972, 47.

"Ragtime Kalamazoo." Kalamazoo, Michigan Public Library, www.kpl.gov/local/arts-entertainment/ragtime-kalamazoo.aspx.

"Rocco Venuto." *In Harmony*, Sheet Music from Indiana, www.dlib.indiana.edu/projects/inharmony/.

Schafer, William J. "Joseph Lamb 'Sensation.'" *The Mississippi Rag*, September 1975, 6–7.

Scott, Patrick. "The Temperanceville Rag." *The Globe Magazine*, March 27, 1965, 12–13, 16.

Shapiro, Elliott. "Ragtime, U.S.A." *Notes*, Second Series 8/3 (June 1951): 457–470.

Shehan, Patricia K. "The Riches of Ragtime." *Music Educators Journal* 73/3 (November 1986): 22–25.

Silverman, Jill. "Villella to Narrate Children's Program." *The New York Times*, Long Island Weekly Section, May 25, 1980, L1.

"Social Doings in Montclair." *The New York Times*, October 6, 1895, www.nytimes.com.

Simms, Dr. Bartlett D., and Ernest Borneman. "Ragtime: History and Analysis." *The Record Changer* (October 1945): 4–9.

Stewart, David. "A Ragtime Pianist Shows Public TV How to Have Fun." *Current*, September 30, 1996, www.current.org/music/music9618ragtime-morath.shtml.

"Teresa Sterne, 73, Pioneer in Making Classical Records," *The New York Times*, December 12, 2000, www.nytimes.com.

Tichenor, Trebor Jay. "John Stillwell Stark, Piano Ragtime Publisher: Readings from *The Intermezzo* and His Personal Ledgers, 1905–1908." *Black Music Research Journal* 9/2 (Fall 1989): 193–204.

_____. "The World of Joseph Lamb: An Exploration." *Jazz Monthly* (four-part series), August-December 1961.

Tjaden, Ted. "Joseph F. Lamb: The Humble Ragtime 'Sensation.'" Classic Ragtime Piano, http://www.ragtimepiano.

Tober, Steve. "May in Montclair to Fete Noted Ragtime Composer." *The Montclair Times*, December 10, 1987.

Tucker, Mark. "Confrey, Zez." *The New Grove's Dictionary of Music and Musicians*, 2d ed., edited by Stanley Sadie, Volume 6, 283.

Tyler, Linda L. "Commerce and Poetry Hand in Hand: Music in American Department Stores, 1880–1930." *Journal of the American Musicological Society* 45/1 (Spring 1992): 75–120.

"Waltzed Facing Death: Titanic Survivor in Hospital Says Music Prevented Panic." *The New-York Tribune*, April 22, 1912, 2.

Wilkes, Galen. "The Black Lamb of the Family: Joseph F. Lamb's Minstrel Shows." *The Rag Time Ephemeralist* I, 1998.

_____. "The Whirlwind Pianist." *The Rag Times*, May 1988.

Wilson, John S. "Records: Lamb's Ragtime." *The New York Times*, October 17, 1973.

_____. "Turn-of-the-Century Music Sparkles." *The New York Times*, September 7, 1963, www.nytimes.com.

Wright, David. "Barbershop Harmony." Articles and Essays, *The A Cappella Foundation*, www.acappellafoundation.org/.

Yagoda, Ben. "Lullaby of Tin Pan Alley." *American Heritage.com*, Volume 34, Issue 6, October/November 1983.

Zakariasen, Bill. "Elite Syncopations." *Daily News*, May 6, 1976.

Additional Sources

Library of Congress, Music Division, Joseph F.
  Lamb Collection.
Montclair, New Jersey Public Library, Local
  History Division, clippings files.
The Music Trade Review (The International Ar-
  cade Museum), www.mbsi.org.
"Patricia Lamb Conn in an interview with David
  Sager" (video recording), Library of Congress,
  2006. http://lcweb2.loc.gov/diglib/ihas/loc.nat
  lib.ihas.200035773/default.html.
A Prairie Home Companion with Garrison Keil-
  lor, National Public Radio, January 29, 2000,
  http://prairiehome.publicradio.org/progra
  ms/20000129/2000129_mu.htm
State of New Jersey Department of State, New
  Jersey State Archives Searchable Database,
  www.state.nj.us/state/darm/links/databases.
  html.
United States Federal Census archives online,
  www.ancestry.com.

Correspondence and Additional Materials

*Copies of correspondence from Joseph
F. Lamb to Allan Meyer of
Orinda, California (courtesy of
Patricia Lamb Conn)*

March 11, 1960
March 31, 1960
April 13, 1960
April 29, 1960
May 12, 1960
May 28, 1960
June 10, 1960
June 16, 1960
June 19, 1960
July 4, 1960
July 13, 1960

*Copies of correspondence from Joseph
F. Lamb to Michael Montgomery
(courtesy of Patricia Lamb Conn)*

October 3, 1957
December 18, 1957
January 25, 1958
April 2, 1958
May 28, 1958
November 3, 1958
January 22, 1959
February 24, 1959
March 26, 1959
October 3, 1959
October 21, 1959
February 16, 1960

*Copies of correspondence from Joseph
F. Lamb to Anastasia and George
Van Gieson, Jr. (courtesy of
Patricia Lamb Conn)*

October 19, 1959
Undated, late 1959
February 2, 1960
February 6, 1960
April 1960
May 11, 1960
May 24, 1960
June 15, 1960

*Copies of correspondence from Joseph F.
Lamb to the following individuals
(courtesy of Patricia Lamb Conn)*

To Arthur Marshall: April 13, 1960
To Trebor Tichenor: April 11, 1958
To Mr. M. Asch of Folkways Records: February
  15, 1960
To "Dear Children": August 28, 1960
To Robert Darch: March 16, 1959; April 3, 1959;
  May 3, 1959 (completed questionnaire); May
  6, 1959; Undated
To Thornton (Tony) Hagert: December 18,
  1958; October 21, 1959; December 21, 1959;
  December 30, 1959; Undated (late 1959)

*Copies of correspondence from
Mrs. Amelia Lamb to Joseph R. Scotti,
and to Joseph R. and Carol Scotti
(courtesy of Patricia Lamb Conn)*

January 9, 1975
March 10, 1975 (with attached answers to type-
  written questions)
October 23, 1975
November 1, 1975
November 5, 1975
November 20, 1975
November 24, 1975
December 8, 1975
January 29, 1976
February 9, 1976
March 8, 1976
July 29, 1976
October 12, 1976
July 11, 1977
August 2, 1981 (attachments)

*Copies of correspondence from Mrs.
Amelia Lamb to Michael Montgomery
(courtesy of Patricia Lamb Conn)*

January 2, 1961

*Copies of correspondence from Paul Van
Gieson (courtesy of Mary Van Gieson)*

To Marjorie Freilich-Den: January 6, 1975
To Joseph R. Scotti: December 8, 1975; January
  27, 1976; Undated (with attachments)

To *The New York Times* "Notes on People" Section: May 31, 1976
To John Hasse, Archives of Traditional Music: March 11, 1978

Copies of correspondence from George Van Gieson Jr. to Joseph R. Scotti (courtesy of George A. Van Gieson III)

January 6, 1975
October 16, 1975
October 31, 1975
December 6, 1975
January 20, 1976
November 30, 1976
July 23, 1977
August 20, 1978

December 17, 1978
December 22, 1978

Copies of written materials by George Van Gieson, Sr. (courtesy of George A. Van Gieson III)

Unpublished autobiography written "to Buckie and Paul" in May of 1947
Letter to Joseph F. Lamb: February 6, 1960
"Recollections of Early Montclair," as presented in eight parts, *The Montclair Times* (September through December of 1955).

Miscellaneous Correspondence

Katherine Schouten to George Van Gieson, Jr., October 12, 1972.

Index

Page numbers in **bold italics** indicate illustrations.

231